MINORITIES: U.S.A.

Research Director:
George Bundy Smith

CONSULTANTS:

Unit 1

Theodore B. Hetzel
Executive Director
Indian Rights Association

Unit 2

Milton C. Lee
Educational Specialist
Department of Social Studies
Public School System,
Washington, D.C.

Unit 3

Mari-Luci Ulibarri
Assistant Professor
College of Education
University of New Mexico

Unit 4

Peter P.S. Ching
Director
Chinese Culture Institute

Hisatane Hatano
President, Japanese-American
Association of New York

Units 5 and 8

Joseph P. Fitzpatrick, S.J.
Department of Sociology and Anthropology
Fordham University

Unit 6

Milton Himmelfarb
American Jewish Committee

Unit 7

Louis Nieves
Executive Director
Aspira, Inc.

Unit 9

Kenneth A. Job
Assistant to the Dean
Paterson State College

The Globe Social Studies Program

MINORITIES: U.S.A.

Milton Finkelstein

Hon. Jawn A. Sandifer

Elfreda S. Wright

GLOBE BOOK COMPANY, INC.

New York—Chicago—Dallas

About The Authors

MILTON FINKELSTEIN is that rare author who is equally at home engaged in scholarly research or dealing with the needs of the disadvantaged student. Dr. Finkelstein has spent more than twenty years teaching and supervising the instruction of disadvantaged students and is coauthor of two New York City curricula in social studies. He was a member of the Joint Committee on Common Learnings of the National Council of Social Studies and National Council of Teachers of English and has published more than two hundred works, including articles in leading educational magazines and several textbooks.

JAWN A. SANDIFER is a Justice of the Supreme Court of the State of New York and has been a judge of the Civil Court of the City of New York. He is a former member of the Advisory Council of the New York State Department of Education. In a long career devoted to the rights of minority groups, he was New York State Legal Redress Chairman of the NAACP, Secretary of the HARYOU Poverty Program and a leading attorney appearing in civil rights cases before the courts of many states and before the United States Supreme Court.

ELFREDA S. WRIGHT is a principal in the New York City school system. Previously she was a music department chairman, instructor in human relations for teachers, Administrator of the Lincoln Center Student Programs, and Associate Director of Junior High School Borough-Wide Chorus. She was consulting editor for THE AFRO-AMERICAN IN UNITED STATES HISTORY and a coauthor of BLACK POETRY FOR ALL AMERICANS, both published by Globe.

GEORGE BUNDY SMITH researched the entire manuscript and enriched it by his wide background in the civil rights movement. He is a former staff attorney for the NAACP Legal Defense and Educational Fund and is a member of the legal staff of the New York State Supreme Court.

Photographs in this text appear with the courtesy of the following:
American Museum of Natural History 5, 6, 7, 8, 18, 19, 20, bot., 21, 25, 30, 31, 32, 42, 43, 45, 71, 75, 98.   Bettman Archive 3, 17, 26, 53, 77, 79, bot., 82, 105, 113, 131, 220, 223, 230, 237, 246, 258, top, 308.   Brown Brothers 15, 29, 41, 67, 94, 97, 161, 166, 194, 199, 207, 221, 227, 233, 271, 276, 289, 311, 313, 374.   Chicago Historical Society 84.   Commonwealth of Puerto Rico 285.   Culver 4, 33, 190, 196, 224, 225, 249, 250.   Ford Motor Co. 259.   Franklin Delano Roosevelt Memorial Library, Hyde Park, N.Y., 314.   Historical Picture Service 33, 35, 79, middle.   Library of Congress 91, 92, 136, 237.   New York Historical Society 13.   New York Public Library 68, 69, 70, 76, 79, top, 89, 112, 151, 343, 345, top.   OEO 316.   San Jacinto Museum 165.   Santa Fe Railroad 5.   Sidney W. Turner, Colonial Williamsburg 65.   UPI 115, 183, 192, bot., 237, 284, 300, 301, 303, bot., 324, top, 325, 362.   U.S. Army 204.   USDA Photo 353.   U.S. Department of the Interior 51, 58.   Wide World 54, 57, 101, 106, 124, 125, 126, 128, 140, 142, 144, 145, 154, 173, 176, 180, 192, top, 200, 209, 211, 212, 213, 219, 235, 237, 255, 258, middle & bot., 261, 262, 264, 275, 279, 291, 292, 302, 303, top, 319, 321, 323, 324, bot., 327, 338, 339, 345, bot., 347, 357, 365, 366, 378, 380, 381, 383, 384, 386.   Woolaroc Museum, Bartlesville, Oklahoma 20 top.
The map on page 43, *Indian Tribes of The United States*, is used by permission of The New Community Press from OUR BROTHERS KEEPER: THE INDIAN IN WHITE AMERICA, edited by S.E. Cohn, published by The New Community Press, copyright © 1969, and distributed by the World Publishing Company.

ISBN: 0-87065-545-0 (softcover edition)
ISBN: 0-87065-546-9 (hardcover edition)

Copyright © 1971, Globe Book Company, Inc.
175 Fifth Avenue, New York, N.Y. 10010

Edited by Marilyn Z. Wilkes
Text and cover design by Arthur Ritter
Illustrations by Sandy Huffaker
Maps and cartoons by Joseph Crowley

PRINTED IN THE UNITED STATES OF AMERICA

Contents

WHAT IS
THIS BOOK
ABOUT?

Minorities: USA explores one of the most serious problems facing our country—the problem of equal treatment for all Americans. Equal protection under the law, civil liberties, civil rights—the United States Constitution guarantees them to all citizens. Yet many have never known equality. Why haven't they? What are they doing to achieve it? These and other questions are asked, and answered, in this book.

The United States is a land of many peoples. They are of different races. They follow different religious ideas. They speak many languages. They live and behave in different ways. Most Americans (the majority) are white, Protestant and English-speaking. Smaller groups within the country (the minorities) may not be white. Most are not Protestant. Many do not speak English. Their ways of living are sometimes different from those of the majority. Our largest minority is almost one-fourth of the whole population. Some of the smallest are only a fraction of one per cent of our people.

Except for the Indians, all Americans came from other parts of the world. Except for blacks, all came willingly and with hope. They became part of a growing, changing land. For years this land was called the "melting pot." All who came here would become Americans like everyone else, it was said. They would be welcomed and given the same rights and chances others had known. This was what made the United States a land of opportunity. All men were equal. All could hope to improve their lives. Other countries denied equality; the United States alone promised it to all!

How strange that this promise of equality should have been stated by the majority for so long! Large groups of Americans were denied promised opportunities by the very people who called this a land of equality. The majority would not consider the minorities equals. It would not permit them to become equal. One minority after another suffered because most other Americans would not grant them the rights they themselves enjoyed—the rights guaranteed by the Constitution.

Prejudice and discrimination have spoiled tens of millions of lives in our country. *Prejudice* is the feeling that someone or some group is not as good as you are. It leads to hatred and often to actions that harm those who are hated. Such actions are called *discrimination*, the things people do to others that deny them equality. A minority that is discriminated against cannot improve its way of living. It is kept from doing so. Prejudiced members of the majority then say that the minority is not as good as the majority—for it has not been able to improve itself!

For most of American history, minorities have suffered, often without hope of improving their situation. Today they are demanding an end to prejudice and discrimination. Many members of minority groups demand the right to live in their own way. Some even want to separate themselves from the rest of the American people.

Minority groups have organized to gain equal treatment. They say that their rights can no longer be denied. They do everything in their power to improve the way they are treated. Bit by bit the majority has come to understand the fairness of many minority demands. Laws and practices have changed. Equality truly has begun to be an American possibility. Cries for equality also grow as more and more groups of people make it their aim. Women demand equal treatment with men. Students ask for a greater voice in their education. Soldiers seek changes in the rules of the armed forces. Groups in every community add their voices to the drive for greater rights.

How did the drive for equality begin? There have always been some Americans who believed in equality for all. But they were few and they were weak when compared with the majority who followed discrimination as a way of life. Today most Americans understand that the "melting pot" was a dream that never came true. Each minority group has begun its own movement for equality. Black Americans led the fight; other Americans later joined them. Blacks, Indians, Mexicans, Puerto Ricans, Asians, Jews, Catholics—these and others have made clear that there are great gaps between the "American dream" and our real way of life.

This book was written to help you understand the story of our country's minorities. Each unit tells the story of a different group. It relates those parts of the minority's history that best explain the great problems each group has faced. It shows what has been done to solve these problems, and what must still be done. *Minorities: USA* includes stories and documents that have never before appeared in a text-book. They were chosen to help you feel close to the events in each minority's history. Some of the documents have been simplified to make them easier to read, although none of the ideas in them have been changed. Some will show you what a minority group felt about a problem. Others will present the thinking of people who did not want that minority to receive equal treatment. Once you know both sides of the story, you can think through the facts to reach your own conclusions.

Laws and court decisions have brought great changes in American life. You will read about many of these in the following pages. They often show that a majority of Americans was ready to accept a change that improved the lives of minority-group citizens. They sometimes show why equality remained impossible at a certain time or place. You will see how communities, states and sometimes the whole country refused to accept change. The new problems that then followed are an important part of *Minorities: USA*.

Minority-group problems are national problems. They affect all Americans, the majority as well as the minorities. Equal treatment for all is a key part of the American dream of a better future. It can make it possible for the members of minorities to add greatly to their country's life. Its absence can make them feel unwanted and apart. In time they may lose interest in their country; some may even want to destroy it.

This book will help you see some of the mistakes of the past. It examines the steps that have been taken to correct them. It presents ideas to solve minority group problems. For these problems have not yet been solved. Active citizens, with you among them, will be making the decisions in the future that lead to new laws and new solutions. Your greater understanding of minority problems will make you a better citizen, better able to work toward greater democracy for all— so that all Americans may some day share equally in the rights for which so much of the world must still struggle.

Unit One

AMERICAN INDIANS

The real story of the American Indian has been hidden by clouds of misunderstanding. At last some of these clouds are being cleared away. This unit begins by explaining how Indians lived when the first settlers from Europe came to the new colonies along the Atlantic Coast. It describes the struggles that followed as these settlers drove the Indians away, taking their lands and their hunting grounds. By the 1830's the United States had forced most of the Indians to move to lands west of the Mississippi. For the next fifty years the Indians were cheated, robbed and murdered. Sometimes they fought back, but they could not win. In the end they were placed on reservations. By 1890 most of them had been killed or had died from the terrible conditions under which they had to live. Congress and the states then did all they could to make the remaining Indians leave their reservations and sell their land to the endless waves of settlers. The Indians grew poorer and poorer. It was 1924 before they became citizens of the United States. It was 1948 before they gained the right to vote in all of the states. Indians still face great problems today. They remain the poorest minority in the country they once called their own land.

Still is our land
& was not called

1

Why Couldn't Indians and White Men Get Along with Each Other?

1 By 1805 most of the Indians of New York State and the other states along the Atlantic Coast had been pushed back into the interior. Indians and white men had not been able to remain neighbors for long. Again and again the white men, hungry for land, had gathered their strength to force the Indians back. One by one the Indian tribes lost at first part and then all of their lands.

Indian leaders were trusting at first. They made treaties in which they gave settlers the use of some land. Then more settlers came; they forgot the treaties as they moved ever farther west. The Indian tribes could do little. Most of them were small. Each had from ten to perhaps a hundred fighting men. These were never enough to hold back the thousands of white men demanding land. Wars were fought but never really won by any Indian tribe. At best a strong tribe, like the Iroquois in New York, could hold back the settlers for a few years.

The land was being stolen from the Indians. The men who were doing it called themselves good Christians. They made excuses for what they were doing, and for the death they brought as they drove the Indians back. They claimed that Indians were savages, not Christians, and deserved whatever happened to them. They pointed out that Indians did not believe in private property and often stole from white settlers. They said Indian women worked hard while their husbands

false

These missionaries hoped to bring Christianity to the Indians. Why might the Indian chiefs refuse to accept it?

2

did little. They were shocked by the way Indians fought, attacking and killing without warning. These excuses remind us strongly of the reasons men gave for trading in and owning slaves.

In 1805 a group of Christian missionaries hoped to bring their religion to the Indians. They met with several Indian chiefs at the edge of a creek near Buffalo, New York. The white men urged the chiefs to save their souls by becoming Christians. Chief Red Jacket of the Senecas answered them. His answer helps us understand why Indians and white men could not remain friends for long in any part of the land.

How Were Indian and White Ways of Living Different?
What Caused Wars Between the Indians and White Men?
Why Did the Indians Lose Most of These Wars?

The first Indians had come to North America ten thousand or more years before Europeans arrived. Archeologists, the scientists who study past civilizations, have learned much about these early Indians. Most agree that the Indians probably came from Asia. They crossed from Siberia to Alaska and then worked their way south over thousands of years. These early people left no written records. Most of what we know about them comes from findings in the places where they lived or hunted. We do know that they were different from the peoples of Europe and Asia. They lived in small groups. Most of them were nomads, people who traveled

50,000 yrs.

Most early Indians were nomads; some remained so. Why did they travel so much of the time?

to wherever there was food. Others were farmers or fishermen. In time they developed weapons; their spears, bows and arrows were as well made as any others in the world. They learned to make pottery. They began to use metals. Yet the tribes of today's United States never built large cities. They never formed powerful empires in which one leader became a king over a large area.

so what? defined in white terms of "advanced"

A large tribe had perhaps ten thousand people. It would gain control over several hundred square miles. The tribe divided into villages, each holding part of the land. All of the land then belonged to the village and the tribe. Each village shared its wealth so that all would have enough. When a village needed food or other aid, it turned to other villages of the same tribe. Life was free and very democratic. Chiefs were elected by their tribe's warriors or by the clan mothers. The word of a chief was law because he carried out the wishes of his tribe. If the people were not satisfied, he could be removed or overruled in a council attended by other leaders of the tribe.

another def – better not true

A village might contain a hundred people. Of these, seven or eight were hunter-warriors, strong young men who had the task of bringing in meat for the village and acting as its defenders. Many of these men died young, in hunting or in war. There were about twice as many women as men, and some men had two or more wives. In 1805 a count of Indians in Canada showed that fewer than 100 of each 1,000 Indians were men. More than 200 were women, and about 700 were children. At one time, more than one million Indians lived in what later became the United States. Most lived by hunting and gathering food. Some raised crops. Some lived in tents made of animal skins; others built strong log houses. Still others built homes and even buildings something like apartment houses, using clay bricks.

low estimate

A Crow chief gives his opinion in a council meeting before calling for a vote. What form of government would this be called?

Different kinds of Indian dwellings: a. Earth and wicker lodge of the Mandans; b. Tepees of the Blackfoot Indians; c. Inside a tepee; d. New Mexican pueblos of the Taos Indians; e. Bark lodge of Wisconsin's Winnebago Indians. Why didn't all Indians build their houses alike?

The Indians built a civilization using many important ideas not yet known in Europe. They began the use of tobacco and developed the cigarette, the cigar and the pipe. They used many medicines made from plants. They developed corn, potatoes and other plants. They invented snow goggles and the toboggan sled. Some Indians knew how to cast metals. Indians made barbed fishhooks, used a scale and built water pumps. Some tribes had systems of writing. Indian fishermen made and used large nets. Indian women spun thread and wove cloth. Indians were certainly not an uncivilized people.

Not a universal

Meat was the most desired food, and each village guarded its valuable "hunting grounds" from all others. Many important products were made from the dead animals brought in by hunters. The skins were used for shoes. We have examples of fine embroidery in which animal hairs were used as thread. The antlers of a deer became tool handles or arrow points.

Many Indians were fine craftsmen. Above: A Seminole silver comb. Right: Beadwork of the Winnebago Indians.

Canoes made long-distance travel much easier. How could this improve Indian life?

Animal bones became weapons, handles or tools. Much of the tool and weapon work was done by women, who were often fine craftsmen.

Indians preferred to remain in their own part of the land. However, the canoe made it possible for them to travel long distances by water. Some canoes were large enough to carry a war party or a group of traders. We know that there was much trading among villages and tribes. Sometimes the villages of a tribe would gather for an important religious or political event. Most of the tribes remained at peace with one another. They quickly found that they could not remain at peace with the white men who poured across the Atlantic from Europe. Columbus and his captains made slaves of some of the first Indians they met. Other Spaniards forced Indians to work (and often die) in mines and on farms. The English were peaceful at first but were soon ready to fight to force the Indians out of the farmlands near the Atlantic. The word spread through the tribes. White men could not be trusted. They might be your friends. They might also steal your land, take your women, make your men slaves and kill you if you tried to resist.

These white men were so different from any people the Indians had ever known. They held black men as slaves—something some of the Indian tribes later did as well. They built towns and filled the land with people. This drove away the game Indians needed for food. The white men did bring the horse. By 1800 Indian warriors were among the best mounted soldiers in the world. White men also brought guns. Until Indians too had them, these weapons brought quick death to the tribes who tried to hold the settlers back. The most horrible "gifts" of the white men were liquor and disease. Liquor drove Indian men mad, or made them so foolish that they gave away all they had, including their lands. Illnesses to which white people had developed resistance could and often did kill whole villages of Indians.

Yet the white men kept telling the Indians of their great and fair God. They swore by this God that they would never break the agreements they made with the tribes. But they did break them, again and again. A tribe might then decide to fight for its lands or its rights. But how much could it do against the many white men with guns and cannon who could destroy any village? Indian villages were often destroyed by fire and gun. Indians in their turn attacked settlers and their homes. Towns such as Schenectady, New York, are today filled

What difference did the white man's gift of the horse make in the Indians' way of life?

with plaques telling of such Indian attacks. The destruction of an Indian village was called a punishment. Indian attacks on settlements have gone down in histories written by white men as "massacres."

good point

Few Indians accepted Christianity. Few of them could understand the white man, who spoke of peace and brought war. Chief Sagoyewatha of the Senecas was called Red Jacket by the settlers. He explained in 1805 why his people could not accept the white man's religion, or his way of life.

Brother, listen to what we say.

There was a time when our forefathers owned this great [land]. Their seats extended from the rising to the setting sun. The Great Spirit had made it for the use of Indians. He had created the buffalo, the deer, and other animals for food. He had made the bear and the beaver. Their skins served us for clothing. He had scattered them over the country and taught us how to take them. He had caused the earth to produce corn for bread. All this He had done for his red children because He loved them. If we had some disputes about our hunting ground, they were generally settled without the shedding of much blood.

But an evil day came upon us. Your forefathers crossed the great water and landed [here]. Their numbers were small. They found friends and not enemies. They told us that they had fled from their own country for fear of wicked men and had come here to enjoy their religion. They asked for a small seat. We took pity on them, granted their request, and they sat down amongst us. We gave them corn and meat; they gave us poison in return.

The white people, brother, had now found our country. Tidings were carried back and more came amongst us. Yet we did not fear them. We took them to be friends. They called us brothers. We believed them and gave them a larger seat. At length their numbers had greatly increased. They wanted more land; they wanted our country. Our eyes were opened and our minds became uneasy. Wars took place. Indians were hired to fight against Indians, and many of our people were destroyed. They also brought strong liquor amongst us. It was strong and powerful and has slain thousands.

Brother, our seats were once large and yours were small. You have now become a great people, and we have scarcely a place left to spread our blankets. You have got our country but are not satisfied; you want to force your religion upon us.

Brother, continue to listen.

You say that you are sent to instruct us how to worship the Great Spirit . . . if we do not take hold of the religion which you white people teach, we shall be unhappy hereafter. You say that you are right and we are lost. How do we know this to be true? We understand that your religion is written in a book. If it was intended for us as well as you, why has not the Great Spirit given to us . . . the knowledge of that book, with the means of understanding it rightly? We only know what you tell about it. How shall we know when to believe, being so often deceived by the white people?

Brother, you say there is but one way to worship and serve the Great Spirit. If there is but one religion, why do you white people differ so much about it? Why not all agreed, as you can all read the book?

. . . We also have a religion . . . It teaches us to be thankful for all the favors we receive, to love each other, and to be united. We never quarrel about religion.

. . . Brother, we do not wish to destroy your religion or take it from you. We only want to enjoy our own . . . Brother, we are told that you have been preaching to the white people in this place. These people are our neighbors. We are acquainted with them. We will wait a little while and see what effect your preaching has upon them. If we find it does them good, makes them honest and less disposed to cheat Indians, we will consider again of what you have said.

I. WHAT ARE THE FACTS?

Write the letter of the choice that best completes each statement.

1. The chief reason for fighting between white men and Indians was that (a) Indians had no religion, (b) white men wanted Indian lands, (c) Indians always broke peace treaties.

2. The first Indians probably came to North America from (a) Asia, (b) South America, (c) Africa.

3. Most of the Indian tribes in the 1500's and 1600's (a) settled in small towns, (b) lived as nomads, (c) lived in small villages within an area belonging to their tribe.

4. The number of people in an Indian village was most often about (a) 100, (b) 1,000, (c) 10,000.

5. The food that men provided in Indian villages was (a) corn, (b) vegetables, (c) meat.

6. The largest group in each Indian village was the (a) men, (b) women, (c) children.

7. The first Spaniards in the New World treated the Indians as (a) equals, (b) slaves, (c) paid workers.

8. The horse was brought to North America by (a) Europeans, (b) Indians, (c) traders from Asia.

9. One of the reasons Indian chiefs gave for refusing to become Christians was that (a) they did not believe in any gods, (b) the Christians they knew did not follow the teachings of Christianity, (c) Christian missionaries were afraid to visit the Indian tribes.

10. In an Indian village (a) each Indian family had to make its own living, (b) all members of the community shared in the village's wealth, (c) most people had to work for a few rich men.

11. The best Indian craftsmen were usually (a) women, (b) old men, (c) young boys and girls.

12. At first settlers and Indians were usually (a) good friends, (b) bitter enemies, (c) frightened neighbors.

13. Quarrels about religion often took place among (a) Christians, (b) Indians, (c) both Christians and Indians.

14. Indians have enriched the world through their (a) novels and plays, (b) new kinds of building, (c) farming.

15. Indian villages of the same tribe often (a) fought bitter wars, (b) helped one another, (c) followed different religions.

II. WHAT DO THEY MEAN?

Explain the meaning of each of these words or phrases in a sentence.

1. living in the interior
2. treaty
3. Iroquois
4. savages
5. private property
6. missionary
7. archeologist
8. tribe
9. council
10. snow goggles
11. toboggan
12. hunting grounds
13. massacre
14. Great Spirit

III. THINKING IT THROUGH!

Discuss.

1. Why were the Indian tribes unable to protect themselves against the white men who settled in North America?

2. Why did white men call the Indians savages? Why do you agree or disagree with this description of the Indians?

3. What proof do we have that Indians were civilized peoples?

4. The white men who settled in North America made slaves of Africans. What was the same about slavery and the poor treatment of Indians?

5. In what ways was the government of the tribes democratic? How was their kind of government similar to or different from the kind found in your own community?

6. How did each of these "gifts" of the white man—the horse, the gun and liquor—change Indian life?

7. Why were the Indians ready to make treaties with white settlers? What did they gain from these treaties? What did they lose? Why did white men break these treaties so often?

IV. RESEARCH PROBLEMS.

1. Check your school or public library to find the names of the Indian tribes that lived in your state when it was first settled. Report to your class on the importance of these tribes in the history of your state.

2. Locate a town, street, river or other place near your home that has an Indian name. Find out what the name means and report to the class.

Should Indians Have the Right to Live Where They Wish?

2 In 1763 twenty Indians of the Conestoga tribe lived near Lancaster, Pennsylvania. These Indians spoke English. Most of them had taken English names. All of them seemed to get along well with their white neighbors. Back in the 1680's, William Penn, founder and first ruler of Pennsylvania, had agreed to peace with the Indians "as long as the sun could shine, or the waters run in the rivers." Penn's settlers could build homes and villages on Indian land only if they had bought it from Indians, and if the Indians had agreed to the sale.

William Penn purchased land from the Conestogas. In the long run, who gained most from the sale?

The settlers had poured in. By the 1760's most of Pennsylvania's Indians had moved west. Some had sold their land; many more had lost it through "sales" made while they were drunk. A great number had fought the large bands of well-armed frontiersmen who just moved into Indian lands and then killed any who refused to give up their hunting grounds. The small group

13

of Conestogas had remained. They felt safe on the good farmland near their tiny village. Their small group contained seven men, five women and eight boys and girls.

At dawn on December 14, 1763, a group of white men called the Paxton Boys surrounded the small Indian village. They attacked without warning and murdered the six people they found there. They said they were getting revenge because some Indians on the frontier had just killed some settlers. The other fourteen Indians, away at the time, were placed in a strong building in Lancaster at the orders of the governor. On December 27, fifty white men broke into that building and killed all fourteen.

Benjamin Franklin wrote about this Conestoga Massacre. His words show the problem faced by many Indians who tried to remain on their land after white settlers had moved into their area.

> The only crime of these poor wretches seems to have been that they had reddish-brown skin and black hair; and some people of that sort, it seemed, had murdered some [white people]. If it be right to kill men for such a reason, then should any man with a freckled face and red hair kill a wife or child of mine, it would be right for me to revenge it by killing all the freckled, red-haired men, women, and children I could afterward anywhere meet with. . . . These people have always been our friends. Their fathers received ours, when strangers here, with kindness and hospitality. Behold the return we have made them! . . . These were not enemies; they were born among us, and yet we have killed them all.

How Did the Indians Try to Keep Their Lands in the Eastern United States?

How Were These Indians Forced to Move to the West?

Trying to Be Friendly. Most of the Indian tribes near the Atlantic had been friendly to the settlers from Europe. Most Indian chiefs saw little harm in sharing their land with the settlers. The Europeans had goods to trade. They bought furs and food from nearby Indians. They accepted help in learning Indian ways of farming. Perhaps Indians and whites could have lived together in peace, except that the numbers of settlers kept increasing. This in turn meant that the Indians were forced to give up more and more of their land. The frontiersmen with their guns, and sometimes with soldiers to help them, moved into Indian hunting grounds and farmlands. Each of the colonies, and later each of the states, found its own ways to take the land.

Fighting Back. Indian weapons were no match for the guns of the frontiersmen. Yet the Indians did try to fight for their lands. Indian attacks were fierce when they came. If white men would not accept Indian ownership of the land, then Indians would treat them like any tribe that moved into their land. They would kill and burn. They would show that Indian rights could not be ignored. A New York poet used these words to describe the fury of an Indian attack on a settlement:

> I will let loose the dogs of Hell,
> Ten thousand Indians, who shall yell
> And foam and tear, and grin and roar,
> And drench their moccasins in gore.

Indian chiefs did not like to join with other tribes. Perhaps the tribes fighting together could have held back the wave of settlers pushing west. Pontiac, chief of the Ottawa Indians, did set up a great union of Indians in 1762. A year later frontier forts were attacked by tribes from the Great Lakes all the way to the Gulf of Mexico. The "uprising" failed, for the Indians could not keep their forces together for the long months of attack needed to take a strong fort.

Tecumseh, chief of the Shawnee Indians, agreed with other chiefs that treaties with the white men could not be trusted. He and his brother, called the Prophet, led the Indians of Illinois and Indiana in 1809 after settlers moved in with support from the United States Army. Tecumseh and his brother moved among the tribes. "Divided we fall" was his cry. In 1811 William Henry Harrison, governor of Indiana Territory, defeated the Prophet in the Battle of Tippecanoe. Harrison became famous as the hero of Tippecanoe and was later President of the United States. However, Tecumseh did not give up his fight. He built up large Indian armies, received guns from England and joined the War of 1812 against the Americans. For a year and a half his forces, working with the English,

"Tippecanoe and Tyler too!" was the slogan that helped William Henry Harrison become President. Why would the hero of an Indian battle have been a popular candidate?

The Battle of Tippecanoe was fought by the Indians to gain back their lands. Can you tell from the picture who won? How?

defeated several American armies and kept the frontier in constant danger. He was killed in 1813 at the Battle of the Thames in Canada. With his death Indian efforts to hold back the settlers seemed to die too.

false other colonial powers used Indians as buffers

Finding Allies. Indian leaders looked for allies to help them keep their lands. In the 1750's Indian tribes had joined the French during the French and Indian War. They fought on the English side during the American Revolution and again during the War of 1812. Spain, which held Florida and Mexico, aided Indian tribes who tried to keep back white settlers. The tribes found that their strongest efforts could never hold back the frontiersmen for long.

By 1820 there were no allies left. The United States had bought the huge Louisiana Purchase from France. It had bought Florida from Spain. Mexico was moving toward its freedom. England had made peace with the United States, and had signed an agreement to keep peace along the border with Canada. From 1820 on, the Indians realized they would have to deal with the white state and federal governments of the United States without any outside aid.

Accepting White Control. The Indians soon understood that they had no choice. They had to give up their lands or die. Some tribes refused to move and were wiped out. Others agreed to take small areas called "reservations." These became Indian property. The state or federal government promised to protect the land from settlers. Yet only a few reservations were really protected. White "agents" were placed in charge. These men often made rules that Indians could not accept. They permitted the sale of liquor. They did little to keep frontiersmen from moving into reservation land.

Indian Removal. The Indians were in the way. By the 1820's the government of the United States had decided to force all of them to move west of the Mississippi River. The Indians were given two choices. If they agreed to break up their tribal lands, each Indian becoming a farmer and an American citizen, they could remain. If they wanted to keep their tribe whole, then all had to move to new land in the West. They would be paid for improvements on their land and helped with the costs of moving. Most Indians agreed to exchange their lands in the East for the promised lands in the West. When they did not, their chiefs were often bribed or made drunk to get them to sign removal treaties.

The name of Andrew Jackson is most closely connected with the removal of Indians to the West. This frontiersman became President in 1829. He had fought Indians for much of his life. Now he decided that they could no longer live in the "settled" areas of the United States. He explained his plan in a message

President Andrew Jackson decided to "remove" all Indians to new lands in the West. Why do you think he did so?

to Congress. The Indians must be removed "to make room for the whites." White people needed all the land east of the Mississippi. The President insisted that he was really helping the Indians when he forced them to leave their homes.

> Can it be cruel . . . to give him a new and extensive territory, to pay the expense of his removal, and support him a year in his new abode? . . . the general government kindly offers him a new home, and proposes to pay the whole expense of his removal and settlement.

long debates

Congress saw no harm in the Indian Removal plan. Indian tribes were moved to the West during the next dozen years. They were "helped" in their move by the United States Army. The soldiers protected them along the way and also made certain that they did not stop for long during their trip. The trip west could be as long as 2,000 miles. Large numbers of Indians died on the way. Cholera and measles wiped out whole tribes. Food ran out; thousands of Indians starved before help could be brought. Some tribes tried to stop long enough to hunt for food or plant a crop. They then found themselves at war with the white people of the area in which they stopped. In 1832 a tribe led by Chief Black Hawk, which had just crossed the Mississippi, came back into Illinois to plant some corn. They would not leave until the corn had grown. Illinois called out its militia and chased the starving Indians north into Wisconsin. Regular troops joined the chase. Most of the Indian men, women and children were massacred at a place called Bad Axe.

The brilliant Sequoyah invented the Cherokee alphabet. How do you think the artist of this portrait felt about Sequoyah?

Choctaws went first

The Indian tribes in the South were really strong nations. The most powerful were the Creek, Cherokee, Chickasaw and Choctaw tribes. All but the Cherokees moved west quickly after 1830. The Creeks suffered most; they had to exchange their good farmland for dry land on the plains. The Cherokees, one of the most advanced of the Indian nations, did not want to leave. They hoped they could be accepted by white people by becoming less "Indian" and more "white." Sequoyah, a brilliant Cherokee leader, had invented a Cherokee alphabet. Cherokee printers published Bibles and newspapers using this alphabet. The tribe accepted the Christian religion, built churches, wrote a constitution and lived in houses similar to those used by white settlers. They did everything possible to be like white men. In 1791 the Cherokees had been promised their lands and their independence in a treaty with the United States. Sequoyah

A front page of the *Cherokee Phoenix*.

and other Cherokee leaders hoped they could remain in their homes forever under such promised protection.

Then, in 1828, gold was discovered on Cherokee land. White miners pushed in. Cherokee territory stretched through parts of Georgia, Alabama and Tennessee. President Jackson agreed with the miners and settlers who wanted this land. He pulled out the soldiers who had been protecting the Cherokees. Meanwhile, Georgia tried to take away Cherokee land within that state. The matter came to the Supreme Court. It decided that Georgia had no power to make laws for Cherokee territory. Jackson made fun of this decision. He knew that the Supreme Court could not enforce its decisions without the help of the President. And he was not going to help any Indians remain east of the Mississippi!

The title of this painting is "The Trail of Tears." Why would the Cherokee Indians have given their westward move this sad name?

Chief Osceola of the Seminoles. He was captured when the Army broke its promise to observe a truce.

In 1838, after they had used up every possible delay, the Cherokees had to move west. The United States Army rounded up the tribe and moved it across the Mississippi. One-fourth of the Indians died along the way. Once in the West, they set up their own government, continued to use their own language and have remained together to this day. Some later returned to North Carolina, where Cherokees still live.

The Seminole Indians of Florida refused to move. Osceola, their chief, took part of his tribe into the swamps of the Everglades. For ten years the United States Army tried to capture Osceola and force the Seminoles out of Florida. Many Indians were captured, but the tribe fought on. The war cost twenty million dollars. Fifteen hundred United States soldiers were killed. Finally Osceola agreed to attend a truce conference. The Army had promised him he would be safe there while peace terms were discussed. Instead he was captured. His people did not give up. Finally the fighting slowly came to an end. The Seminoles remain in the Everglades today, still a proud people who have never made peace with the United States.

Some Voices of Justice. Most white leaders agreed that Indians had no rights. By the 1840's political speakers were telling

Seminole Indians remain in the Everglades today. How would you guess from this picture that they live in a warm climate? Compare their home with those on page 5.

Americans that they would sweep ahead in the West until they had settled all the land between the Atlantic and the Pacific. President John Quincy Adams did what he could to ease the problems of the Indians. However, he was the only President to defend their rights in any serious way. From time to time some minister or other leader might cry out that Indians should have rights and justice. Henry Clay, a leading member of the United States Senate, did speak out once against the stealing of Indian lands. It was wrong, he said. It showed no love of justice. It denied respect for the rights of others. It was reported that Clay's speech brought tears to the eyes of some Senators. However, they did not end their policy of Indian removal.

The promise by the United States government had been clear. The tribes could keep their new lands "as long as grass grows and water runs." Yet the promise proved false. The tribes were able to hold their new lands only until settlers again pushed west. The United States government then made its choice. The settlers were more important than the promise to the Indians. Let white settlers take the lands; force the Indians to give them up. Between 1853 and 1856 alone—only twenty years after the Indian Removal—United States officials made 52 new treaties with Indian tribes in the West. In each of these the Indians lost part or all of their land.

William H. Seward was governor of New York State in 1841. Seward spent most of his life in public service and was later a member of Abraham Lincoln's Cabinet. He saw what was being done to the Indians and cried out against it. Here are some thoughts he wrote in a letter on June 15, 1841.

Each nation has in its turn been surrounded and crowded by white men. White men have always wanted more room. . . . It is a fearful thing to uproot a whole people and send them, regardless of their own rights, interests, and welfare, their feelings and affections, into a distant and desolate region. . . . The removal of the Indians [is] a great crime against an unoffending and injured people.

I. WHAT ARE THE FACTS?

Answer each question in a sentence or two.

1. Who were the Paxton Boys?

2. What did the Paxton Boys do to six Conestoga Indians in 1763?

3. Why did the Paxton Boys attack these Indians?

4. What did Pontiac do after he united the tribes in 1762?

5. Explain Tecumseh's warning, "Divided we fall."

6. How did William Henry Harrison become a national hero?

7. When did the Indians lose their French and Spanish allies?

8. What decision did President Andrew Jackson make regarding the Indians in 1829?

9. How did Chief Black Hawk become the target of an Indian war?

10. Why was Osceola considered an enemy of the United States?

11. Explain the meaning of the phrase "as long as grass grows and water runs."

12. Explain one way in which Chief Sequoyah changed the life of the Cherokees.

13. What did Governor William H. Seward of New York say about the Indian Removal plan?

14. How did Henry Clay's statement about the Indians show that he agreed with William H. Seward?

15. How did treaty changes weaken the power of tribes on the reservations?

II. EXPLAINING WHY.

Why did each of these happen?

1. Indians often made fierce attacks on white settlements.

2. Pontiac could not keep his Indian armies together.

3. White settlers were permitted to move into Indian reservation land.

4. Andrew Jackson and Congress decided to "remove" all Indians to land west of the Mississippi.

5. The Cherokees tried to live like white men.

6. The Cherokees had to move, even though the Supreme Court had decided they had the right to remain on their land.

7. The Seminoles have never made peace with the United States.

8. Few political leaders in the United States defended the rights of the Indians.

9. The United States government changed its treaty agreements with Indian tribes.

10. William H. Seward opposed the Indian Removal plan.

III. THINKING IT THROUGH!

Discuss.

1. How good was Benjamin Franklin's argument against the hatred many frontiersmen held for the Indians? Why?

2. Why did the Indians take sides in the wars between European countries over control of North America?

3. Why did so many Indians die on the trip west in the 1830's?

4. Some people said that the Indians were in the way of progress. How did this idea seem to excuse the way Indians were treated?

5. Describe a motion picture or television program you have seen that takes the side of the white settlers in a conflict with Indians. Describe another that takes the side of the Indians. How much truth do you find in each story? Why?

How Were the Indian Tribes Destroyed?

3 The last massacre of American Indians took place at Wounded Knee, South Dakota, in 1890. Since then no Indian tribe has used force against the power of the United States government. Sitting Bull, leader of the Teton Dakotas, was 56 years old in 1890. For most of his life he had led Indian tribes who fought to keep their lands. He had been one of the leaders of the Indian army that wiped out Colonel George Custer's forces in 1876. Five years later he had agreed to take his people into a reservation. He had kept peace among the tribes from then on. "Keep the land," he had said. "Do not sell it to the white men." The tribes followed his advice. But by 1890 the frontier was gone. The only new lands white men could settle were those owned by the Indians.

In that year as well a new religious movement spread among Indians from Nevada to North Dakota. White men called it the Ghost Dance religion. It taught that the day would come when the white men would be gone. Then the Indians would own the land once more. The buffalo herds would return, and peace would arrive for all time. Those who accepted the new religion prayed and danced to show their hope for a better

"The Ghost Dance by the Ogallala Sioux," painted in 1890 by Frederic Remington. What is happening in the painting? What is the mood that is created?

future. They dressed in the old costumes—feathered headdresses, bows, spears—and danced the old dances until they were nearly fainting. Many reported that they had spoken to great dead heroes of the tribes during the long dances.

Some white leaders began to say that the ghost dancers were really preparing for a new Indian war. They were believed, and troops moved into the lands of the Sioux. Orders were given to arrest Sitting Bull. When he refused to go with the soldiers, he was killed. A large number of soldiers surrounded a group of Sioux at the Pine Ridge Reservation, near Wounded Knee. The Indians did not want to fight; they were cold, hungry and ragged. They surrendered on that cold December day without any hint of what would happen. The soldiers opened fire with cannon! Shells swept through the unarmed Sioux. The troops charged, killing men, women and children with rifle fire and bayonets. The United States government called this massacre "The Battle of Wounded Knee."

With Sitting Bull's death, religion and the old Indian pride seemed to die among all the Indian tribes. They were a completely defeated and destroyed people.

The death of Chief Sitting Bull. What does this painting tell you about the way he died?

What Is the Meaning of Genocide?
How Did Genocide Destroy the American Indians?
Why Did This Genocide Take Place?

The Meaning of Genocide. The United Nations began its work in 1945. World War II had just ended. Millions had been killed during the war because of their race, religion, culture or nationality. This was *genocide*, the murder of a people. In 1946 the United Nations agreed that genocide would from then on be a crime under international law. Since 1951 most of the countries in the world (but not the United States) have accepted an agreement to end genocide. They promised to pass laws to punish any persons who planned or carried out genocide against any group.

The memories of World War II were still fresh in 1951. Adolph Hitler and his Nazi Party in Germany had used genocide against all who opposed them. They had made and carried out a plan to kill every Jew they could find. Six million Jews—

men, women and children—had been shot, buried alive, starved to death, burned alive, gassed and killed in medical experiments. The Jews had been called enemies of Germany. They were placed in concentration camps—death camps where most of them died. The Nazis also killed six million other people who were not Jews. Some of these were labor leaders. Many were religious leaders who would not follow Nazi orders. Any person who did not accept the ideas of the Nazis could be sent to a camp. Few people left these camps alive. Between 1945 and 1950 many of the Nazi leaders who had ordered or carried out such "crimes against humanity" were sent to prison or hanged after public trials.

A Short History of Genocide. Genocide was not new. It had happened on every continent and in every century. Turkey had almost wiped out the Armenians in its lands. In 1890 this minority made plans to gain freedom. The Turks massacred about 200,000 Armenians between 1894 and 1896 alone. Troops attacked Armenian towns and villages without warning and killed everyone they found there. Massacres took place each time Armenians spoke out against the way they were treated. In 1915 the Turkish government made plans to get rid of all Armenians, and tens of thousands were killed.

Most cases of genocide in European history were begun to force people to accept the religion favored by a country's rulers. Many of these massacres were directed against Christians who opposed the Catholic Church. They took place in France, Germany, Spain, England, Czechoslovakia and Russia. Jews were killed in country after country for more than 1,500 years. Arab Muslims killed Christians or made them slaves for hundreds of years—chiefly in North Africa. Christians in their turn killed Muslims in the Crusades.

Genocide was a way to control conquered peoples in the ancient world. Rome defeated Carthage in a long, bitter war. The Romans then destroyed the city and killed or made slaves of all of its people. Many rulers treated conquered people in such ways. Mongols, Indian rulers, Chinese emperors, African kings, South American tribes—the list of those who have been guilty of genocide could go on and on.

The Only Good Indian. Genocide also destroyed the Indians. In the year 1500 there were more than a million Indians in the land that became the United States. By 1890, when the murder of Indians came to an end, there were only a little more than 200,000 left. They were killed by frontiersmen, by miners and settlers and chiefly by the United States Army. The Indians fought back as savagely as they could. Hatred between whites and Indians grew so fierce that Americans began to say, and believe, "The only good Indian is a dead Indian." Most Americans lived in the East. Newspapers there told daily tales of death caused by Indian attacks. They did not say much about the troubles white men brought to the Indians whose lands they wanted. As late as 1886 Theodore Roosevelt, later President of the United States, used these words in a speech in New York City: "I don't go so far as to think that the only good Indians are the dead Indians, but I believe nine out of every ten are, and I shouldn't like to inquire too closely into the case of the tenth."

The chief problem facing every Indian tribe was to hold the lands it had been promised in its treaties with the United States government. By 1860 most Indian leaders realized that the promises would not be kept. Settlers were pouring across the Mississippi and pushing west. Other white men were pushing east from California. Texas was filling with white men who had begun to move north toward Indian Territory—Oklahoma and parts of the states near it.

The Civil War began in 1861. It seemed to offer some hope to the Indians. Both sides in this war wanted help from the tribes. Indian armies could help win battles in the West. Indian scouts could find enemy forces and report on their movements. Some tribes joined the Northern armies; others fought for the South. A few of the tribes fought both sides. They wiped out settlements that could not be defended once soldiers were pulled east to fight in the war. The Civil War gave the Indians the guns and horses they needed to defend their own lands. Each side—Union and Confederacy—gave guns and supplies to those Indians who would agree to use them against the other side. For a while, the "good Indians" were the ones on your side!

The Battle of Pea Ridge. In the 1830's the Five Civilized Tribes (Cherokees, Chickasaws, Creeks, Choctaws and Seminoles) had been driven across the Mississippi from their homes in the South. Some of these Indians were rich slaveholders. Most were farmers or herdsmen. There were about 70,000 people in the tribes. They could raise an army of 10,000 men. The Confederacy promised them the right to keep their black slaves and their lands. It told them they could always rule themselves in their own ways. Most of the warriors of the Five Tribes, led by Chief Stand Watie, joined an army to fight for the South. Watie became a general in the Confederate Army. When the war ended in 1865, he was one of the last Southern officers to surrender.

Indian soldiers fought on both sides in the important Battle of Pea Ridge (Arkansas) in March, 1862. The Confederate armies lost this bitter battle. They would have been captured as well, except for the defense of their rear by the Indian horsemen under Stand Watie. Pea Ridge meant the end of Confederate hopes to hold the Southwest. Settlers from the North continued to move into Indian Territory in large numbers.

The Homestead Act. Congress passed a law in 1862 to give free land to those who would settle on it and remain there. A homestead is a farm owned by the family that farms it. The new law became known as the Homestead Act. It gave each new settler in the West 160 acres of land. This was one-fourth of a square mile. This meant that every four families of settlers would need a square mile of land. Four hundred families would take one hundred square miles! In less than thirty years all the land in the West had been settled. Much of this land belonged to the Indians. Part of it was open land on which great herds of buffalo had long roamed. Buffalo gave food, clothing, shelter and trade goods to the Indians of the Great Plains west of the Mississippi. White settlers quickly learned that the Indians on the plains could not make a living without the buffalo. Whole herds were destroyed, the animals left to rot in the sun after their hides had been removed for sale. Twenty years after the Civil War, the buffalo herds were almost gone.

Years Without Hope. One by one, the Indian tribes saw settlers, well armed and ready to kill, moving into their lands. They tried to keep the settlers out. The United States Army was supposed to help carry out the treaties that had promised these lands to the tribes. Most often these soldiers helped the settlers who had moved in. Indian agents were placed in charge of the reservations. It was their duty to help the Indians, and to keep

Shooting buffalo from a train was a popular sport around 1870. How must this slaughter have affected the Indians' food supply and way of life?

out the settlers. Many of them helped themselves instead. They ran trading posts in which Indians were cheated. They kept the supplies the government sent out for the tribes. They did not permit Indians to leave the reservations to hunt for food. Again and again Indians were ordered to camp near the agency trading posts, where troops forced them to remain for months at a time.

Many of the tribes had guns. They got some of them during the Civil War. They bought others from traders or Indian agents. The Indians had plenty of horses. With them they became great fighting horsemen. One tribe after another came to see

Sioux warriors of a South Dakota reservation plan a raid. What chance for success do you think they would have?

that there was little hope. They would soon lose their lands and homes. They met in council and decided to fight back. The fight was also without hope; the large armies of white men sent against them were better armed. The Indians could charge, but they had no defense against the early machine guns soon used by the Army. The Indians lost most battles, and then found themselves hunted by the stronger forces of the United States Army. Their chief victories came when an ambush took place, or when a large number of Indians could attack a small number of soldiers.

Chief Joseph and the Nez Percés. The first great Indian massacres came in the Northwest. Settlers in Oregon, Washington and Idaho, with Army aid, wiped out the power of the Indians in the Columbia River valley after 1855. Many of the chiefs were killed. Their people were then placed on small reservations, while white people took their lands.

The best known of the Northwest tribes was the Nez Percés, led by Chief Joseph. In 1863 some Nez Percé chiefs were tricked by government agents and agreed to give up most of the tribe's lands. Chief Joseph and some other chiefs would not accept this new treaty. They refused to move their people to the small new reservations set up for them. In 1877 the United States Army went to war against the Nez Percés. The Indians fought their way north from Idaho into northern Montana. A battle took place in the Bear Paw Mountains. The Nez Percés were defeated; most of their chiefs were killed. Chief Joseph decided to surrender. His words at that time help us understand how hopeless the Indian fight had become.

> I am tired of fighting. Our chiefs are killed. . . . The old men are all dead. It is the young men who say yes or no. He who led the young men is dead. It is cold and we have no blankets. The little children are freezing to death. My people, some of them, have run away to the hills, and have no blankets, no food; no one knows where they are—perhaps freezing to death. I want to have time to look for my children and see how many I can find. Maybe I shall find them among the dead. Hear me, my chiefs, I am tired; my heart is sick and sad. From where the sun now stands I will fight no more forever.

Chief Joseph of the Nez Percés. ". . . I am tired; my heart is sick and sad. From where the sun now stands I will fight no more forever."

From Texas to California. The land from Texas to California is called the Southwest. The most important tribes there were the Comanches, Kiowas and Apaches. These tribes refused to give up any of their land. Texas gained its independence from Mexico in 1836. Twelve years later the rest of the Southwest was taken from Mexico. War against the Indians followed. White men pushed west, as the Indians fought back from mountains and desert. The plan of the United States government was to place as many tribes as possible in the large area then called Indian Territory. Most of this territory later became the state of Oklahoma. Chief Quanah Parker became the most important leader as the Indians of the Southwest fought to keep their lands. By 1867 the tribes had been defeated and moved into reservations in Indian Territory.

In 1848 gold was discovered in California. White settlers poured in. Miners and armed farmers massacred village after village, taking Indian lands simply by killing the Indians. In the 1850's alone, 70,000 California Indians were killed by such murders, by disease and by forced slave labor in mines. The remaining Indians were placed on small desert reservations. Thousands more soon died there.

The Apache Indians kept white men out of most of Arizona. Its mountains are rugged and gave Indians bands good hiding places. Apache chiefs fought to keep their lands from 1862 until 1871. The two most important chiefs, Mangas Colaradas and Cochise, learned that their men could fight on and on if they were divided into small groups. Apache raids kept settlers out of most of Arizona for years. The attacks were as savage as the Indians could make them. The United States Army also learned to fight in small groups. It used its greater numbers to track and defeat one Apache band after another. Mangas Colaradas was killed by the Army when he agreed to meet for a peace talk. Cochise finally surrendered and led his people to their reservations. Later, Apache chiefs such as Geronimo, who could not accept life on a reservation, broke out and raided settlements from mountain hideouts for years. In the end all of these war chiefs were killed or captured.

From Colorado to Minnesota. The Cheyenne and Sioux were the most important tribes in the land north of Indian Territory. They had fought short wars against the Army and the settlers but had usually pulled back to lands farther west. In 1864 the Cheyenne came to Sand Creek, Colorado, prepared to make a lasting peace. There, a colonel hoping for glory attacked them. About 300 men, women and children were killed. The news of this massacre spread among the Sioux; they decided to go to war. Red Cloud, chief of the Sioux, refused to permit a new trail to be built through his lands. Sioux and Cheyenne fighting men fought the Army for two years. Red Cloud then agreed to place his people on a reservation so that his remaining men would not be killed. A few weeks after Red Cloud signed a peace treaty, Colonel George Custer massacred a Cheyenne tribe in Indian Territory.

The Last Great Indian War. The Black Hills of South Dakota had been promised to the Sioux in their peace treaty. But in 1874 gold was discovered in this sacred Indian land. Colonel

The Apache chief Geronimo raided settlements for years until his capture. What does his face reveal about the kind of life he led?

Custer's massacre of the
Cheyenne at the Washita
River took place a few weeks
after the signing of a peace
treaty.

George Custer became the Army commander in the area. He
did not keep the miners out. Soon they were fighting the
Indians. Custer's men helped protect the miners. It seemed a
new Indian war would begin at any moment.

How was this war to be prevented? The United States government ordered all Indians to move to the agency posts. Those
who did not would be considered to be at war with the United
States. Army groups were sent out to make all Indians move
to the agencies and forts without delay. The Cheyenne and
Sioux leaders knew that they would lose their lands once they
moved their men out of the hills. The chiefs met and agreed
that they had to fight. Chief Sitting Bull made the plans for
this last great defense. Chief Crazy Horse, his general, led the
Indian armies to war.

Crazy Horse knew the hills and mountains better than the
Army did. He gained some victories, even though his men could
not match the power of the large Army groups sent against
him. One of these victories was the killing of Custer and about
225 of his men in the short battle called "Custer's Last Stand."

The Battle of the Little Big
Horn, known as "Custer's Last
Stand," was one of the few
Indian victories. From this
painting, can you tell why the
Indians won?

After this battle the full power of the United States Army was organized to destroy the tribes. Crazy Horse surrendered in 1877. A few months later a soldier killed him. He is remembered as the last and perhaps the greatest of Indian military leaders.

The Cheyenne were placed on poor reservation land in Indian Territory. They decided to return to their own homes in Montana in 1878. They moved north for months, fighting off the armies of soldiers sent to make them return. When the Army did catch up with them, most of the Cheyenne were massacred. Indian hopes for fair treatment had been crushed again. For the next ten years most Indians suffered on their reservations. The last blow came when their new religion was viewed as a danger by the white men. Then Sitting Bull was murdered in 1890, and the Sioux were massacred at Wounded Knee, South Dakota. The American Indians had been destroyed as a people.

A Voice for Justice. The Indian wars had lasted for more than 200 years. Most white people in the United States had come to hate all Indians. Thousands of soldiers volunteered to serve in the Army units that massacred hundreds of thousands of Indians. White men might remember a friend or relative who had once suffered in an Indian attack. Many of the soldiers after 1865 were black freedmen. Some of them may have entered the Army because they knew some Indians held black people as slaves. Others may have joined because the Army gave a secure life at a time when so many freedmen were starving. Many Indians worked for the Army, as scouts or soldiers. They often joined to fight old enemies of their own tribes. The Army killed Indians in battle, by massacre, by planned starvation and sometimes by the accidental spreading of disease.

Helen Hunt Jackson was one of many Americans who were shocked by this genocide. She wrote a book in 1881, *A Century of Dishonor*, in which she described what had been done to the Indians. She reported that there were only about 250,000 Indians still alive. Most were on reservations; a small number were in the few places not yet settled by white men. There they lived by hunting and fishing. This was all that remained of a proud people who had once held all the land in the United States!

It makes little difference . . . where one opens the record of the history of the Indians; every page and every year has its dark stain. The story of one tribe is the story of all, varied only by differences of time and place; but neither time nor place makes any difference in the main facts.

What had happened? Mrs. Jackson took the story from a report made to President Grant. He had set up a commission to study Indian problems in 1869. Here are some of the findings of this group:

> The history of the government connections with the Indians is a shameful record of broken promises and unfulfilled promises. The history of the border white man's connection with the Indians is a sickening record of murder, outrage, robbery, and wrongs committed by the [white men] as the rule, and occasional savage outbreaks and unspeakably barbarous deeds of [revenge] by the [Indians] . . .
>
> . . . in our Indian wars, almost without exception, the first [attacks] have been made by the white man . . .
>
> . . . there is a large class of . . . men who use every means in their power to bring on Indian wars for the sake of the profit to be realized from the presence of troops and the [spending] of government funds in their midst. They [call for] death to the Indian at all times in words and publications, making no distinction between the innocent and the guilty.
>
> . . . Every crime committed by a white man against an Indian is [not punished]. Every offense committed by an Indian against a white man is borne on the wings of the [mails] or the telegraph to the remotest corner of the land, clothed with all the horrors which the reality or imagination can throw around it.

The Secretary of the Interior in the President's Cabinet was in charge of the Bureau of Indian Affairs. Carl Schurz held this post in 1881. In that year he presented the government's defense to the kind of attack made by Helen Hunt Jackson and others. Here are the ideas he used to explain what had happened to the Indians.

— The government had not planned the Indian wars. They came because there was no way to prevent white men from moving into Indian lands.
— The United States had made a great mistake when it promised the tribes that they could keep their lands forever.
— The government had no choice except to attack Indians who attacked settlers. Indians were placed on ever smaller reservations because white men needed their land.

Secretary of the Interior Carl Schurz felt the government had no other choice but to conduct the Indian Wars and Removal program. Do you agree? What might it have done instead?

— Now it was time to make the Indians give up the remaining reservations. They had to become farmers, learn the way of life of the white men and then become American citizens.

Few Indians were ready to accept such changes in 1881. Ten years later, with their last great leaders gone and their military power only a memory, they had no choice. Genocide had ended their strength as a people. Long years of war and suffering had killed most of their culture. Now the power of the United States government would be used to take away their very right to remain Indians.

I. WHAT ARE THE FACTS?

In each group below, match the event in COLUMN A with its cause in COLUMN B.

COLUMN A

1. The Sioux and Dakotas refused to sell their land because . . .
2. The United Nations decided to make genocide a crime because . . .
3. Indian tribes took sides in the Civil War because . . .
4. Indians rarely defeated soldiers in battle because . . .
5. Chief Joseph decided never to fight again because . . .

COLUMN B

a) . . . they hoped to keep their lands and freedom.
b) . . . they could not win against machine guns and cannon.
c) . . . millions had been killed because of their race or religion.
d) . . . they followed Sitting Bull's advice.
e) . . . the Nez Percés had been completely defeated.

6. California's Indians were killed because . . .
7. Indians thought of Colonel George Custer as their enemy because . . .
8. The stories of Sitting Bull, Mangas Colaradas and Crazy Horse ended in the same way, because . . .
9. Many black freedmen fought the Indians because . . .
10. Many white men wanted Indian wars because . . .

f) . . . they were killed by soldiers during a truce or in a time of peace.
g) . . . they made profits from the wars.
h) . . . he massacred a peaceful tribe.
i) . . . some Indians were slaveholders.
j) . . . white farmers and miners wanted their land.

II. PEOPLE, TIMES AND PLACES.

Answer each question in a sentence.

1. In what year did the last massacre of Indians take place? Where?

2. What tribe was led by Sitting Bull?

3. What American leader was killed by Indians led by Chief Crazy Horse?

4. Why did Adolph Hitler use genocide as a weapon in the 1930's and 1940's?

5. How many people were killed by Nazi genocide?

6. What opinion did Theodore Roosevelt hold about Indians?

7. In what part of the United States had the Five Civilized Tribes been forced to settle?

8. What group of Indian tribes held black slaves?

9. Name one Indian who became a general in the Confederate army during the Civil War.

10. What state has been made from the land once called Indian Territory?

11. From what country did Texas gain its independence?

12. What tribe was led by Cochise?

13. When was the last great Indian war?

14. Who was the author of A *Century of Dishonor?*

15. Who was President of the United States in 1869?

III. THINKING IT THROUGH!

Discuss.

1. *The events of the last few years show that genocide is still used by some countries or groups as a way to control people.* How true would this statement be if applied to Southeast Asia (Vietnam, Laos, Cambodia), Nigeria (Biafra) and Communist China (Tibet)? Before

discussing this question, check recent events in each of these countries in encyclopedia yearbooks.

2. What might explain the failure of the United States to sign the United Nations convention against genocide?

3. Why do many people say that slavery was a kind of genocide against black Africans?

4. Why has genocide continued in the world, even though it is recognized as organized murder?

5. Describe any conversations you have heard in which people have suggested that a group of people should suffer because of their race, religion or beliefs. Why do some people feel this way?

6. Show how the Homestead Act benefited some people while harming others.

7. Why do most Americans believe it was the Indians who were at fault in most of the Indian wars?

8. Why did so many thousands of Americans volunteer to fight in the United States Army against the Indians?

What Rights Did Reservation Indians Have?

4 The land west of the Mississippi was divided into territories. Each territory later became one or two states. Each territory sent a delegate to the House of Representatives in Washington. These men took part in the work of the House but did not have a vote. However, their speeches on topics like the Indian problem were important. They came from the West. They knew such problems from their own experience. But they did not always agree on what the problems were.

The House heard many such speeches in 1869 and 1870. Some Western delegates wanted to see all Indians destroyed. Others called for justice and fair treatment for the tribes. W. A. Burleigh, delegate from Dakota Territory, told the House, "We have hunted them down and murdered them like wild beasts of the forest." It was time to end such actions. "Instead of sending soldiers, let us send food and clothing." R. C. McCormick, Arizona's delegate, would have none of this kindness. He wanted Congress to take away all reservation lands. The tribes had no right to keep any property from which white men could benefit. The "mineral, agricultural and pastoral wealth" of the reservations was needed, he said, to make the United States a richer nation.

The United States in 1870. In what ways do you think territories were different from states?

The Indians had no real voice in Congress. They could do nothing against the power of the white armies that forced them from place to place. During the last Indian wars, which brought tribe after tribe to destruction, a song spread among the tribes. Translated into English, it gives some idea of the pain they suffered.

O why does the white man follow my path
Like the hound on the wildcat's track?
Does the dust on my cheek make him angry?
Does he want the bow at my back?
He has rivers and seas where the waves and winds
Bring riches for him alone.
And we sons of the wood never seek land or water
Which the white man calls his own.

What Was Life Like on the Reservations?

How Did the United States Government Treat the Tribes?

Size of the Reservations. By 1880 most of the Indians had been defeated and placed on reservations. Each of these areas was "reserved" for Indians only. Sometimes a large tribe was placed on two or more reservations. Sometimes several small tribes shared one reservation. There were then between 250,000 and 300,000 Indians still alive.

Most of the reservations were in the Southwest—Oklahoma, Arizona, New Mexico, Nevada and Utah. Others were scattered through other western states and territories. The tribes were often given large stretches of land, though it was usually unfit for farming. In 1887 the total amount of reservation land was more than 230,000 square miles. This was more than one-twelfth of all the land then in the United States.

Most of the Indians placed on reservations felt that they had been put into a kind of prison. They were on poor land that they could not leave. They were in great camps where they could never improve their lives. The land of a reservation belonged to the tribe, not to each Indian who lived on a part of it. Some of the reservations were very large. The Navaho tribe held about 25,000 square miles. This was half the size of New York State. However, almost all of this land was desert. Some reservations were tiny—only a few acres! By the 1880's

most of the tribes were small. Some were left with only two or three hundred people. A few tribes still had thousands. The number of reservations changed from year to year, as tribes were again and again forced to move. Today there are about 300 areas still held by Indian tribes.

A group of homes on a Hopi reservation. What is the land like? Would you like to live here?

Life on the Reservations. Each reservation was a little different from every other. Yet all were alike in some ways. Each was under the control of an official of the United States government. These men were sent by the Department of the Interior and were under the orders of the Department of Indian Affairs (now called the Bureau of Indian Affairs). Most of these "Indian agents" had a small staff to aid them. Each reservation had its government clerks, blacksmiths, farmers to train the Indians, telegraph operators, one or more postmasters and a doctor. The Indian agent was in complete charge. He gave the orders and carried them out. He had power as judge and jury over the Indians. When he wanted it, he had the help of United States Army troops on or near the reservation.

It was each agent's job to keep peace on his reservation. Most of them did this well. Yet they had so much power that many wrongs took place. Indians did not always obey orders they believed were wrong, or that they did not understand. The agent could then put them in prison, and they could not appeal his decision. An agent could break up a family by ordering a father to move to another part of the reservation, or by ordering children sent to special schools. No matter how much land a reservation contained, only the agent could decide where each Indian could live.

Most of the agents had had no experience with Indians. They got their positions because they had political friends in Washington. Such agents did not understand the many differences between the cultures and ways of living of Indians and white men. Many agents saw their jobs as ways to grow rich quickly. The government would send them money to buy supplies, food, horses, cattle and farming equipment for their Indians, and to build roads or buildings on the reservation. Agents often stole much of this money. Each agent was allowed to set up trading posts where Indians could buy and sell goods. An agent might put his friends in charge of these posts, or sell them the right to open stores. The traders could then charge high prices, or steal from the Indians who traded with them. They could refuse to pay for goods made by Indian craftsmen—and then escape punishment. The same agent who protected them would receive part of the profits. Most agents left their jobs after a few years and returned to the East as rich men.

Congress seemed to want the Indian problem to disappear. It hoped this would happen if the Indians lived and acted like white men. Agents tried to get tribes to build houses and live in them. They tried to get Indians to wear white men's clothing. They ordered Indian men to cut their hair (although most of them refused to do so). Indian men were told to become farmers. This might have eased the problem of feeding their families. But few of them accepted this order. They had lived so long by hunting that many starved rather than do the "women's work" of farming.

Inside the trading post on a Navaho reservation in Arizona. Why do you think reservations have their own stores?

Indians felt much as black slaves had felt when they first arrived in the New World. They were powerless. They had once lived freely, had traveled where they wished and had known that the tribe would help care for any member in need. Now they were being forced into a new way of life. Rules were being made that they hated and often did not understand. Some Indians killed themselves rather than live under such rules. Some ran away from the reservations. They became "bandits" and were hunted down and killed by the Army. Many became ill of the diseases brought by the white men who ran the agencies. Tuberculosis, for example, spread through many tribes and killed thousands.

Each tribe still chose its own leaders. These men tried to keep the tribe together. They spoke for the tribe when an agent did wrong. Sometimes chiefs even went to Washington to ask for needed changes on their reservations. They kept the old

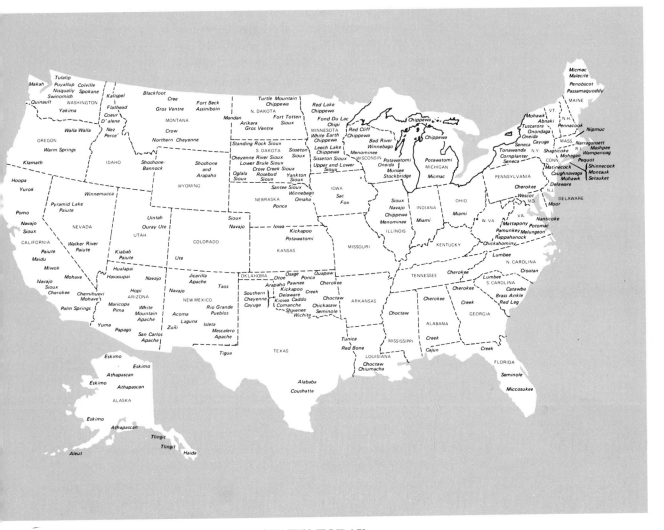

INDIAN TRIBES IN THE UNITED STATES TODAY.
How many are here? Which ones are familiar to you?

religions and customs when they could, even when agents brought in Christian missionaries to convert them. No chief could do much to improve the way his tribe lived; he did what he could to help it stay alive.

Congress and the Reservations. Many political leaders hoped to get the reservation lands for white settlers. Members of Congress from the South opposed most plans to improve the lives of reservation Indians. Jim Crow laws in the South, and Jim Crow customs in other parts of the country, were directed against

Indians as much as against black Americans. The racism that made white men hate Indians for more than two hundred years remained alive as late as the 1920's. It is alive in some areas today. No President of the United States did much to change the way reservation Indians were treated until the 1930's. Instead Congress voted money to keep the reservation system as it was, and the Presidents then signed the laws. Some of these laws did help Indians who needed food and clothing. The laws also helped Indians against white settlers who continued to steal tribal lands. However, there was no change in the fact that Indians were treated as a conquered people.

The Dawes Act. In 1887 Congress passed a law that it expected would break up most of the reservations. The law took reservation land and divided it into "farms." Any Indian man who agreed to leave his tribe could receive 160 acres of land. He could receive eighty more acres for each of his young children. An Indian with two children could in this way receive half a square mile of land. If he remained on the land for 25 years, it would become his to sell or keep as he wished. After all the men of a tribe received their land, the remaining land of the reservation could be sold to settlers by the government.

Many of the members of Congress who voted for the Dawes Act believed they were helping the Indians. They thought the law would help make each Indian more like other Americans. The Indians did not agree. They were not farmers and did not want to become farmers. The land they received was not good farmland anyway. Many of them rented their land to white men at once and remained even poorer than they had been on the reservations. Once the land was legally theirs, most of them sold it quickly. Many signed sale agreements while they were drunk and received little or nothing for their land. Indians who had been cheated of their land had no real protection. The judges before whom they appeared almost always ruled against them. In one way or another, the ownership of land Indians received under the Dawes Act passed into the hands of white men. By 1932, 45 years after the law was passed, they had lost almost two-thirds of all the land the law had given them.

Suffering and Poverty. Life on the reservation was marked by great poverty. Indians had little except what the government might give them. Most of them refused to learn English. They

not true

did not want and rarely received schooling. Each year a few thousand boys and girls were sent to "Indian schools," where they were taught English and other subjects thought important to make them give up their old ways of living. Most of these children left school as soon as they could. Their different culture made most of what they were taught meaningless to them. However, in time each reservation had a group of Indians who could speak English well enough to speak for their tribe in its dealings with the agent. Some tribes used these "educated" Indians in tribal police forces, as traders for others and as teachers of trades they had learned in the schools.

Poverty has forced thousands of Indians in the Southwest to live in "pit houses" such as these.

pit houses? hogan natural house for desert

Most Indians stayed on or near the old reservation lands. The largest number of Indians lived in the Southwest. There white man's customs kept them from most kinds of work. They became the poorest group of people in the United States. As late as the 1950's most Indian families earned an average of only $20 a week; many earned less. States often kept them from relief aid. In states such as Arizona and New Mexico, thousands of Indians have had to live in "pit houses"—holes dug in the ground covered by a roof reaching a few feet above the soil. Others have lived in tents or wooden shacks. Whole reservations remained without electricity. Indians had to shop in stores on the reservations, where they paid high prices. When they tried to shop in nearby towns, storekeepers cheated them or refused to sell to them.

Escaping the Tribe's Problems. The Indian had no rights. He might leave the tribe and try to live in a town or city. There he found himself at the mercy of any white man. He was not a citizen. It was 1924 before the United States made him a citizen, and 1948 before the last state agreed he was one. The Fourteenth Amendment to the United States Constitution stated that all persons born in the United States and under its laws and control were citizens of the United States and their states. The Fifteenth Amendment declared that the right of citizens to vote could not be denied because of their race or color. It seemed to many Indians that they therefore could become the equal of other Americans once they left the reservation. Didn't the Constitution protect them as it protected others?

Many Indians tried to escape the problems they knew on the reservations. One of these was named John Elk. He moved to Omaha, Nebraska. There he found work and a place to live. He learned to speak English well and got along well with the white people around him. In April, 1880, John Elk wanted to vote in the town's elections. He was told no Indian could register. When he later tried to vote, he was prevented from doing so. John Elk then sued Charles Wilkins, the official who had kept him from voting. In 1884 the case of *Elk v. Wilkins* came to the United States Supreme Court.

The Court agreed with Mr. Wilkins. John Elk was not a citizen. He could not even become a citizen. This is what the court said:

—Indians are born in the United States. However, they are ruled by their tribe, not by the United States. They owe their allegiance only to the tribe.
—They are like the children of foreign visitors to the United States who are born here.
—The only way John Elk could become a citizen would be for Congress to pass a law setting up ways to make Indians citizens, or by a treaty that agreed they were citizens.

Justice John Harlan dissented from this decision. He stated that John Elk had every right to be a citizen, for he had been born in the United States and, like every other Indian, he was certainly under the control of the United States government. These facts made him a citizen of the United States and also of Nebraska.

Forty years later Congress passed the law the Supreme Court had said was necessary. The 1924 Indian Citizenship Act was one of the shortest laws ever passed by Congress. Some states had agreed to treat Indians as citizens. Now the United States government would do so as well.

> *Be it enacted* . . . That all non-citizen Indians born within the territorial limits of the United States be, and they are hereby declared to be, citizens of the United States; Provided, That the granting of such citizenship shall not in any manner impair or otherwise affect the right of any Indian to tribal or other property.

Some Americans saw this law as a joke. They laughed at political leaders who called the Act a great democratic gift to the Indians. When Columbus first came to the New World, it had been the Indians who greeted him. Now, more than 400 years later, the United States had finally agreed that Indians were Americans!

I. WHAT ARE THE FACTS?

Write the letter of the choice that best completes each statement.

1. Most of the Indian tribes had been placed on reservations by (a) 1800, (b) 1840, (c) 1880.

2. The word "reservation" describes (a) land, (b) a treaty, (c) a tribe.

3. Between 1800 and 1880 the number of Indians in the United States (a) grew larger, (b) remained the same, (c) grew smaller.

4. Most Indians were forced to live in the (a) Rocky Mountains, (b) Southwest, (c) Mississippi Valley.

5. The most important task of an Indian agent in 1880 was to (a) teach English to Indians, (b) keep peace on the reservation, (c) help white settlers find land in the reservation.

6. Few Indian men became farmers because (a) they knew nothing

about farming, (b) they thought farming was "women's work," (c) Indian agents did not permit them to farm.

7. Indian chiefs on reservations had (a) more power than agents, (b) the same power as agents, (c) less power than agents.

8. Until the 1930's, most Indian tribes were treated as (a) conquered people, (b) equals with the rights of citizens, (c) prisoners of war.

9. The Dawes Act gave Indians who left their tribes (a) money, (b) land, (c) cattle.

10. Most young Indians refused to continue their education in government schools because the work was (a) too hard for them, (b) too easy for them, (c) without interest or meaning to them.

11. Today most Indians in the United States are (a) members of the middle class, (b) among the poorest Americans, (c) richer than other minority groups.

12. Congress made Indians United States citizens in (a) 1887, (b) 1924, (c) 1970.

13. John Elk never voted because he (a) could not read or write, (b) lived on a reservation, (c) was an Indian.

14. Many Indians were jailed because they (a) did not understand the rules made by Indian agents, (b) killed Indian agents, (c) had no money.

15. The poor treatment of reservation Indians continued because (a) they never told Congress their problems, (b) Indian leaders grew rich by sharing power with Indian agents, (c) Congress would not pass laws to protect Indian rights.

II. WHAT DO THEY MEAN?

Explain the meaning of each of these words or phrases in a sentence or two.

1. the Indian problem
2. pastoral wealth
3. "sons of the wood"
4. Department of the Interior
5. trading post
6. bandit
7. tribal police force
8. pit house

III. THINKING IT THROUGH!

Discuss.

1. Why was life on the reservations between 1880 and 1900 called "hopeless"?

2. How did the Dawes Act help Indians? How did it harm them?

3. In 1883 the United States Supreme Court ended the Civil Rights laws passed during Reconstruction. In 1884 it decided John Elk was not a citizen under the 14th and 15th Amendments. In 1896 it approved Jim Crow laws through the Plessy decision. What do these decisions tell you about the Supreme Court's view of equal rights during these years?

4. Why did it take the United States government until 1924 to make Indians American citizens?

What Problems Do American Indians Still Face Today?

5 The President of the United States sends a message to Congress each year in which he discusses the country's problems and needs. Part of Lyndon B. Johnson's 1967 message told of the conditions Indians lived with each day of their lives. The President reminded Congress that Indians had been forced to become "strangers" in their own land. After two hundred years of poor treatment, they were the poorest of all Americans. One-third of them did not even have fit homes. Many had to live in "huts, shanties, even abandoned automobiles." Two of every five Indians had no jobs—"more than ten times the national average." Half of all Indian children dropped out before completing high school. Great numbers had never learned how to read and write. Their "rates of sickness and poverty are among the highest." Life was so hard on the reservations that thousands of Indians had left their tribes and families to move to the cities. There, however, they found themselves "untrained for jobs and unprepared for urban life."

How Has the United States Government Tried to Help the Indians?

What Have the Indians Themselves Done to Solve Their Problems?

What Problems Keep Indians from Improving Their Way of Life?

The Allotment Policy. The Dawes Act of 1887 was the beginning of a government plan to break up the tribes. Each Indian would be turned into a farmer. When he left his tribe, he received land (called an *allotment*). We have seen how most Indian farmers later lost their land. This meant that by the 1920's tens of thousands of Indian families had no land and no jobs. They did not even have the help they might have received if they were still with their tribes. Many of them starved. Men without work or hope turned to drink. Drunkenness be-

An Indian home on an Arizona reservation. Why do you think there are so many water containers? How might such conditions affect the health of the family who lives here?

came a serious Indian problem—so bad that laws were passed in state after state making it a crime to sell liquor to any Indian.

Those Indians who kept their farms made poor livings. They never had the money for tools or modern farming equipment. In 1970 many of them were still pulling simple plows by hand or with the help of one or two farm animals. They were lucky to grow enough to feed their families. They never had money for proper clothing, medical care or better housing. The diseases that come with poverty hit them harder than most other Americans. Tuberculosis is under control in most of our country. It still kills thousands of Indians or destroys their health each year.

Many Indians came to believe that their lives would improve if they had the same rights other citizens enjoyed. They became citizens of the United States by an act of Congress in 1924. Perhaps if they could vote in their state elections they could use that power to gain better treatment. But they soon discovered that they could not have the rights of citizens unless the white people who ruled their state agreed. Most states quickly passed laws to give Indians more rights. Arizona was one of those that refused. Two important court cases, twenty years apart, spelled out the problem.

Gaining the Right to Vote. The case of *Porter v. Hall* was decided by the Supreme Court of Arizona in 1928. Peter H. Porter and Rudolph Johnson were Indians who tried to register to vote. Mattie Hall, the election official, refused to register them. The two men were citizens of the United States. They had always lived in Arizona. They could read and write and could pass any test for voters. The court admitted these facts but said that the two Indians could not vote because they were Indians.

The United States government had treated defeated Indians as "wards" of the country. This meant that they did not have the same rights any adult American could have—to own land, to sue in court, to make legal agreements, to decide how to make a living or where to live. The Arizona court said that Indians were therefore not really full citizens. No Indian could vote so long as he was not a full citizen.

It was 1948 before Arizona's Indians did gain the right to vote. Frank Harrison and Harry Austin were Apaches who lived on a reservation. Roger Laveen, an election official, would not permit them to register. A new court case followed—*Harrison v. Laveen*. This time the Supreme Court of Arizona held a different view about Indians. Frank Harrison was one of the 25,000 Indians who had fought for the United States during World War II. Many of these men had won awards for their bravery. Ira Hamilton Hayes of Arizona had become a national hero; he was one of the squad of men who raised the American flag on the Japanese island of Iwo Jima. Ernest Childers and Jack Montgomery received Congress' Medal of Honor. Indian soldiers had been important members of radio teams. They had used Indian languages to send messages between army groups. American generals never had to worry about an enemy hearing such messages, for only the members of the same tribe could understand what they meant!

The state court in Arizona agreed that men like Frank Harrison should no longer be treated as second-class citizens. They and all other Indians had earned the right to vote. People who had served their country so well could not be kept "wards" of the government, without the same rights other

"Raising the Flag on Iwo Jima," a statue in Washington, D.C. One of the soldiers it honors was Indian Ira Hamilton Hayes.

Americans had. The court reversed its earlier rule. Since 1948 every Indian in the United States has been able to vote in state elections.

New Laws in the 1930's. Indians had gained from President Franklin D. Roosevelt's New Deal laws. In 1934 an Indian Reorganization Act was passed. It tried to end the allotment policy of the Dawes Act. The tribes would be helped to keep their reservation lands. Some of the land that had been taken from them would be returned. Each tribe could set up its own government, like a town or county government, on the reservation. Led by the Navahos and Apaches, tribes learned how to set up their own tribal councils. Such a council ran businesses that gave jobs to Indians on its reservation. It opened courts that heard the cases Indians brought to them. Tribal police systems enforced the laws made by the council. Some councils provided relief for the poorest members of their tribes. In other words, these were real governments that had the power of governments, even though Indian agents remained "in charge" of the reservations. Chee Dodge, first chairman of the Navaho Council, kept in touch with other tribes, trying to get them to follow the lead of his people.

B.S. had to based on fed. gov't.

tribal council decisions are still approved by agent

53

Chee Dodge, "head chief of the Navahos" and first chairman of the Navaho Council.

The Navahos were the most successful in bringing the modern world to their people. They began to use a new alphabet. They printed newspapers and worked to teach every Navaho to read and write. Many Navahos had long refused to learn English; they were ready to learn to read and write in their own language. Chee Dodge had to teach his people to be concerned about the politics of Indian life. One of his ideas was the use of pictures and Indian signs in elections, so that people who were not able to read were still able to vote.

John Collier was Indian Commissioner in the Department of the Interior from 1933 until 1946. He helped the country's Indians form their first truly national group. It was called the National Congress of American Indians. Since 1944 it has given the Indians a single voice to which Congress had to listen.

The Termination Policy. World War II marked an end to the spending of large amounts of government money to aid the Indians. The war was so costly that Congress cut down its spending on most minority-group needs. Without such aid, the tribes had to lessen their self-help activities. Their people were too poor to improve their lives without outside help. New problems began to face the tribes after 1946.

World War II had cut down foreign supplies of oil. Oil companies explored every part of the United States in the search for oil and other mineral wealth. They found great deposits of oil and other resources on reservation lands. Congress decided to open these lands to oil drilling. The Hopi Indians of Arizona held some of the richest oil lands. They knew that oil companies could destroy their farmland and grazing land. In 1949 the chiefs of the Hopi sent a letter to President Truman telling how shocked they were at this termination, or ending, of their rights in their own lands. The ideas in the letter also show how much the Indians considered the United States to be an enemy rather than a friend.

— This land is a sacred home of the Hopi people and all the Indian Race in this land. . . . We are still a sovereign [self-ruling] nation. Our flag still flies throughout our land. . . . We have never [given up] our sovereignty to any foreign power or nation. We've been self-governing people long before any white man came to our shores.

—We will not ask a white man, who came to us recently, for a piece of land that is already ours. We think that white people should be thinking about asking for a permit to build their homes upon our land.

—Neither will we lease any part of our land for oil development at this time. This land is not for leasing or for sale. This is our sacred soil. . . . Any prospecting, drilling and leasing of our land that is being done is without our knowledge and consent.

—Are you ever going to be satisfied with all the wealth you have now because of us, the Indians? There is something terribly wrong with your system of government because after all these years, we, the Indians, are still licking on the bones and crumbs that fall to us from your tables. . . . Have the American people, white people, forgotten the treaties with the Indians?

—All the laws under the Constitution of the United States were made without our consent, knowledge and approval, yet we are being forced to [accept them].

The termination policy was a way to end the self-government of the tribes. It became the official policy of the government under Presidents Truman and Eisenhower during the 1950's. Federal aid to Indian tribes came to an end. State governments received the power to rule over their state's Indians. These state governments quickly gave control of the resources on the reservations to white-owned corporations. The companies stripped away valuable wealth on the land that Indians had preserved. In Oregon the Klamath tribe had protected the great forests on their reservation. They soon found private lumber companies cutting the trees and destroying the forests. This and other tribes received little from the use of their lands. They might get some payment, which they could then divide among the members of the tribe or use for tribal projects. Just as often they received little or nothing unless they were able to win long, expensive lawsuits.

The termination policy tried to break up the tribes. The Indian Bureau sent thousands of Indian families to the cities. An Indian man might be trained for some trade. The Bureau found him a job and a place to live in a large city. However, its interest in him and his family then seemed to end. Some Indians succeeded in the cities; there they became much like

Relocation

other Americans. New York State's Iroquois tribes were soon providing the country's best "high steel" bridge and construction workers. Those men never seem to lose their balance on the most dangerous high construction jobs. They receive high pay for this work. Today they are among the most desired of all construction workers. Some Indians have found that their skill with their hands makes them valuable in jobs requiring delicate handling of small tools. They have gained good jobs in the electronics industry. But other Indian workers, without special skills, soon found themselves out of work. They were treated as members of minority groups have long been treated in the big cities. They became the last hired and the first fired. Many of them found their reservations had been broken up under the termination policy. They had to remain in the cities, where they became part of the unemployed poor living on welfare aid.

One part of the termination policy did help some Indians. A government commission was set up in 1947 to hear Indian claims for payment for lost lands and rights. In its first ten years it paid Indian tribes $40,000,000. This money helped keep many of the tribes from breaking up. These payments have continued. In 1964, for example, Indian tribes received more than $38,000,000 to settle claims against the United States. The Navaho tribe is the largest in the United States today. Its 125,000 members have gained most from the work of the claims commission. Some tribes have received little or nothing.

Changes Under President Kennedy. Presidents John F. Kennedy and Lyndon B. Johnson tried to end the termination policy. However, they did not end the leases and sales of land that had already weakened the tribes. Instead, they had companies pay more money for the use of Indian land. The weakened tribal councils did not always use this greater income for the tribe's needs. When the money was divided among a tribe's members, it was soon spent without improving the life of the tribe as a whole.

Most of the laws passed by Congress had tried to make Indians live and act like white people. Most Indians wanted to remain Indians. They did not want to leave their tribes. They were proud of their language and customs. From 1961 to 1966 a new Indian Commissioner, Philleo Nash, tried to help the tribes remain alive. He saw to it that Indians were

On her first day of school, 300 miles from her reservation home, this 14-year-old girl looks at a Navaho-English textbook she can't understand. How do you think she feels?

aided under the War on Poverty that began in 1964. The National Indian Youth Council was begun. It worked among young Indians, trying to get them to accept the need for education.

Indian Schools. Most Indians attend segregated schools, open only to Indian boys and girls. These schools are run by the Bureau of Indian Affairs. Most of the 225 schools in 1970 were in Alaska, Arizona, New Mexico, North Dakota and South Dakota. About 100 schools for Indian children are on the great Navaho reservation. There are also Indian schools in the twelve other states in which tribes remain together. Usually a school is built on the land of the reservation. Many of these schools are boarding schools; the Indian boys and girls leave their families and live at the schools. Some schools draw children from several reservations. High schools are also boarding schools. All education is free for Indian children until they finish high school. Many of them are then helped to go on to college. This college group has remained small. In 1970 only about 4,000 Indians were in colleges. There was only one college in the country for Indian students—Navaho Community College.

The number of Indians in the United States, as reported by the United States government, has grown to more than 600,000. Some Indian leaders say children of marriages between Indians and members of other races are also Indians. If all these are counted, then there may be more than one million Indians living today. More than 100,000 Indian children are

Young Indian men learn how to repair appliances at this job training center. How can such training help them improve their lives?

in the schools run by the Bureau of Indian Affairs. Until the 1960's these children were taught by English-speaking teachers, even though most Indian children know no English when they begin school. Today educated Indians often return to the reservations to become teachers. They have brought important changes. They teach in the Indian languages as well as in English. Indian boys and girls learn more this way. Each year more of them can be transferred to public schools, where they mix for the first time in their lives with children who are not Indians. Perhaps this is one reason for their lower high school drop-out rate beginning in 1969.

By 1970 many Indian communities had gained the power to manage their own schools. They placed Indian parents in the classrooms, on school boards and in decision-making positions at each school. A National Indian Education Conference has been organized to work for even greater Indian control of the education of their children.

Many Problems Remain. The work to improve the lives of the country's Indians has only begun. They are still the poorest group in the United States. Their children are still the least educated. They still find it harder than other Americans to find jobs. Their rights as citizens are still more limited than those of any other minority. In 1965 the United States Senate described some of the rights still denied to Indians.

—Each tribe that governs itself runs its own courts. Indians cannot appeal the decisions of these courts except in criminal cases.

—When a white man commits a crime against an Indian, the case is heard in a white court near the reservation. Indians feel that they do not always receive justice in such a court.

—Indians who live under a state's laws do not always receive equal protection of the laws.

—A tribe cannot use the courts to protect its rights until the United States government approves its choice of lawyers and gives it permission to begin a lawsuit.

The great problem remains unchanged. The white people of the United States have not been ready to accept the right of Indians to remain different from other people. Vine Deloria, head of the National Congress of American Indians in 1965, told Congress what his people wanted. His words remain true today.

All we basically ask is justice, the consent of the governed, time to develop what we think should be developed in our own way. You cannot . . . try to turn the Indian into a white man or anything else.

I. WHAT ARE THE FACTS?

Answer each question in a sentence or two.

1. How did the decision in *Porter v. Hall* limit the rights of American Indians?

2. How did the decision in *Harrison v. Laveen* enlarge the rights of American Indians?

3. What is a tribal council?

4. How did Chee Dodge help the Navaho Indians?

5. What position did John Collier hold?

6. Why did aid to Indians lessen between 1941 and 1945?

7. Why did the Hopi chiefs send a letter to President Truman?

8. What made the "termination" policy different from the way Indians were treated under President Franklin D. Roosevelt?

9. In what trades have Iroquois Indians been most successful?

10. How did Indians benefit from the War on Poverty?

11. What is the purpose of the National Indian Youth Council?

12. Where are the largest Indian groups living today?

13. Why do Indian parents desire "community control" of schools?

14. What is the National Congress of American Indians?

15. Why have Indians failed to get equal justice in the courts near their reservations?

II. UNDERSTANDING WHY.

Explain why each of these happened.

1. In 1967 two of every five Indians had no jobs.

2. In 1967 half of all Indian children dropped out before completing high school.

3. Few students drop out of Navaho Community College.

4. The Hopi Indians refused to lease their land to oil companies.

5. In the 1950's the United States adopted the termination policy for dealing with Indian tribes.

6. Congress tried to make Indians live and act like white people.

7. Many Indian children have attended segregated schools for Indians only.

8. Indians could not appeal the decisions of their tribal courts.

III. THINKING IT THROUGH!

Discuss.

1. What do you feel have been the chief reasons for the failure of American Indians to improve their ways of living as other minority groups have done?

2. Why do you think Arizona refused to permit Indians to vote until 1948?

3. Prepare a class list of the chief problems facing American Indians today. How are these different from the problems of other minorities?

4. How has control of the tribes by state governments helped or harmed the Indians?

5. Why do you think black Americans adopted more of the white man's customs and culture than the American Indians did?

Unit Two

BLACK AMERICANS

This unit deals with some of the great steps in the struggle of black Americans for freedom and equality—a struggle that is still going on. Blacks were the only group brought to the United States as slaves. They lived without rights, treated as property more often than as people. A movement to end slavery began in the early years of the United States. It did not succeed until the end of the Civil War. The freed slaves then knew a few years of hope during Reconstruction. Hope ended after 1877, when the crushing, unequal treatment called Jim Crow came into being. Jim Crow prejudice and discrimination damaged the lives of black Americans in every part of the country. Black leaders appeared who offered ways to overcome Jim Crow. Black organizations began to use the courts to gain equal rights. Their greatest success came in 1954. In that year the United States Supreme Court ruled that separate schools for black children were not permitted by the Constitution. A national drive for greater rights grew stronger. Congress and some of the states took steps to end discrimination. The country's laws changed slowly. Some parts of the country refused to accept change. However, the nation seemed to have taken on a new goal—to use its power to increase the rights of all.

Views of Slavery

1 In 1757 slavery was already a way of life for many American colonists. John Woolman was visiting friends in South Carolina, Quakers like himself. He saw his white friends living well while their slaves suffered. He felt this was wrong. He knew all men had the right to be free. People who kept slaves were crushing the rights of others. The slaveowners listened politely, but in the 1750's men like John Woolman could not change many minds. The slave trade was too good a business for too many people. They refused to worry about what was right and what was wrong!

How Did Slavery Come to the Americas?
What Excuses Did the Slave Traders Give?
What Did Those Who Opposed Slavery Do?
What Was It Like to Be a Slave?

Slavery in the Old World. There had been slaves for thousands of years. Egypt, Greece and Rome built much of their power on the work of their slaves. At one time the Romans were said to have had three slaves for every free man! About 1,500 years ago Rome lost most of its power. The tribes from Asia who conquered it brought a different kind of "slavery." We call it feudalism. People became serfs rather than slaves. They were not allowed to leave the land on which they worked. Their masters, or lords, took most of what the serfs grew. The older kind of slavery, in which a person becomes the property of another, continued in Africa and Asia. Muslim slave traders captured tens of thousands of white Christians and black Africans each year. These people were made slaves for life. The black tribes and kingdoms of Africa also had slavery. Many of these slaves were people captured in war. Some became slaves in other ways.

Slavery Comes to the Americas. The Portuguese and then the Spaniards began to trade in black slaves in the 1400's. They bought or captured most of them in West Africa. They got some from Arab slave traders and some from African kings and chiefs. At first the slaves were taken to Europe. From 1500 to 1700, Spanish and Portuguese landowners bought uncounted shiploads of black slaves for their American lands.

Virginia was the first English settlement in North America. The Englishmen who began coming there in 1607 needed more workers to farm their land. They used a plan called *indenture* to get these workers. A person would agree to work without pay for as long as seven years. He was then brought across the Atlantic to Virginia to be a servant or farm worker. He was treated much like a European serf. After he had finished his years of service, he was freed and given some land. Many Englishmen came to America as indentured servants.

Slavery in the English Colonies. The growing colonies needed still more workers. In 1619 a Dutch ship with twenty blacks on board came to Virginia. The captain offered to "sell" them as indentured servants. Virginia farmers saw nothing wrong in this idea. They bought the services of the twenty "servants." In later years, other ships came with more blacks for sale. However, they were sold as slaves, not as servants. In the 1600's laws were passed in Virginia to give slaveowners greater power over their slaves. The children of any slave woman would also be slaves. A slave who became a Christian would still remain a slave. Masters had the right to whip their slaves. If a master killed a slave while punishing him, the master would not be

The first blacks to be brought to the United States were sold as indentured servants.

punished for what he had done. Slavery soon spread to the other English colonies.

Defending the Slave Trade. The slave trade was the biggest business the world had ever known. It came to be controlled by the English. Englishmen who had settled in North America became slaveowners. Their slaves—men, women and children brought from Africa—were called Negroes, from the Spanish word *negro*, or black.

In America men like John Woolman spoke out against slavery. So did many people in England. In 1746 an Englishman named Malachy Postlethwayt wrote a defense of the slave trade. The ideas he presented were used by slaveowners and traders to defend slavery for more than a hundred years. His pamphlet was called *The National and Private Advantages of the African Trade Considered.* Here are the ideas it offered:

— Our American colonies are valuable chiefly because of our trade with Africa. That trade gives American planters the Negro servants they need to raise the crops they send us from across the Atlantic. England's trade with America keeps our sailors at work and helps our manufacturers.
— The African trade is all profit to England. We bring Negroes to our own colonies. We also sell them to the Spaniards. And how little it costs to get Negroes in Africa! We just trade our manufactured goods for them. No other part of England's trade is so favorable to us.
— Many say that it is wrong for our country to carry on this Negro trade. They say we are making the Negroes slaves. This is not true. They are not slaves; they are servants. They are well treated. The planter's profit depends on it!
— Besides, the black rulers in Africa are always at war. They now sell their prisoners instead of killing them. These slaves are going to a Christian country—better than living among savages!

Attacking Slavery. The ideas of people like Postlethwayt were all most Englishmen knew about slavery. But people in the American colonies saw slavery all around them. They saw how the slaves were treated. Many of them began to work for an end to slavery. Groups began to meet in Philadelphia, New

York and Boston. It was 1775 before they found a leader. His name was Thomas Paine.

Paine came to America from England in 1774 at the age of 37. His friend Benjamin Franklin placed him in a job with a Philadelphia newspaper, the *Pennsylvania Journal and the Weekly Advertiser*. Paine helped organize the first anti-slavery society in the English colonies. He spoke for the thousands of white people in the colonies who opposed slavery. These people could do little, for the businessmen of England and the planters of the South were making too much money from the slave trade and slavery. On March 8, 1775, Paine offered an answer to those who defended slavery:

— Those who steal men and make them slaves are wretches. How can other people approve of this and then make money from it? Those who buy or sell other persons must know how wicked this is. Yet they do it, all in search of money.

— The men who carry on the slave trade know what evil they are doing. They give the Africans liquor. They pay them to steal other Africans. They pay kings to sell their own subjects. They hire one tribe to war on another so as to bring back prisoners who can be made slaves. In such wicked ways the English take 100,000 slaves a year from Africa to America. More than 30,000 of these die in their first year of slavery.

— We hear many excuses for this slave trade. Some say there is nothing wrong in slavery. Men, they say, are punished for crimes and jailed. No man can excuse slavery by saying a slave is like a man being punished for breaking laws. Others say that no wrong is being done, for the Negroes were already slaves when the traders bought them. Such men may as well join with a band of robbers, buy their stolen goods and then claim they did no wrong. Freedom, like any other stolen property, belongs to the man from whom it was taken.

— The most shocking excuse of all is to say that the Bible approves the holding of slaves . . . Christians are taught to call all men their neighbors; to love their neighbors as themselves; to do to all men as they would be done by; to do good to all men. To make a neighbor a slave; to treat him like a wild beast, has nothing to do with Christianity!!

Thomas Paine said, "Freedom, like any other stolen property, belongs to the man from whom it was taken." What did he mean?

For and Against Slavery. Malachy Postlethwayt and Thomas Paine had presented the chief arguments for and against slavery. The arguments did not change much in the next hundred

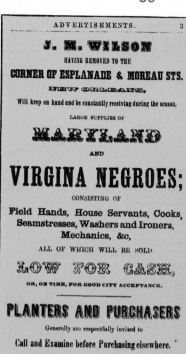

A poster advertising slaves for sale.

years. Those who defended slavery spoke of the money it could make for the slaveowners. They said that there was no other way to work the farms and plantations of the South. They insisted that slaves were property, and that no man could take away another's property. Their slaves, they said, were better off than they had been in Africa. Finally, they turned to religion. Were they not making Christians of their slaves? The souls of these black men, women and children would be saved no matter what happened to their bodies on earth.

The attack against slavery followed the ideas of such men as Thomas Paine. No man had the right to own another man. It was evil to make money from slavery. It was wrong to say that a slave was just another kind of property. No human being could be property. It mattered little how well a master treated his slave. The slave still had a right to his freedom, as all men do. And talk of helping slaves by making them Christians was nonsense. What Christian would try to save a soul by destroying a life?

Kindness or Cruelty? There were only a few thousand slaves in the colonies when Virginia made slavery legal in 1661. The number reached and passed one million by 1800. It grew to four million in the 1850's. If a master was cruel, a slave might be beaten, starved or worked to death. If the master was kind, the slave might be treated well. There was no protection from a cruel master; there was no promise that a kind master would not change. Most masters cared little about the way their slaves were treated. After 1800, stories of how slaves had to live spread across the United States.

The Slave Codes. Slavery was protected by law. Slaveowners made these laws. The judges who decided cases involving slaves were also slaveowners. Sets of laws called *slave codes* were passed in the slave states of the South. Let's look at some of the ideas in the slave codes. They will help us understand how helpless any slave must have felt in a world ruled by slave-holders.

— A slave was not permitted to leave his master's land without a pass. If he was caught without a pass, he could be ordered whipped.
— If a Negro gave a pass to a slave without the consent of his

owner, both could be punished. The one who gave the pass could receive up to 39 lashes on his bare back. (More than forty lashes could kill a slave.)

— Slaves who held a meeting without the consent of their masters could be whipped.

— If a free Negro fought with a slave, the free Negro could receive up to 39 lashes.

— Slaves who met in a school to learn reading or writing could be given up to twenty lashes.

— A Negro who used abusive language to a white person or lifted his hand against a white person could receive up to thirty lashes on his bare back.

— A Negro who plotted to kill any free white person would be killed. He would not be permitted the help of a minister before or after death.

— All cases against slaves were decided by judges and never by juries.

— Any slave who stole could receive up to forty lashes on the bare back. He might also be branded with the letter T (for THIEF) on his left cheek.

Whipping was a common punishment for slaves who broke the slave codes. Why was it often done in public?

Attacks on Slavery. Such laws were real. They were enforced. Life under slavery grew worse as the years passed. One of the most shocking descriptions of slave life appeared in the book *American Slavery As It Is,* written by Theodore Weld in 1839.

Theodore Weld of New York, a white man, was a leader in the struggle to end slavery. His book was based on thousands of stories told by slaves and slaveowners. Many of them had been printed in newspapers in the South. Weld told how slaves were overworked, underfed, poorly dressed and poorly housed. Men and women worked from dawn to dark and did not get enough sleep. Many were made to wear iron collars around their necks. Some had to drag heavy chains and

Some slaves were forced to wear bells, iron collars or heavy chains. What was the purpose of such things?

weights attached to their feet while working in the fields. Some had to wear bells so that their master would always know where they were. As punishments, some had to wear gags in their mouths for hours or days at a time. A master might have a slave's front teeth torn out or broken off. If the slave then ran away, he could be recognized more easily. It was common for slaves to be whipped. A really cruel master would then have red pepper or hot salt water rubbed into the torn flesh.

Theodore Weld was describing the horrors that were part of slavery. He told how runaway slaves could be hunted with bloodhounds. When caught, they might be shot or torn to pieces by dogs. He told how some slaves had been hung by the arms and beaten until they fainted. Sometimes, he said, they were then beaten again until they died. Such things, Weld said, happened to many slaves in many places. They were done in the open. They happened in all of the slave states. They were done by slaveowners who were the leaders of their towns.

A Defense of Slavery. Slaveowners said that such reports were not true. In 1849 Solon Robinson, a visitor from the North, wrote an article for the Southern magazine *De Bow's Review*. Robinson did not agree that slaves were badly treated. He called them happy and contented. He said they were well clothed, had enough to eat and were cared for by their masters when sick, weak or old. He claimed that slaves in the South had better lives than the farm workers of Europe.

Robinson told how slaves had become good Christians. In all his tour of the South, he wrote, he had heard of only two cases of whipping. He said that the Negroes he had seen wore better suits than he did. They also had plenty of spare money. Masters who starved or mistreated their slaves, he reported, were hated by other slaveowners.

The Question of Right and Wrong. What was it like to be a slave? Who was telling the truth? Had men like Theodore Weld described what was really happening, or were men like Solon Robinson telling the real facts about life under slavery? Whatever any man might think, he still had to answer two of the questions raised by men like Thomas Paine: Could any man have the right to own another? Wasn't slavery wrong?

Jefferson's Thoughts on Slavery. Slaveowners had been leaders in the struggle for freedom from England. Four of the first five Presidents of the United States came from Virginia. They were George Washington, Thomas Jefferson, James Madison and James Monroe. All were slaveowners. These men were members of the Founding Fathers, the men who organized the first government of the United States. They have been praised by Americans since then for making their country free and for building it into a democracy. However, most of these men worked for freedom for whites only. The laws they wrote were fair to white men. Some of them, such as Washington and Jefferson, were ready to keep slavery out of the new states that would be added to the United States. They were not willing to end slavery.

Thomas Jefferson had placed the words "all men are created equal" in the Declaration of Independence. Still, he kept his own slaves until he died. In 1782, eighteen years before he was elected President, he stated his doubts about slavery in his *Notes on the State of Virginia:*

— The fact that we have slaves must have an unhappy influence on the manners of our people. To be a master, or to be a slave, means great strain at all times. The master cannot help being cruel; the slave cannot help bowing down before the master's power.
— Our children see this and learn to imitate it. Black and white, the children do as their parents do.
— Indeed I tremble for our country when I remember that God is just. His justice cannot sleep forever. One day he may make white men slaves and black men masters! If this happens, God will not help the whites.

Slavery and the New Government. The new nation—the United States of America—was ruled chiefly by white slaveowners, lawyers and businessmen. These men did not share Jefferson's thoughts about the coming end of slavery. In 1787 fifty-five of them, representing their states, met in Philadelphia. There they wrote a new Constitution for the country. It shows that they were not willing to take steps to end slavery. The attacks on the slave trade had grown stronger. The men in Philadelphia did agree to allow Congress to pass laws to end this trade after twenty years. One question about slavery was settled in a way that greatly pleased the slaveowners. Should the slaves in the South be counted as people when each state was assigned its number of votes in the new Con-

Thomas Jefferson knew slavery was wrong, yet freed his own slaves only when he died. Why?

gress? The more people in a state, the more votes it would have. The men who wrote the Constitution wanted each state to approve it. They feared that the states of the South would not agree to the Constitution unless they were given greater power. The Constitution therefore allowed three-fifths of the slaves to be counted as people. This gave the slave states more votes in Congress, and a firm grip on the new country's government.

Madison's Thoughts on Slavery. James Madison has been called the Father of the Constitution. This Virginia slave-owner went from state to state speaking in favor of the new plan of government. He and others wrote a group of articles to show the advantages of the Constitution. These became known as the Federalist Papers. Number 54 of these papers gives us Madison's answer to the question, are slaves people or property?

— Slaves are both property and people. In some ways the laws consider them to be people. In other ways the laws consider them to be property. In some ways a slave is not different from an animal. He is forced to work for his master, not for himself. He can be sold by one master to another. He can be locked up at any time, or chained. He can be beaten or otherwise punished. All of these things can happen whenever his master so decides.

— There are also ways in which a slave is a person. The law protects him against harm from the violence of others—even from his master. The slave can be punished for what he does to others. A slave is a moral person, one who is made by law to do right rather than wrong.

— This is why the new Constitution views slaves as both persons and property. . . . Suppose that one day we end slavery. Could we then refuse to give the freed slaves their share in government? We could not.

Slavery Continued. Slavery remained part of life in the United States under its new government. Jefferson had hoped for a change. He had said that masters were becoming kinder and that the hopes of slaves were "rising from the dust." As the number of slaves increased from year to year, these hopes seemed to drop back into the dust.

I. WHAT ARE THE FACTS?

Write the letter of the choice that best completes each statement.

1. John Woolman believed in (a) slave trading, (b) freedom, (c) slaveowning.

2. Malachy Postlethwayt defended (a) slavery in Africa, (b) the freeing of slaves, (c) the slave trade.

3. Thomas Paine is remembered as (a) an enemy of slavery, (b) a believer in slavery,(c) one who thought white men should also be slaves.

4. Slaveowners said that owning slaves was approved by (a) the Bible, (b) the slaves, (c) all governments.

5. The word Negro comes from a Spanish word meaning (a) black, (b) slave, (c) prisoner.

6. Thomas Jefferson freed his slaves when he (a) wrote the Declaration of Independence, (b) became President, (c) died.

7. The purpose of the Federalist Papers was to (a) protect slavery, (b) get people to vote for the Constitution, (c) give black people equal rights.

8. The daily life of slaves was controlled by (a) the Constitution, (b) state and local laws called slave codes, (c) fair laws passed by the national government.

9. The writings of Theodore Weld tried to show Americans that (a) slavery helped the country grow rich, (b) slavery was evil, (c) it was possible to make slaveowners treat their slaves fairly.

10. Solon Robinson tried to show that (a) slavery would soon end, (b) slavery was evil, (c) slaves were well treated.

II. EXPLAINING WHY.

Answer each question in a sentence or two.

1. Why did slaveowners keep slaves even when they knew it was wrong to take away another person's liberty?

2. Why did Thomas Paine think it wrong for a Christian to own a slave?

3. Why did Malachy Postlethwayt think the slave trade was a good business for England?

4. Why did James Madison want slaves to be considered both property and people?

5. Why did the slaveowners need slave codes when they already had control of their slaves?

III. OPINIONS AND REASONS.

Explain why you agree or disagree with each of these statements.

1. Thomas Jefferson was right when he said that a slaveowner must be cruel to his slaves.

2. The Founding Fathers wanted all Americans, black and white, to have equal rights.

3. Once slaves were declared property by law, no man was doing wrong when he owned slaves.

IV. THINKING IT THROUGH!

Discuss.

1. Why was it necessary for white slaveowners to find excuses for slavery? What were these excuses?

2. Why did slavery grow so rapidly in the colonies and then in the United States?

3. How did the fear of punishment make many slaves appear to be loyal to their masters?

How Could Slavery Be Ended?

2 Until 1848, Henry Brown was a slave in Richmond, Virginia. That year he made one of the most daring escapes of all time. A white friend nailed him in a box and sent him by train to Philadelphia. He was squeezed into a space three feet by two feet, breathing through three small holes in the box. He was tossed about, moved from the train to a steamboat, from there to a wagon, to another train, and finally to a delivery wagon.

Henry "Box" Brown escaped to Philadelphia, and freedom. How do you think he got his nickname?

This wagon took him—still in the box—to the home of a white man who was waiting for him with some of his friends. They opened the box. Henry "Box" Brown was still alive! He had feared the box might become his grave. Instead, it had brought him to freedom.

In What Ways Did Slaves Escape to Freedom?
Who Were the Abolitionists?
How Did the Abolitionists Help Slaves Become Free?
How Did the Abolitionists Plan to End Slavery?

Opposing Slavery. Henry Brown was one of tens of thousands of slaves who ran away from their masters. Those who were caught were returned to slavery. Those who reached free states in the North could begin new lives, unless they were caught by slavecatchers. Slavecatchers were men who hunted down runaway slaves and returned them to their owners for money. Many escaped slaves changed their names and moved often. Others kept going north until they reached Canada. Slavery was not permitted there, and no slavecatcher could force a person to leave Canada. In the years after 1820, white people organized help for escaping slaves. They set up the Underground Railroad, the secret routes to the North by which escaping slaves were helped to freedom. Soon thousands of whites and blacks were working as "conductors" on the Railroad.

The men who helped Henry "Box" Brown escape were *abolitionists*. They hoped to end, or abolish, slavery. White people had set up anti-slavery societies in the 1770's. These groups had spread to every state, in the South as well as in the North. It even seemed for a while that slavery might be ended, as more and more people turned against it.

Cotton and Slavery. Then, in 1793 Eli Whitney invented a machine called the cotton engine, or cotton gin. Whitney's machine cleaned more cotton in a few hours than a dozen slaves could pick in a day. Cotton was suddenly cheap and easy to prepare for sale. Farmers made cotton their chief crop and

Slaves worked from dawn to dark in the cotton fields. Why did they work such long hours?

grew rich. They bought more land and used it to grow cotton. For all this they needed great numbers of slaves. The success of cotton planting was the single most important reason for the growth of slavery after 1800.

Slaveowners controlled every state government in the South. They soon forced anti-slavery groups to stop meeting. Laws were passed to protect slavery. Terrorism was used to silence those who dared speak out against it. Each year the number of slaves grew. Each year the power of the slaveholders seemed greater.

Abolitionist Efforts. Boston, New York and Philadelphia were the centers of abolitionist activity. Abolitionist leaders vowed to liberate, or free, as many slaves as possible. They studied the legal ways of doing this; they held meetings and made speeches all over the North. They tried to get state laws passed to help freedmen and escaped slaves. They wrote pamphlets, plays, books and magazine articles. Tens of thousands joined the movement. But this was in the North, where there were no slaves. The abolitionists grew stronger, but they could not free the slaves.

William Lloyd Garrison, one of the most famous abolitionists. How is he an example of the saying, "The pen is mightier than the sword"?

William Lloyd Garrison of Boston became one of the best-known abolitionist leaders. On January 1, 1831, he published the first issue of his newspaper, *The Liberator*. The lead article told his readers what he hoped to do. He would turn the minds of his fellow Americans against slavery.

> I will work to free the slaves at once!
> I will be as harsh as truth and as stubborn as justice.
> Some people say it is better to end slavery slowly. No! No!
> Would you tell a man whose house is on fire to move slowly?
> Would you tell a man slowly to rescue his wife from the hands of an attacker? Would you tell a mother to take her baby slowly from the fire into which it has fallen?
> I mean what I say—I will not turn away—I will not excuse—
> I will not retreat a single inch—AND I WILL BE HEARD.

These were bold words. Yet Garrison must have known that there was little he could really do to end slavery. Congress was controlled by Southerners. They would never permit a law to weaken or end slavery. Some people talked of changing the Constitution of the United States to end slavery. But this required the approval of three-fourths of the states. There were too many slave states for this to happen.

If Garrison and those who agreed with him hoped to weaken slavery, they would have to accept illegal actions. They would have to steal slaves to freedom on the Underground Railroad, even though this was against the law. They would have to help runaway slaves, even though they might be jailed for doing so. Some of them would even have to consider helping slaves revolt. *The Liberator* and other abolitionist writings spoke of these things.

Fighting the Abolitionists. The white slaveowners of the South were shocked and frightened by the abolitionists. This talk of freedom could not be permitted to continue! They passed new laws to hold down their slaves. They made plans to keep abolitionist writings out of the mails. They prevented abolitionist meetings in the South. At the same time they made plans to keep these ideas from their slaves. Laws against teaching slaves were strengthened and enforced. As late as 1853, Mrs. Mary Douglas, a white woman of Norfolk, Virginia, was found guilty of the charge of "Teaching Colored Children to Read":

— You have been charged with meeting with Negroes to teach them how to read and write. You have been found guilty, and will now be fined.
— Our laws are fair. Every citizen should respect them. You have failed to do so. This Court orders you to pay your fine and the costs of this trial. You will also have to spend one month in the city jail.

David Walker's Advice. The greatest fear of Southern whites was that their slaves might revolt. There had been slave revolts since the first slaves were brought to the New World by the Spaniards. Records were kept of only a few of these, but stories of what might happen if slaves rose up against their masters were told again and again all over the South. David Walker, a free Negro living in Boston, wrote four articles in 1828 and 1829. They were printed as a pamphlet called *Walker's Appeal.* He told the slaves to be ready to revolt. If necessary, they should kill their masters. This was a frightening answer to slavery!

Oh, my colored brethren, all over the world! When shall we

arise . . . and be MEN! ! ! For you must remember that we are men as well as they. God has been pleased to give us two eyes, two hands, two feet and some sense in our heads as well as they. They have no more right to hold us in slavery than we to hold them.

Now, I ask you, had you not rather be killed than to be a slave to a tyrant, who takes the life of your mother, wife and dear little children? Look upon your mother, wife and children, and answer God almighty, and believe this, that it is no more harm for you to kill a man, who is trying to kill you, than it is for you to take a drink of water when thirsty.

No Wicked Acts! Was this the best way to free the slaves? David Walker's words shook most abolitionists, just as they frightened the slaveholders of the South. William Lloyd Garrison found that people were still talking about *Walker's Appeal* in 1831. He had to tell his readers his thoughts on slave revolts:

— I believe that men should never do evil so that good may come. A good goal is not enough reason for wicked acts. I am against the spirit of *Walker's Appeal*.
— I want to see slavery end. I do not want this to happen by having slaves fight to get revenge. The idea of a bloody revolt in the South fills me with uneasy thoughts.

The abolitionists did not end slavery. But they did turn millions of people against it. Frederick Douglass, an escaped slave whose life story was a sharp view of the truth about life under slavery, spoke at their meetings. So did Harriet Tubman, another escaped slave who became the most successful of all workers on the Underground Railroad. A group of abolitionists helped John Brown, who tried in 1859 to free the slaves by invading Virginia with a handful of followers.

For thirty years they pressed on for freedom. They never agreed on what the best road to freedom might be. But they did speak and write and act in their effort to make all men free. Henry "Box" Brown's escape was one of the thousands of acts of bravery by whites and blacks in the long years of working for freedom.

Top: Frederick Douglass, escaped slave and Negro leader. Middle: Harriet Tubman, famed "conductor" on the Underground Railroad. Bottom: John Brown, who tried to free slaves at Harper's Ferry, Virginia.

I. WHAT ARE THE FACTS?

Answer each question in a single sentence.

1. How did Henry Brown escape from slavery?

2. What does the word *abolitionist* mean?

3. What machine led to an increase in slavery?

4. What three cities became the centers of abolitionist activity?

5. What happened to Mary Douglas because she taught black children to read?

6. What was David Walker's advice to the slaves?

7. What is the difference between legal and illegal actions?

8. What group of people controlled all state governments in the South?

9. How was William Lloyd Garrison important in the fight against slavery?

10. What was the greatest fear of the slaveowners?

II. WHAT DOES IT MEAN?

Explain each of these ideas in the story of the abolitionists.

1. Why is truth sometimes *harsh*?

2. Why is justice *stubborn*?

3. What did Garrison mean by "AND I WILL BE HEARD"?

4. What did Garrison mean when he said that men should not do evil so that good may come?

III. THINKING IT THROUGH!

Discuss each of these questions in class. If you find you need more information, decide where to look for it and then use it to help you reach your conclusions.

1. Many Negro spirituals were really secret messages about the

Underground Railroad. What special meaning can you find in "Swing Low, Sweet Chariot," "De Gospel Train," "Down by the Riverside" and "O My Good Lord, Show Me de Way"?

2. Why do you think people join movements such as the abolitionists'?

3. How would you compare David Walker's way of ending slavery with the views of some young black militant leaders today?

4. Would you break the laws to help a person in trouble? Explain when you would and when you wouldn't. Why have leaders of minority groups sometimes "broken the law" to help the cause of their groups?

5. Explain your views about using violence to achieve a goal. What dangers do you see in accepting violence as a way to bring changes?

IV. USING THE LIBRARY.

Use your school or public library to find the answers to one of these questions. Then report your findings to your class.

1. What is the story of John Brown's Raid? What later happened to Brown? What reasons did he give for his actions?

2. How was each of these persons important in the struggle against slavery?
    a) Frederick Douglass
    b) Harriet Tubman
    c) Sojourner Truth

What Rights Could a Black Person Hope to Have in the 1850's?

3 In 1857, at last, the Supreme Court had to decide a case in which the power of slaveowners was challenged. A group of abolitionists had paid the costs of a law case that would become one of the most important in the country's history. A slave named Dred Scott had been taken by his master from a slave state to one where slavery was not permitted. The abolitionists claimed this made him a free man. If it did, then every slave who escaped to a free state could be legally free too! The Chief Justice of the Supreme Court, Roger B. Taney, was a Southerner. So were four of the other justices. How would they decide?

Could a Black Person Become a Citizen in the 1850's?

Could He Sue in a Federal Court?

Did All Slaves Who Reached Free States Become Free?

Could Congress Pass Laws to Keep Slavery Out of Some Parts of the Country?

How Did the White Leaders of the North Feel About Slavery?

What Was the Emancipation Proclamation?

Dred Scott. Abolitionists claimed he was free in a state that did not allow slavery. Do you think they were right?

A Time of Despair. In 1857 black Americans had little hope. Slavery was stronger than ever in the South. There was little equality in the North. In most places white people could not forget that each freedman had once been a slave. Most white people could not rid themselves of the feeling that any white person was somehow better than any black. There were few places where a black man could hope to vote, find a good job or give his children an education equal to that received by white boys and girls.

Life was worse in the South. The slaveowners who ruled there used their power to make certain that black people were never given equal rights. Meanwhile, the United States was growing. New states were forming in the West. Southern leaders, helped by many politicians in the North, worked to spread slavery to these new states. Stephen Douglas, Senator from Illinois, said slavery should be allowed in any new state whose white citizens wanted it! In 1854 Congress had passed the Kansas-Nebraska Act, which seemed to open a great new area to slavery. The whole country was waiting for the Supreme Court's decision in the Dred Scott case. It would decide many questions at the same time.

The Dred Scott Decision. Chief Justice Taney read the court's decision. Everything he said seemed to weaken the position of the abolitionists. Dred Scott didn't even have the right to sue for his freedom, for he was a Negro. No Negro could be a citizen. Only citizens had the right to sue in court.

Slaves were property. Property could be taken anywhere. Congress could not take away any man's property. Therefore it could not pass laws to end slavery or to limit the areas in which slavery could exist. Any laws it had passed to limit slavery were not allowed by the Constitution. Dred Scott, then, was still a slave. He could never become a citizen. No black man or woman in the United States had any rights that could not be taken away!

Was there any hope left? The abolitionists turned to a new political party, the Republicans. The party was led by men like Abraham Lincoln. The Republicans said slavery was a moral wrong. They did not call for abolition, but they did speak for human rights. They did not try to end slavery or the selling of slaves in the South, but they did try to keep slavery out of the new states being formed in the West.

Lincoln and Douglas. The new party grew rapidly. In 1856 it won control of some parts of the North. In 1858 it sent many men to Congress. In that year its ideas reached the minds of people all over the United States. Stephen Douglas, the Democrat, was a Northern leader who seemed close to the Southern politicians in Washington. Abraham Lincoln, the Republican, ran against Douglas for Senator from Illinois. The two men offered different answers to the question of Negro rights. Douglas explained his views in a speech on August 21, 1858. A hundred years later, black Americans were still hearing such ideas in much of the South.

> We are told by Lincoln that he is opposed to the Dred Scott decision. He says it takes the rights of citizens from Negroes. I

The Lincoln-Douglas Debate argued the question of Negro rights in 1858. What does Lincoln's statement, "A house divided against itself cannot stand," mean?

ask you, are you in favor of giving Negroes the rights of citizens? Do you desire to change our state constitution to allow slaves and free Negroes to come into Illinois? . . . Do you want these Negroes to become citizens and voters equal to yourselves? Do you want them to be able to hold public office and serve on juries? Do you want them to decide on the rights of white people? . . .

I am opposed to Negro citizenship in any and every form. I believe this government was made by white men, for the benefit of white men. I am in favor of permitting only white men to be citizens, instead of making citizens of Negroes, Indians and other inferior races.

Douglas was answering the very different ideas Lincoln had expressed two months earlier. Lincoln's speech when he accepted the nomination of the Republicans to run against Douglas is known as the "House Divided" speech. In it he stated the highest hopes black men had left in the 1850's.

A house divided against itself cannot stand. I believe this government cannot last half slave and half free. I do not expect the country to break up; I do not expect the house to fall; but I expect it will cease to be divided. It will become all one thing, or all the other. Either the opponents of slavery will end the further spread of it, or it shall become lawful in all the states, the old ones as well as the new ones, in the North as well as in the South.

Could Changes Come? Lincoln lost to Douglas after a campaign that excited the whole country. The next elections would come in 1860. A new President would be elected in that year. Meanwhile, men from the South still seemed to be in command of the national government. There they worked to save slavery. A large number of Republicans had been sent to Congress from the North. These men worked just as hard to stop the spread of slavery. They talked of giving equal rights to Negroes. The few black men in the North who could be active in politics turned to these Republicans. Whatever hope black Americans might have for a better life had to begin with changes in government. Would the Republicans be the ones to make those changes?

Lincoln and the Republicans won the election of 1860. Eleven states of the South left the Union, forming the Confederate States of America. A bitter civil war then followed. One of the first questions facing Lincoln was the matter of freeing the slaves. Americans in the North had grown up listening to the teachings of the abolitionists. Now they waited for President Lincoln to take steps to free the slaves. A year passed, and then another. When would Lincoln act? When would all black Americans become citizens and free men?

The President was waiting for a victory. Only a victor could make decisions about how people on the losing side were going to live. It was not until the summer of 1862 that Union armies began to win battles. Now the order could come. Lincoln announced his plan in September. He would free all the slaves in states still at war with the Union! If Union victories continued, he could enforce such an order all over the South. He issued his Emancipation Proclamation on January 1, 1863. These words were part of it:

I do order and declare that all persons held as slaves within said [rebel] states and parts of states are, and henceforward shall be free; and that the . . . Government of the United States . . . will recognize and maintain the freedom of said persons.

And I further declare and make known, that such persons . . . will be received into the armed services of the United States. . . .

The Proclamation could free only those slaves in the states still fighting against the Union. The Constitution would have to be amended to free *all* slaves forever. This happened in December, 1865, when the Thirteenth Amendment was added to the Constitution. Legal slavery had come to an end in the United States.

I. WHAT ARE THE FACTS?

Write the letter of the choice that best completes each statement.

1. Dred Scott was (a) a lawyer, (b) an abolitionist leader, (c) a slave.

2. Senator Douglas believed slavery should be permitted (a) only in the South, (b) wherever white people wanted it, (c) only in the new territories of the West.

3. Douglas believed Negroes (a) should have the same rights as whites, (b) should be citizens, but should not serve on juries, (c) should not be citizens at all.

4. Abraham Lincoln believed (a) the United States would soon break up, (b) slavery could never be ended, (c) the United States would become all slave or all free.

5. Slavery was ended (a) before the Civil War, (b) during the Civil War, (c) after the Civil War.

II. HOW TRUE IS IT TODAY?

Each of these statements was true before the Civil War. In a sentence or two for each, explain how true the statement is today.

1. Only white people could be citizens of the United States.

2. Most black people favored the Republicans over the Democrats.

3. The Supreme Court had the power to decide whether a law was permitted by the Constitution.

III. THINKING IT THROUGH!

Discuss.

1. How was the Dred Scott Case important to:
— the slaves?
— the slaveowners?
— the abolitionists?

2. Why were white men in the South willing to die to keep slavery? Why were other white men in the North willing to die to end slavery?

3. Lincoln had told the North that saving the Union was more important than freeing the slaves. What do you think he meant by this statement?

4. Why was it necessary to amend the Constitution to free all of the slaves?

How Were the Freedmen Helped and then Harmed During Reconstruction?

4 Congress set up a special committee in 1866 to find out what was happening to the freed slaves, or freedmen. It heard from many witnesses. One of them was T. W. Conway, a minister from the North who had been in charge of helping the freedmen in Louisiana. He feared that the work of helping freedmen would be ended before they had gained the rights of citizens and the training they needed to make a living. He feared that the white leaders of the South would keep Negroes from gaining equality. Conway said these leaders had told him that "the Negro must be gotten rid of in some way." They had promised to destroy all black people within ten years. "They will be murdered by wholesale," said Conway. "It will be slaughter." Freedmen would have no hope unless "the strong arm of the government" protected them.

J. D. B. De Bow of Louisiana was a well-known editor. He had once been an important official in the national government. He told a very different story.

> I think if the whole regulation of the Negroes, or freedmen were left to the people of the communities in which they live, it will be . . . for the best interests of the Negroes as well as of the white men. I think there is a kindly feeling on the part of the planters toward the freedmen. . . . Leave the people to themselves, and they will manage very well.

What Problems Faced the Freedmen After the Civil War?

How Was the Constitution Changed to Help the Freedmen?

How Did Congress Try to Help the Freedmen?

What Was the Work of the Freedmen's Bureau?

What Did the Ku Klux Klan Try to Do?

Hope for Equality. The years 1865–1877 have been named the Reconstruction Period. It was during these years that four million freed slaves learned what freedom meant. Schools and hospitals opened their doors to black men, women and children for the first time. Black men gained the right to vote; many of them became officials of Southern state governments. Some were elected to the House of Representatives and the Senate. For a while it seemed that the doors to equality would open. Instead they soon closed, leaving black Americans on the outside.

Senator Hiram Revels and Representatives Benjamin Turner, Robert De Large, Josiah Walls, Jefferson Long, Joseph Rainy and R. Brown Elliott. All were elected to Congress during the brief period known as Reconstruction.

How could this have happened? A chief reason was that Southern state governments soon returned to white control. White leaders passed new "black codes" that took away the rights black citizens had begun to gain in the South. At the same time, groups of white men began to use force and murder as weapons to keep Negroes in bitter poverty and hopeless political weakness.

The leaders of Congress had not expected such things to happen. When the Civil War ended, three amendments to the Constitution seemed to give Negroes freedom, the rights of citizens, equal protection of the laws and the right to vote. The Thirteenth Amendment was obeyed; no person was held a slave after 1865. The Fourteenth Amendment made several promises that would have meaning only if white people were ready to carry them out.

> All persons born . . . in the United States . . . are citizens of the United States and of the State wherein they reside. No States shall make or enforce any law which shall [lessen the rights] of citizens of the United States; nor shall any State deprive any person of life, liberty or property, without due process of law; nor deny to any person . . . the equal protection of the laws.

The Fifteenth Amendment promised that the freedmen would have the right to vote.

> The right of citizens of the United States to vote shall not be denied or [lessened] by the United States or by any State on account of race, color or previous condition of servitude.

The Black Codes. It took little time for the white leaders of the South to show that they would not permit black Americans to have such rights. Mississippi passed a law in 1865 setting up a state code for black citizens. Here are some parts of this "black code."

—No white person may marry any Negro.
—Freedmen who agree to work for a white person and then leave the job for any reason will receive no pay for the work they have already done.
—If a Negro quits his job, the police can arrest him and bring him back to the person for whom he has been working.
—A freedman under 18 can be made an indentured servant of his former master. These children must work for these former masters until they are 21; or, if they are females, until they are 18.
—Any freedman who does not have a job will be fined $50. If he does not have the money for the fine, he will be "hired

out" to any white person who will pay this fine in exchange for the freedman's labor.

— Each person in the state must pay a tax of $1. Any Negro who cannot pay this tax can be hired out to any white person who pays the tax for him.

— No black person may keep a gun or knife.

— All the laws in the old slave codes describing and punishing the crimes of slaves or other Negroes are still in effect, except that the trials and punishments will now be changed.

Thaddeus Stevens wanted Congress to protect the freedmen. What would happen to them otherwise?

Laws like this "black code" would bring the freedmen back to the kind of life they had known under slavery. The Republican leaders of Congress understood this. One of them, Thaddeus Stevens of Pennsylvania, spoke out about the problem:

> We have turned loose four million slaves without a hut to live in or a cent in their pockets. Congress must care for them until they can take care of themselves. If we leave them to the laws made by the white people who used to be their masters, the freedmen will be treated like slaves again! Today black citizens do not even have the right to vote in the South. I am for Negro voting in every rebel state!

In 1865 Congress passed one of the most important laws of the Reconstruction Period—The Freedmen's Bureau Act. The law set up the Freedmen's Bureau, headed by General Oliver O. Howard (Howard University was named after him).

Inside a freedmen's school in Vicksburg, Mississippi. Why were there old and young alike in the classroom?

The Freedmen's Bureau. Bureau offices were opened all over the South. Their work went on for five years. The Bureau built more than 4,000 schools. It helped set up the first Negro colleges—Howard University, Fisk University, Hampton University and Atlanta University. General Howard and those working with him built more than forty hospitals. These were different from any other hospitals in the South, for they admitted black patients as well

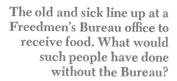

The old and sick line up at a Freedmen's Bureau office to receive food. What would such people have done without the Bureau?

as white ones. For many black Americans their visits to such hospitals were the first medical care they had ever known!

Congress also passed laws to protect the civil rights of freedmen, to try to give them the same rights other citizens had. The Freedmen's Bureau was given the power to set up special courts. Here the rights of black Americans under these laws were protected for the first time. Poor white citizens were given the same protections.

The first of the civil rights laws was passed in 1866. It said no state of the South could enforce laws directed against Negroes. Black men gained the right to vote and hold public office. The President could use the army to protect the rights of Negroes. One law gave black Americans equal rights in all public places—hotels, theaters, ships, etc.

Attack and Defense of the Bureau. White leaders from the South asked Congress to close down the Freedmen's Bureau. Their attack moved against General Howard. Southern politicians said he was not honest. They insisted he was trying to make himself rich through the work of the Bureau. These and many other charges were made again and again. In 1870

Congress investigated the work of the Bureau. It heard many witnesses. One of them was Sidney Andrews, a newspaperman from New England. He reported what he found during a tour of the South:

> Of the thousand things that the bureau has done no balance sheet can ever be made. How it helped the ministers of the church, and saved the blacks from robbery! How it made all show respect for the Negro's rights! How it taught all the people the meaning of the law! It settled neighborhood quarrels, brought about friendly relations between employers and workers, improved education, helped freedmen become landowners, broke up bands of outlaws, taught equal rights, and in such ways carried the light of the North into the dark places of the South. . . .

The end of the Bureau came in 1870. It had given great assistance to four million black Americans. Some of them had become independent of their old masters for all time. They had found the beginnings of real dignity in their daily lives. They had learned trades and had begun their education. For the first time, they had gained the right to vote.

Voting could lead to equality. Southern whites took steps to deny this right to all black Americans. One group in South Carolina sent this protest to Congress in 1868 to explain why it was ready to do anything to prevent Negroes from taking part in government.

> The low slaves of yesterday are the freedmen of today. . . . We do not mean to threaten resistance by arms. But the white people of our state will never allow Negro rule. We will keep up this contest until we have won back control. We owe this to the proud white race, whose rule on earth God has ordered.

Years of Terror. Groups of white men in the South took steps to regain full control. Organizations like the Ku Klux Klan were soon feared all over the South. The Klan, or KKK, had begun in Tennessee a few months after the end of the Civil War. Its members wanted to return Negroes to a life close to slavery. Their method was terror. They burned, whipped and killed.

The KKK and groups like it could destroy the hopes that black Americans had found in Reconstruction. The Fourteenth Amendment had promised "equal protection of the laws." This equal protection depended on the power of the federal govern-

After Reconstruction the Ku Klux Klan and other groups used violence and terror to maintain "white supremacy." Where do you think these men are going? Why do you think they are dressed in this way?

ment. The Freedmen's Bureau was gone after 1870. By 1877 all Northern soldiers had left the South. A new agreement seemed to give the South back to its old white leaders: The North would keep control of the national government; the white men of the South would do as they pleased in their own states. "White supremacy" became the rule—the white race controlling the black race and keeping its power in every way possible.

The use of force against Negroes became part of everyday life in most of the South. Lynching, or murder by mobs, took the place of law in town after town. This remained true for more than sixty years! "Lynch law" stole justice from black Americans, and sometimes from whites. In 1899 the National Afro-American Council made these points against the long years of lynching:

1. Negroes are dragged before the courts by thousands and sentenced to every form of punishment, and even killed, without proper trials.
2. Negroes in some parts of the country are arrested and jailed just because they are suspected of crimes.
3. Mobs then form, made up of ignorant, vicious and drunken men. They are given the keys of the jails. The accused

Negro is then tortured, hanged, shot or cut up in the most horrible ways. This has happened thousands of times!
4. Such mobs have even walked into courtrooms to take their prisoners.

As late as 1930 twenty Negroes were killed by mobs. In each case a man was accused of a crime. He did not get to trial. Instead, a mob of angry white men killed him. None of the men in these mobs were ever punished for what they had done.

Failure or Success? How can we judge the success of Reconstruction? It had proved that black people in the South could be the equals of whites in politics, education and skills. These were among the goals of the Freedmen's Bureau. But these goals were not fully reached. The white men who had fought the Civil War for the South came back into power. Groups like the KKK grew strong. They used terror to return black Americans to a life almost as bad as that under slavery. Terror turned Reconstruction from a success into a bitter failure. Yet it had been shown that freedmen could succeed, and could really improve their lives—if the power of the federal government was used to protect them. Without this power they could never know equality!

I. WHAT ARE THE FACTS?

Answer each question in one or two sentences.

1. What does the phrase "Reconstruction Period" mean?

2. How many slaves were freed at the end of the Civil War?

3. What rights did freedmen gain from the Fourteenth Amendment?

4. What rights did freedmen gain from the Fifteenth Amendment?

5. How did the black codes bring freedmen back to the kind of life they had known under slavery?

6. Who was General Oliver O. Howard?

7. Name four famous Negro universities begun by the Freedmen's Bureau.

8. What is the KKK?

9. Explain two of the chief goals of the KKK.

10. What is the meaning of "lynch law"?

II. WORDS TO KNOW.

Match each word with its definiiton.

1. Lynching	(a) the same laws for all people
2. Amendment	(b) having more power than other groups
3. Equal protection	(c) murder by mobs
4. Code	(d) the rights of citizens
5. Civil rights	(e) rights having to do with government
6. Political rights	(f) a set of laws
7. Supremacy	(g) a change in a constitution or law

III. THINKING IT THROUGH!

Discuss.

1. Why couldn't the freedmen improve their lives without the aid of the national government?

2. How did the Freedmen's Bureau change the lives of white and black Americans in the South?

3. Black men held such offices as governor, Senator, Congressman, sheriff and member of state legislature during Reconstruction. Why did this end after Reconstruction?

4. Why have so many white men in the South joined groups like the Ku Klux Klan in the more than 100 years since the Civil War?

5. Explain the statement: "White supremacy is the key to understanding the last 100 years of Southern history."

How Did the Idea of "Separate but Equal" Affect Black Americans?

5 The case really began on June 7, 1892. People were boarding a train in New Orleans. White passengers climbed into the front cars. Black passengers went into the rear car. Homer Adolph Plessy entered one of the "white" cars. He looked like a white man but was known to have had a black great-grandparent. The conductor told him he could not remain there. Mr. Plessy refused to move to the "colored" car and was arrested. A Louisiana law stated that white and colored passengers on trains in that state had to be separated. Plessy was taken before a white judge, John H. Ferguson. Judge Ferguson ordered him jailed for breaking the law. Mr. Plessy's lawyers appealed the sentence. Four years later the case reached the United States Supreme Court.

Homer Plessy refused to move to the "colored" car. What would you have done?

What Is Meant by the Term "Colored"?

Who Was to Decide That a Person was "Colored" or "White"?

How Do Cases Come to the United States Supreme Court?

What Was Meant by "Separate but Equal"?

What Power Did "Separate but Equal" Give to State Governments?

97

The Meaning of "Colored." We have been using several different words to describe the people who were brought from Africa, became slaves and were later freed. *Negro*, the Spanish word for *black*, was the first word used to describe the slaves. *Blacks* was a word used by many white slaveowners. Some also said *Africans* or *Afro-Americans*. After 1800 the white people of the South began to use the word *colored* to describe their slaves. The word is still used today. But what does it mean?

Scientists tell us that there are three chief races of man. These divisions are based largely on skin color. The names that have been given to the races are Caucasian (for white), Negroid (for black or dark brown) and Mongoloid (for yellow). However, within each race there are great differences in skin color. Some Caucasians have dark skins; some Negroids have light skins; some Mongoloids have skin that is not yellow.

These races have so much variety because they have mixed with one another for thousands of years. Tribes and whole peoples have moved from place to place. They have then married members of the group already in the area. This has happened so often in history that there are no longer any "pure" races. Most people cannot be certain that they did not have ancestors of more than one race. In the New World, many slave children had white fathers. There were soon large numbers of light-skinned slaves in the Americas.

Who Was "Colored"? The white people of the South said that any person with one black ancestor was black. Soon they began to use the word *colored*, for some slaves had skins that were not black. In fact, many were as fair as most "whites."

Examples of Caucasian (left), Mongoloid (middle) and Negroid (right) features.

Those who had one or more white ancestors, and whose skin was fair, became known as *mulattoes*. They were treated like Negroes and were also called *colored*. It did not matter how "white" a person's skin might be; if he had one *colored* ancestor, he was *colored*.

White Supremacy Laws. By 1877 Reconstruction had ended. The South was again under the control of its white leaders. These men wanted white supremacy. Any white person, they believed, was better than any colored person. They quickly passed laws to treat the two races in different ways. Within twenty years Southern states had passed laws to keep black farm workers on the land, to keep their wages low and to punish them for any word or action against a white person. In these and other ways, black Americans were kept as close to slavery as possible. Many special laws were also passed to keep whites and blacks apart. People all over the country, whites as well as blacks, began to question laws that were so clearly directed against black people. The Fourteenth Amendment had promised all citizens equal protection of the laws. Were the laws of the South giving black citizens equal protection?

The Supreme Court and Laws. The Supreme Court is the branch of our national government that decides what the Constitution means. Suppose a law (local, state or federal) seems to take away a right guaranteed by the Constitution of the United States. A person who feels he is treated unfairly by that law can sue a public official, in order to get a judge to rule that the law is improper. The case is decided in favor of one side or the other. The loser can then appeal the judge's decision. This means he can take the case to a higher court, called an appeals court. It may or may not agree with the lower court. The decision of an appeals court can also be appealed. If the case involves the Constitution, it can come finally to the United States Supreme Court.

The lawyers for both sides present their case to the Court. The justices ask questions and discuss the case. They vote to decide which side is correct. Then the Chief Justice assigns to one of them the task of writing the opinion of the majority of the Court. This opinion explains the reasons for the Court's decision in the case. Any justice may write a different opinion in which he *dissents*, or disagrees, with the majority.

The Constitution is the highest law of the land. The decisions of the Supreme Court are based on the Constitution. The Court may find that the law questioned in a case was proper. Then the law remains in force. If the Court finds that the law was not proper, then the law should end at once.

The Supreme Court After Reconstruction. Supreme Court decisions on the same problem or question of law have been changed (lawyers say "reversed") many times. Yet until a decision is changed, it remains the law of the land unless the Constitution itself is changed. The Dred Scott decision said that slavery was legal and could not be limited. The Thirteenth Amendment ended slavery. This erased the Dred Scott decision.

Most justices of the Supreme Court in the 1880's and 1890's believed the federal government had no power to pass laws increasing the rights of citizens. They felt this was a power of state and local governments. In 1883 the Court ruled that the federal government could not pass and enforce civil rights laws. Such laws were part of a state's "police power"—the power to make laws and rules to protect its people. So long as a state did not take away rights promised to all people by the Constitution, it could pass *any* laws about the rights of citizens. The Supreme Court in this way ended key civil rights laws Congress had passed during Reconstruction. It also made each state its own judge of its need for other civil rights laws.

The Plessy Decision. The case of *Plessy v. Ferguson* (*v.* means *versus*, or against) was one of the most important cases ever decided by the Supreme Court. Homer Plessy asked for the answers to two questions: (1) Since his appearance was white, could the state of Louisiana treat him as it treated its colored people? (2) Didn't the Constitution also protect a colored man against unequal treatment, such as being forced to sit in a separate car on a train?

The Supreme Court does not have to rule on all the questions lawyers raise in the court. In 1896 it refused to answer Plessy's first question. The Court ruled that each state could decide for itself who was "white" and who was "colored." This meant that each state in the South could continue to divide its people into the two groups—as part of a state's police power.

The Court's answer to the second question showed that it believed forced separation of white and colored people did not deny the right to fair and equal treatment promised by the Constitution:

> . . . we cannot say that a law which . . . requires the separation of the two races . . . is unreasonable.

The Plessy decision became known as the "separate but equal" decision. It meant that a state could pass laws to keep white and black citizens separate. The Court had ruled that this was proper so long as each race had "equal" facilities. However, each state kept the power to decide for itself what kinds of separation it wanted, and how "equal" its separate facilities would be. The national government did little for almost sixty years to make the life of black Americans in the South "equal" to that of whites.

Justice John Marshall Harlan opposed the Supreme Court's decision to allow "separate but equal" facilities in the Plessy case. Why is Harlan called "a lonely voice in his time"?

Justice Harlan's Dissent. Justice John Marshall Harlan did not agree with the other members of the Court in the Plessy case. He wrote a dissent strongly attacking the idea of "separate but equal." His thinking was similar to that accepted by the Supreme Court more than fifty years later! He was a lonely voice in his time, a man speaking out clearly for equality. Here are the ideas in his famous dissent:

— To force people to be separated on trains just because they are of different races is like marking some of them as slaves. The Constitution does not allow this. No laws should be allowed to do this.
— A person should have certain rights because he is a citizen, not because he is a member of a certain race. We boast of the freedom enjoyed by our people. Then how can we let any state take away this freedom? Just by saying railroad cars are "equal," we do not fool anyone into thinking we are giving people equal treatment.

Years of Suffering. The Plessy decision remained the law of the land for more than fifty years. "Colored" Americans had to live under special state laws that denied their rights. The government of the United States seemed to remain under Southern control, even though Southern members of Congress were always a minority. The national government would not pass laws to improve the rights of all Americans. The Supreme Court would not prevent laws that took away the rights of colored people. In fact, its "separate but equal" rule seemed to approve such laws in advance.

I. WHAT ARE THE FACTS?

Write the letter of the choice that best completes each statement.

1. Homer Plessy tried to take a seat in a railroad car reserved for (a) white passengers, (b) black passengers, (c) soldiers.

2. The case of *Plessy v. Ferguson* was decided by the (a) governor of Louisiana, (b) President of the United States, (c) Supreme Court of the United States.

3. "Equal protection of the laws" is promised by the (a) Thirteenth Amendment, (b) Fourteenth Amendment, (c) Fifteenth Amendment.

4. A *dissent* is an explanation of why a justice (a) agrees with the majority, (b) disagrees with the majority, (c) refuses to vote.

5. The famous phrase used to describe the rule made by the Court in the Plessy case is (a) "giving people equal treatment," (b) "equality under the laws," (c) "separate but equal."

II. EXPLAINING WHY.

Answer each question in a sentence or two.

1. Why was Homer Plessy called a "colored" man rather than "Negro" or "black"?

2. Why did the civil rights laws passed by Congress during Reconstruction end?

3. Why have we given the Supreme Court so much power in our government?

III. THINKING IT THROUGH!

Discuss.

1. How have people decided who is white and who is black? Has this way of deciding been fair?

2. What is meant by a "double standard"? How did the Plessy decision set up a double standard for white and black Americans in the United States?

3. Why did the white people of the South want to keep the races separate in every possible way?

4. Why has the Plessy decision been called the greatest blow against equality of the races since slavery?

How Did Jim Crow Treatment Change the Lives of Black Americans?

6 In 1902 W. E. B. Du Bois, a young professor at Atlanta University, tried to use the public library. He was completing his book, *The Souls of Black Folk*. There were still a few points he had to check. The books he needed were not in the library of the Negro college. He went to the Atlanta Public Library. The books were there, but he could not use them. No black person was permitted to read or even examine any of the books in this or most other public libraries in the South. A year later, when his book was published, Dr. Du Bois explained that he wanted it to be "possible for a man to be both a Negro and an American, without being cursed and spit upon by his fellows, without having the doors of opportunity closed roughly in his face."

> The nation has not yet found peace from its sins; the freedman has not yet found in freedom his promised land.
>
> . . . the very soul of the toiling, sweating black man is darkened by the shadow of a vast despair. Men call the shadow prejudice. . . .
>
> . . . before that nameless prejudice . . . he stands helpless, dismayed, and well-nigh speechless. . . . Work, culture, liberty, all these we need . . . and all striving toward that vaster ideal that swims before the Negro people, the ideal of human brotherhood.

No black person was allowed to use a public library in the South.

How Did Jim Crow Laws and Customs Harm Black Americans?

What Excuses Did White Men in the South Give for Jim Crow?

What Did Black Leaders Ask the Country to Do About Jim Crow?

Jim Crow Laws. Once the United States Supreme Court had made its decision in the *Plessy v. Ferguson* case, each state could make its own laws about its black citizens. Every state in the country was ruled by white people. States in the South were ruled by white people who believed in white supremacy. They passed law after law to keep the races separate and to

This one-room segregated school in Georgia was an example of Jim Crow in action. Why were separate schools set up?

prevent black people from bettering their lives. They set up separate schools for black children. These were taught only by black teachers and received a small fraction of the money white schools were given. White and colored people were separated in every public place. Black workers received lower wages than whites for the same kind of work. Black people were

White and "colored" people were kept separate in all public places, such as this railroad station waiting room.

denied the right to vote. In Louisiana, for example, a law provided that no man could vote unless his grandfather had also had the right to vote. Since no black person had voted before Reconstruction, this meant no black person could ever vote! This became known as the "grandfather clause."

Such laws as these came to be called "Jim Crow" laws. "Jim Crow" was a song sung in the South as early as the 1830's. It mocked Negroes. The words came to describe all laws and customs that kept black people from gaining equality. Jim Crow laws were passed in every state in the South—some of them as late as the 1960's! Jim Crow customs still keep black Americans from equality in much of the United States.

Congressman White's Speech to Congress. Black men from the South had been members of Congress during and after Reconstruction. George H. White of North Carolina was the last of this group. For the next 28 years there would be no black members in Congress. On January 29, 1901, a few weeks before he left, Congressman White made a long speech about the problems and needs of the country's black people. He told of problems for which he could see no solution, and of what it was like to be a black American at the beginning of the twentieth century:

— The Negro vote in the State of Alabama has been eliminated to a large extent.
— The men who do such things are like highwaymen who are caught and then say: "Let me alone; I will not be arrested;

I will not be tried. I'll have none of your execution of your laws, and if you try to carry out these laws, I will see to it that many more men, women or children are murdered."

—The Negro should not be measured by what he was in 1868, but by what he is today. Half of us can read and write. We have written and published nearly 500 books. We have nearly 300 newspapers. . . . We have now in practice over 2,000 lawyers and an equal number of doctors. . . . We own about 140,000 farms. . . . We have 32,000 teachers, 20,000 churches. . . .

—All this we have done under the worst possible conditions. We have done it in the face of lynching, burning at the stake . . . Jim Crow cars, the loss of the right to vote, poor treatment of our women, with the factories closed against us, no Negro permitted to be conductor on the railway cars, no Negro permitted to be a locomotive engineer and the mines closed against us. Labor unions have been formed all over the country; all but a few have kept black faces out. Negroes cannot get jobs in stores.

—After thirty-five years of struggling against such high odds, the black man asks a fair and just judgment. He asks no special favors, but simply demands that he be given the same chance for existence, for earning a living, for raising himself, that other groups have. Treat him as a man.

—I am pleading for the life, the liberty, the future happiness, and the right to vote for one-eighth of the people of the United States.

The Excuses for Jim Crow Laws. What excuses could the white leaders of the South give for their actions against Negroes? Senator Benjamin R. Tillman of South Carolina was one of the South's best-known spokesmen. On January 21, 1907, Tillman made a long prepared speech in which he defended Jim Crow and all else that the white people of the South were doing to black citizens. Here are parts of what he said:

It was in 1876, thirty years ago, and the people of South Carolina had been living under Negro rule for eight years. . . . They were taxing us to death and taking away our property. . . . Life ceased to be worth living on the terms under which we were living, and in desperation we determined to take the government away from the Negroes.

We reorganized the Democratic party with one idea, namely,

that "this is a white man's country and white men must govern it." Under that banner we went to battle. . . . It was then that "we shot them"; it was then that "we killed them"; it was then that "we stuffed ballot boxes." Desperate diseases require desperate remedies, and having resolved to take back the government of the state, we hesitated at nothing.

The race question is being discussed all over the country. The real question is whether or not the races are equal. If the majority of the white people make up their minds that the Negroes are not their equals, they will sooner or later put it into law that Negroes shall not have a part of the inheritance of the white race. We shall take care of ourselves in the South, helped by all who believe in white supremacy and white civilization.

Was There Any Hope? White leaders of government in parts of the South were saying that they had to keep black citizens from taking part in government. They said Negroes did not understand how to rule. They believed whites were better than blacks. This helped excuse lynch law and rule by mobs. These white people also claimed to be protecting themselves against terrible danger from Negroes. They welcomed Jim Crow laws and customs. They permitted lynchings to continue. It was clear that white Americans in the rest of the country would not take action to end either Jim Crow or lynchings. How, then, were black people to escape from the kind of life in which most of them were trapped?

I. WHAT ARE THE FACTS?

Write the letter of the choice that best completes each statement.

1. W. E. B. Du Bois was a famous (a) Senator, (b) scholar, (c) librarian.

2. The last black member of Congress in 1901 was (a) Benjamin Tillman, (b) George H. White, (c) W. E. B. Du Bois.

3. Jim Crow laws were directed against (a) black people, (b) all poor people, (c) whites in the South.

4. In 1901 the part of the country's population who were Negroes was (a) one-half, (b) one-eighth, (c) one-thirtieth.

5. In 1876 most white people in the South were (a) Republicans, (b) Democrats, (c) non-voters.

II. WHAT DO THEY MEAN?

Explain each of these statements in a sentence or two.

1. The freedman has not yet found in freedom his promised land.

2. The ideal of human brotherhood is before us.

3. The Negro vote has been eliminated.

4. All but a few unions have kept black faces out.

5. We stuffed ballot boxes.

III. THINKING IT THROUGH!

Discuss.

1. Why has the term "Jim Crow" continued in use in the United States for about 150 years?

2. Why couldn't black Americans hold the gains they had made during Reconstruction?

3. How did the *Plessy v. Ferguson* decision help bring about the conditions described by George H. White?

4. How did the Jim Crow laws "shut the doors of opportunity" to black Americans?

5. Why did the people who favored Jim Crow laws also believe that Negroes were not their equals?

Should Black Americans Live with Discrimination, Oppose It—or Escape It?

7 The Cotton States and International Exposition was held in Atlanta, Georgia, in September, 1895. Southern businessmen had organized this great fair to show the world that their part of the country was not backward. On September 18 the speaker at a large meeting at the fair was Booker T. Washington, director of Tuskegee Institute. Washington had been born a slave. After the Civil War he had become a teacher and then a well-known Negro leader. This was the first time a black man had been invited to speak to an audience of leading white Southerners. Thousands gathered in the hall. What would Washington say?

. . . .

The convention of the Universal Negro Improvement Association took place in 1921, 26 years later. Fifty thousand members and friends joined the grand march from Harlem to New York City's largest hall, Madison Square Garden. With bands playing and flags

Fifty thousand Negroes marched from Harlem to Madison Square Garden in support of Marcus Garvey.

flying, Marcus Garvey, leader of the Association, led the march. The crowds cheered as he came into view. Madison Square Garden was filled to overflowing. The crowd roared as Garvey was named President of all Africa. His words brought shouts and screams of joy. Afro-Americans were going BACK TO AFRICA!!

What Was Booker T. Washington's Proposal?

What Effect Did the Atlanta Compromise Have on Negro Life?

How Did W. E. B. Du Bois and the National Association for the Advancement of Colored People Plan to Solve the Problems Facing Black Americans?

What Was Marcus Garvey's "Back-to-Africa" Plan?

Jim Crow in the South. Jim Crow laws and customs were found all over the South in the 1890's. Black men were denied their right to vote. Lynchings went on openly. In 1896 alone 86 black men were lynched; the number grew to 123 in 1897. White men in thousands of Southern towns used violence to keep equal rights from Negroes. From the day they were born to the day they died, black Americans were made to feel in-

ferior in every possible way. But these were not the problems Booker T. Washington would discuss in Atlanta in 1895.

A Compromise, Not a Struggle. A compromise is an agreement in which each side gives up part of what it wants so that both sides may get part of what they want. Black Americans had been asking for full equality. White Southerners had been trying to take away all forms of equality. Booker T. Washington offered a compromise. Negroes would give up the struggle for equality until they were trained and ready for it.

Washington began his speech with the story of the captain of a ship that had no water. He asked the captain of a passing ship for help and was told to "Cast down your bucket where you are." The first captain did so, and found fresh water! His ship was near the mouth of a great river pouring fresh water into the sea.

> To those of my race . . . I would say: "Cast down your bucket where you are"—cast it down by making friends in every manly way of the people of all races by whom we are surrounded.
> Cast it down in agriculture, mechanics, in commerce, in domestic service and in the professions. . . . No race can prosper until it learns there is as much dignity in tilling the field as in writing a poem. It is at the bottom of life we must begin, and not at the top.

The Atlanta Compromise. Booker T. Washington was telling black Americans to accept the life of a worker in the South. Frederick Douglass, the most important Negro leader in the United States until his death that same year, had always fought for equality. He had told black people to accept nothing less. He had reminded white people again and again that it was wrong to try to prevent that equality. Now Washington was telling Southerners that black people had changed their goals. It was time for white people to trust their Negro workers.

> Cast down your bucket among those people who have, without strikes and labor wars, tilled your fields, cleared your forests, built your railroads and cities and brought forth treasures from the bowels of the earth. . . . In our humble way, we shall stand by you with a devotion that no foreigner can approach, ready to lay down our lives, if need be, in defense of yours. . . .

Booker T. Washington said, "Cast down your bucket where you are." What does that mean?

But what of equality? Washington went on, making the statement that became known as the Atlanta Compromise:

> In all things that are purely social we can be as separate as the fingers, yet one as the hand in all things essential to mutual progress. . . . The wisest among my race understand that the agitation of questions of social equality is the extremest folly. . . . It is important and right that all privileges of the law be ours, but it is vastly more important that we be prepared for the exercise of those privileges. The opportunity to earn a dollar in a factory now is worth infinitely more than the opportunity to spend a dollar in an opera house.

Booker T. Washington, Leader. For the next twenty years Booker T. Washington was the most important black man in the United States. White people in the North and the South considered him the spokesman for all black Americans. They sent him large amounts of money for schools and colleges for thousands of black students. Presidents asked his advice; few Negroes were given government jobs without his approval. He traveled all over the country, speaking again and again to spread the ideas in his "compromise."

W. E. B. Du Bois—A Different Goal. New black leaders became important after 1905. They began to disagree openly with Washington. Perhaps the most important of these men was W. E. B. Du Bois. It was 1915 before he was able to get American Negroes to turn to the program he wanted them to follow. Its goal was immediate equality:

> We need not waste time by seeking to deceive our enemies into thinking that we are going to be content with a half loaf, or by being willing to lull our friends into a false sense of our . . . present satisfaction.

> The American Negro demands equality—political equality, industrial equality and social equality; and he is never going to rest satisfied with anything less. He demands this . . . as an absolute measure of self-defense and the only one that will assure to the darker races their . . . survival on earth.

> The Negro must have political freedom. . . . American Negroes of today are ruled by tyrants who take what they please in taxes and give what they please in law and administration, in justice and in injustice; and the great mass of black people must stand helpless and voiceless before a condition which has time and time again caused other peoples to fight and die.

W. E. B. Du Bois (pronounced doo boys') wanted immediate equality for all. How was that goal different from Washington's?

> . . . the Negro laborer is the most exploited class in the country, giving more hard toil for less money than any other American, and has less voice in the conditions of his labor.

What should black Americans do? Dr. Du Bois did not expect them to cast down their buckets where they were. Instead, he hoped black people could move forward to improve their standards of living. He believed they should develop black art and literature. He wanted them to be more active in politics. He urged all Negro parents and children to get as much education as possible. It was time for black Americans to refuse to be servants to whites. Most important, perhaps, was his call for strong Negro organizations to work for the most important goal of all—equality. In such ways, at last, true freedom might come to every black American citizen.

Which Road to Follow? Here, then, were two different programs to end the Jim Crow conditions of American Negroes. Should black people wait until they had more education and were well-trained workers before they demanded equal rights? Or should they press for equality at once? These two approaches to Negro rights continued to separate black Americans for another forty years.

Who Was Marcus Garvey? Marcus Garvey was born in 1887 in Jamaica, then a British-owned island in the West Indies. The Englishmen who ruled Jamaica often treated dark-skinned Negroes more harshly than those with fair skin. Marcus Garvey, himself very dark in color, grew bitter toward white people and fair-skinned Negroes. In 1914 he proposed the ideas of the Universal Negro Improvement Association. This would be a movement to solve the problems of *black* people. Garvey would not permit any Negroes with fair skin to join.

Garvey's Plan. Marcus Garvey came to the United States in 1916 and quickly spread the ideas of his Association. His chief idea was that all black Americans go back to Africa! They had no hope in the United States. White Americans would never give them equal rights. Why should they remain there? The Universal Negro Improvement Association became known by its initials, the UNIA. It planned to take control of as much of Africa as possible. Garvey founded the Black Star Steamship Line. Its ships would belong to American Negroes. They

Marcus Garvey's plan was to go BACK TO AFRICA! Can you think of some weaknesses of such a plan?

would carry the black people of the United States back to their homeland.

This was a plan for the separation of the races. It required a great deal of money. Some of its came from white groups who already believed in separating the races. Members of the Ku Klux Klan sent money to support this idea of removing black people from the South. However, Garvey raised most of the UNIA's money from black Americans. He sold shares in the steamship line. He organized the African Orthodox Church. He set up a Black Cross organization to take the place of white men's Red Cross. He began an African Motor Corps and a Black Eagle Flying Corps. He set up businesses run by black people to serve black communities.

Garvey seemed tireless. He went from city to city preaching the glory of being black. Negroes, he told his audiences, should be proud of their color. Black people, Garvey said again and again, should know and be proud of the glorious history of Africa. BACK TO AFRICA! His words excited millions.

There were many weaknesses in Garvey's plan. Almost all of Africa was ruled by European nations. They would never give up their colonies. Billions of dollars would be needed—even if the land for settlement somehow could be obtained. Most black Americans were not willing to begin life over in a strange, new land. The United States was their home; they would remain and fight for their rights.

The UNIA Fails. The UNIA gained more than a million members in less than five years. Its busy branches worked in every large city. Garvey collected at least $10 million for his activities. His followers were tired of being second-class citizens. Marcus Garvey's dream was better than the life they were living. No wonder they cheered his words, such as these from his best-known speech on November 25, 1922:

> . . . at this time, among all the peoples of the world, the group that suffers most from injustice, the group that is denied most of those rights that belong to all humanity, is the black group. . . . We of the UNIA believe that what is good for the other folks is good for us. . . . We [want] a kind of government that will place our race in control, even as other races are in control of their own government. . . . You and I can live in the United States of America for 100 years, and our generations may live for 200 years or for 5,000 more years, and as long as there is a black and white population, when the majority is on the side of the white race, you and I will never get political justice or get political equality in this country. . . .

In 1923 the United States government brought the work of the UNIA to a sudden end. It charged Marcus Garvey with using the mails to steal money from his followers. He insisted on acting as his own lawyer at his trial, even though he had no training as a lawyer. The case dragged on for two years; finally, Garvey was found guilty. After two years in jail, he was sent back to Jamaica. The UNIA died. Yet its plans for a "Back to Africa" movement lived on in the minds of millions.

A Different Road. Most American Negroes did not join the UNIA. They turned to W. E. B. Du Bois and the new National Association for the Advancement of Colored People. Dr. Du Bois and others believed that men of good will, black and white working together, could take steps to end segregation and discrimination. They believed that the Constitution could be the wedge to hold open the door to equality. Du Bois felt Jim Crow laws denied the equal protection and the rights that the Constitution promised all Americans.

In July, 1905, Dr. Du Bois and 28 other black leaders met in Niagara Falls, Canada. They began a new group called the Niagara Movement. Their chief demand was clear: "We will not be satisfied with less than our full manhood rights." The Niagara Movement issued a statement of its goals.

Here are some of them:

—We believe all men have the right to vote.
—All American citizens have the right to equal treatment in public places.
—We especially complain against the denial of equal opportunities to us to make a living.
—We want equal education in elementary schools and high schools, with college training open to all. Education in the South must be improved.
—We want honest judges, fair juries and the same laws and punishments for blacks and whites.
—We plead for action to give us better health.
—We want labor unions to admit black workers.
—Jim Crow laws must be ended.
—It is time for the federal government to pass laws to enforce the Thirteenth, Fourteenth and Fifteenth Amendments to the Constitution.
—While demanding our rights, we also accept these duties:
   The duty to vote.
   The duty to respect the rights of others.

The Niagara Movement was started in 1905 to call attention to the needs and rights of black Americans. Why was this the beginning of the modern civil rights movement?

The duty to work.

The duty to obey the laws.

The duty to be clean and orderly.

The duty to send our children to school.

The duty to respect ourselves, even as we respect others.

The N.A.A.C.P. The Niagara Movement spread its ideas to many white and black Americans. Then in 1909, the National Association for the Advancement of Colored People—the N.A.A.C.P.—was born. It was headed by Moorfield Storey, a white lawyer from Boston. The N.A.A.C.P. was interracial— for blacks and whites. Its goal was complete equality within the United States. Its methods were slow. It would use the courts. It would work patiently in each community. It would make all people understand Negro problems and needs. The most important leader of the N.A.A.C.P. was W. E. B. Du Bois.

Which Road to Follow? Where was the future for black Americans? Was it in Africa, as Garvey said? Or was it in the United States, as Du Bois insisted? Here are some of the demands the N.A.A.C.P. made in 1919:

—A vote for every Negro man and woman on the same terms as for white men and women.

—An equal chance for a good education.

—A fair trial in the courts for all crimes, by judges Negroes have helped elect.

—A right to be on juries.

—Defense against lynching and burning at the hands of mobs.

—Equal service and treatment on railroads and other public carriers.

—Equal right to use public parks, libraries and other community services for which Negroes too are taxed.

—An equal chance to make a living.

I. WHAT ARE THE FACTS?

Answer each question in a sentence.

1. Who was the first black leader to speak before a large white audience in the South?

2. In what part of the United States were Jim Crow laws strongest?

3. State an important difference in the membership rules of the UNIA and the N.A.A.C.P.

4. Who were the leaders of the UNIA and the N.A.A.C.P.?

5. What did Booker T. Washington mean by "cast down your bucket where you are"?

6. What did W. E. B. Du Bois mean by the statement: "We will not accept half a loaf"?

7. What did the leaders of the Niagara Movement mean by "rights" and "duties"?

8. Why did Marcus Garvey believe black Americans should return to Africa?

9. What is the meaning of the word *compromise?*

10. What was W. E. B. Du Bois's chief goal?

II. THREE POINTS OF VIEW.

Write WASHINGTON if the statement might have been made by Booker T. Washington. Write DU BOIS if the statement might have been made by W. E. B. Du Bois. Write GARVEY if the statement might have been made by Marcus Garvey.

1. Black Americans should not expect full equality until they know as much as white people do.

2. We cannot expect to improve our condition in the United States.

3. Black people are proud to work for white farmers.

4. Black workers should not take jobs as servants to white people.

5. Black Americans should demand equality at once!

III. WHAT DID THEY MEAN?

Explain the meaning of each of these sentences or phrases.

1. Make the great leap from slavery to freedom.

2. There is dignity in tilling the field.

3. We must begin at the bottom of life, not at the top.

4. . . . an equal chance to make a living.

5. . . . denial of equal opportunities.

6. . . . a kind of government that will place our race in control.

IV. "JIM CROW"—A PROBLEM IN MANY PARTS OF THE WORLD.

Laws very much like the Jim Crow laws have appeared in other parts of the world. Class committees can check these examples in the library. Then report to class. Compare each to Jim Crow treatment of black Americans in the United States.

1. The government of the Republic of South Africa follows a policy called *apartheid*. What is apartheid? Who suffers from it? In what ways?

2. About one-fifth of India's people, the group called the Untouchables, had no hope for equality for hundreds of years. How were they treated?

3. In the 1930's the German government passed the Nurenberg Laws, directed chiefly against the Jews. What did these laws try to do?

V. THINKING IT THROUGH!

Discuss.

1. Why did Marcus Garvey conclude that there was no hope for black Americans in the United States?

2. Would you have agreed or disagreed with Booker T. Washington; with W. E. B. Du Bois; with Marcus Garvey? Why?

3. Why did the N.A.A.C.P. decide to use the courts as a key part of its drive to gain complete equality for black Americans?

4. What do the eight demands of the N.A.A.C.P. in 1919 tell you about the problems facing black Americans at that time?

5. What problems caused by the desire of minority group workers to be admitted to trade unions have been important in the news in recent years?

How Did the Supreme Court Begin to Weaken Jim Crow Laws?

8 The *Henderson v. United States* case began on May 17, 1942. President Franklin D. Roosevelt had done much to bring Negroes into government service. Elmer W. Henderson was one of those who had found good jobs in Washington, D.C. He was on a government trip from Washington to Alabama. He bought a first-class ticket. About 5:30 P.M. he heard the first call to dinner. He hurried to the railroad dining car. The two tables nearest the kitchen were used for Negro diners. Curtains were drawn to separate them from the white people in the rest of the car whenever black people ate at these tables. The curtains were not drawn when white passengers used the same tables.

The two special tables were filled with white diners when Mr. Henderson reached the dining car—except for one seat. The man in charge of the dining car refused to seat Mr. Henderson. Jim Crow rules did not permit white and colored persons to be served at the same table. Mr. Henderson returned to the dining car two more times, but could not be served there. At 9:00 P.M. the dining car was taken off the train.

Elmer Henderson knew he had been denied equal treatment only because he was a black man. He complained to the government agency that makes rules for all railroads. He later went to court, aided by Alpha Phi Alpha Fraternity (a national group founded by black students at Cornell University). The fraternity's lawyers fought the case for him. Eight long years passed before the Supreme Court announced its decision—in 1950!

How Could a Court Case Change the Way Millions Live?

How Did Negro Civil Rights Groups Plan to Fight Jim Crow Laws?

What Success Did This Plan Have?

Why Was Progress So Slow?

Judicial Review. *Judicial review* is the power of the Supreme Court of the United States to decide whether a law is permitted by the Constitution. If the Court finds that a law is not permitted, or is *unconstitutional,* then that law should end. But the Court does not judge all the laws passed in this country. A court can make a ruling only when a case is being decided. Most of the cases that come to the Supreme Court reach it as an appeal of the decision of a lower court. This takes time and money. A case can begin in a state court or federal district court. The judge makes a decision. If the losing side is unhappy with his decision, they can then appeal to a higher court. Years may pass as the case moves through the lower courts to the Supreme Court of the United States.

A Plan to Use the Courts. By the 1920's the N.A.A.C.P. and other civil rights groups had decided to use the courts to change the way minority groups were treated. A grand plan was worked out:

— Choose a law that denies a group a right they should have equally with all other citizens.

— Find some person who has suffered from this unfair law. He must be ready to spend years fighting for justice through the courts.

— Find the money to pay all the costs of taking the case from the lowest courts through appeals and up to the United States Supreme Court.

— If you win the case before the Supreme Court, be ready to have your lawyers represent other people in lower courts until the Supreme Court's decision is obeyed all over the country.

— Work at many such cases at the same time. This will bring many court decisions. Each one will bring equality a little closer.

Such a plan called for great patience. Civil rights groups would have to raise millions of dollars. Years would pass before cases were decided. More years would follow while the changes were brought to the whole country. Only real faith in justice and the courts could have kept so many people working at such a plan. Yet they worked hard, and their plan succeeded! The lawyers of the N.A.A.C.P. and other civil rights groups

A NAACP lawyer giving testimony to the United States Supreme Court. How have NAACP court victories helped other minority groups achieve more equality?

won most of the important cases they brought to the Supreme Court. One early victory was an order by the Supreme Court that ended the grandfather clauses that had kept Negroes from voting in some states of the South since the end of Reconstruction. (See p. 106.)

The Attack on Jim Crow. A decision by the Supreme Court stands until the court changes it. The Court may refuse to hear new cases about any matter it has already decided. In 1896 it had decided in the case of *Plessy v. Ferguson* that "separate and equal" treatment of Negroes was proper. The white people of the South had used the Plessy rule to force this separation—but clearly without treating whites and blacks equally. Now N.A.A.C.P. and other civil rights lawyers decided to use the Plessy ruling as their weapon too. They would demand that the United States government and each state in the South *prove* that Negroes were being treated equally. For if the treatment was not equal, then it could not be separate! That in turn would mean that blacks and whites would have to live under the same laws rather than under laws that kept them apart. Bit by bit, the laws that made the Jim Crow world possible would be destroyed!

Elmer Henderson's case shows us how the plan worked. Mr. Henderson had been traveling on the Southern Railway Company. The federal government had approved its rules about dining cars.

—Curtains were placed around the tables at which Negroes could be served. When a white person was served at one of these tables, the curtains were kept open. When a black person was served, the curtains were closed.

—White passengers had first use of these tables and of all other tables in the dining car. When a white person was seated at one of these tables, and there was an empty seat at the table, only another white person could be placed there.

—These rules meant that no black passenger could ever eat in a dining car unless all white passengers were served first!

The Supreme Court agreed that this was not equal service. It ruled that any passenger on a train had the same right to be served in the dining car. He had the same right to take any empty seat. It was wrong to set aside special seats for Negroes, with signs on the tables and curtains around them. The Court ordered that new railroad rules be made so that black passengers would receive equal treatment.

Elmer Henderson orders a meal in a dining car after the Supreme Court decided that separate seating in such cars was not "equal."

Elmer Henderson and his two Alpha Phi Alpha lawyers, Belford V. Lawson and Jawn A. Sandifer, had worked for almost eight years to end this one Jim Crow rule. Was this small change worth all the cost and effort? The men who worked on the case knew it was. If it became the law of the land that all people should be treated equally on railways, then all Jim Crow laws would be a little weaker. Other men could fight other cases, each leading to another kind of equal treatment. Each case could bring all Americans closer to the goal—equality.

Many Cases and Many Changes. Dozens of cases reached the Supreme Court. Let's look at three of them.

The states of the South had set up separate school systems for whites and Negroes. Black boys and girls were separated from whites in elementary schools, in high schools and even in colleges. Schools that offer training after college, such as law and medical schools, are called graduate schools. They are open only to college graduates.

1) The University of Missouri (for whites only) had a law school. Lincoln University (for Negroes only) did not have a law school. In 1935 Lloyd Gaines, a student at Lincoln, made plans to go to law school. He asked to be admitted to the University of Missouri. The State of Missouri offered to pay for his education at a law school of another state. Gaines refused. Instead, he sued to be permitted to attend the University of Missouri's law school. Three years passed before the Supreme

Lloyd Gaines sued for admission to the University of Missouri law school. Why do you think he would not accept a free education at another school instead?

H. Marion Sweatt sued to attend the all-white University of Texas law school, even though there was a black law school. How was this case an additional step toward equality?

Court heard and decided his case. Was he getting "equal" treatment? The Court found that he was not. Missouri had to give him the same kind of education it gave its white law students. He had the right to attend the University of Missouri's law school. The only way Missouri could keep him out would be to build another law school for Negro students equal in every way to the one at the state university.

2) Texas tried to do this. It built a law school for its Negro students. Yet another case, begun in 1946, ended this plan to keep white and black students separate. H. Marion Sweatt was helped by N.A.A.C.P. lawyers as he sued to be admitted to the all-white University of Texas Law School. The Court found that the white law school was better than the new law school Texas had built for Negro students. The new law school could not give its black students an equal education. Texas was ordered to admit black students to the University of Texas Law School.

3) Another case came from Oklahoma. George McLaurin was admitted to the graduate school of the state university. However, he was forced to remain separate from the white students. He was placed at a desk in the doorway rather than in the classroom. When he used the library, he had to take his books to a separate desk on a balcony. When he ate in the student cafeteria, he had to sit at a separate table. His treatment was so different that his education could not be equal to that received by the white students.

N.A.A.C.P. lawyers sued for him. The years passed, and the Supreme Court made its decision. It agreed that George McLaurin had not received equal graduate training. All students had to receive the same treatment in any state's graduate schools.

The Supreme Court decided the Sweatt case, the Henderson case and the McLaurin case on the same day in 1950. Black and white people who hoped for equality cheered these decisions. Segregation and discrimination had been weakened a little more. But the Supreme Court had not given up its Plessy rule. "Separate and equal" was still the law of the land.

I. WHAT ARE THE FACTS?

Answer each question in a sentence or two.

1. Why did Elmer Henderson sue the United States?

2. What group provided help to Mr. Henderson in his lawsuit?

3. Why wasn't Lloyd Gaines admitted to the University of Missouri Law School when he first applied?

4. State one example of the unfair treatment given to George McLaurin in the graduate school of the University of Oklahoma.

5. Name the national civil rights organization that was most active in bringing cases of "unequal treatment" to the Supreme Court.

II. EXPLAIN THE FACTS.

Write the letter of the statement in Column B that best explains the reason for each event described in Column A.

COLUMN A	COLUMN B
1. Elmer Henderson missed his dinner.	a) The school had to obey the ruling of the Supreme Court.
2. The Supreme Court heard the "equal treatment" cases.	b) Those who ran the school believed in Jim Crow.
3. Lloyd Gaines was told to study law in another state.	c) The railway followed Jim Crow rules.
4. H. Marion Sweatt was admitted to the University of Texas Law School.	d) The Supreme Court has the power of "judicial review."
5. George McLaurin sat in the doorway of the classroom.	e) Missouri had no law school for black students and would not admit a black student to its "white" law school.

III. THINKING IT THROUGH!

Discuss.

1. Re-read the five steps in the plan to weaken Jim Crow laws through the courts (page 122).
a) What happens to a case if the person in whose name it was begun later changes his mind and refuses to continue?
b) What happens to a case if the lawyers or group involved in it run out of money?
c) What happens if the case is won, but local cases based on it are not fought?

2. Why was it necessary to use the courts to weaken Jim Crow laws? What would have happened if black Americans had simply refused to obey these laws?

What Rights Could a Negro Have in a Southern Court?

9 The first shots were fired on September 30, 1919. Bullets tore into the church. A mob of white men was attacking! This was the first of several attacks on groups of Negroes in Phillips County, Arkansas.

The real reason for the attack on black farmers in Hoop Spur, Arkansas, was to keep them from joining a union. Why would this have been so important to their attackers?

Most black farmers in Phillips County were sharecroppers who farmed land rented from white landowners. The landowners received a large part of all crops raised on their land. The share left to each Negro farmer was small. He had to live in great poverty. Finally, some of the farmers joined a farmers' union. On this evening in 1919 they met in a church at the village of Hoop Spur to talk over their problems. Suddenly they were attacked! Three days later more than 200 people—men, women and children—were reported dead. The white men who had made the attack said they feared a black revolt was being planned. What they really wanted was to keep Negroes from gaining the protection of a union.

Two white men were killed during the attacks. Seventy-nine Negroes were arrested. Twelve were charged with murder, the others were charged with other crimes. Quick trials followed, and all 79 were found guilty. The N.A.A.C.P. entered the case to save the lives of those wrongly convicted. The case moved up through the courts. In 1923 the Supreme Court made a final decision.

What Rights Should a Person Have When Charged With a Crime?

Why Haven't Black Americans in the South Had Such Rights?

Why Was the Decision in Moore v. Dempsey *Important?*

LANGUAGE OF THE COURTROOM

Judge — In charge of the trial. He rules on all questions of law that come up during the trial. He explains to the jury the points of law that can affect their decision.

Defendant — The person on trial, charged with having committed a crime.

Defense Attorney — The lawyer for the defendant.

District Attorney or State's Attorney — The lawyer for the state. He tries to prove that the defendant is guilty of the charged crime.

Jury — The group of citizens, usually twelve, who decide whether or not the defendant is guilty as charged.

Evidence — Information offered during the trial to prove that the defendant is guilty or innocent.

Confession — A written or oral statement made by a defendant in which he admits his guilt.

Appeal	— Taking a case to a higher court, which has the power to order a new trial or to change the decision of the lower court.
Witness	— A person who gives information or evidence in court.
Testimony	— The sworn statements of a witness in court.

Trials in the United States. The Constitution of the United States guarantees each person a trial whenever he is charged with a crime. He should have a speedy trial. It must be a public trial. The trial must take place in the state and county in which the crime was committed. The defendant must be told exactly what crime he has been charged with. He can be present to hear the evidence of all witnesses against him. He must have the right to call witnesses in his defense. He has the right to have a lawyer to defend him. The court must see to it that these rights are not taken away.

Most crimes and punishments are defined by state laws. Sometimes courts and juries do not always provide fair trials. Let's look at some of the ways in which a trial can become "unfair."

Unfair Trials. Sometimes a defendant wishes to act as his own lawyer. He has a right to do this. Or he can ask for a lawyer's help. The judge can appoint a lawyer to provide this aid if the defendant does not have one of his own. Such court-appointed lawyers have not always tried very hard to help defendants, especially in the South and other areas where poor people are charged with crimes.

The Constitution guarantees a trial by an *impartial* jury, one that has not made up its mind about a case before the trial begins. Yet fair juries are hard to obtain in some parts of the country. In the South, for example, the members of juries have almost always been white men. Blacks have been kept off. When a black person was charged with a crime against a white person, the members of these juries were often prejudiced against the defendant. They would quickly find him guilty, no matter what evidence was given. Members of other minority

groups, chiefly Indians and Mexican-Americans, have also suffered greatly in this way.

The judge does have some power to help the defendant get
a fair trial. He can order that the trial be held in another town
if he and the lawyers agree that a fair trial is not possible in
his court. He might do this if there was a great danger of mob
violence during the trial. He can do it if there has been so
much publicity that he feels a fair trial is no longer possible.
He can do it if the members of the jury admit that they cannot
be impartial. Finally, the judge can declare a *mistrial*. This
means that something has happened during the trial that denied
the defendant his rights. The district attorney may have said
or done something not permitted by state laws. Jury members
may have broken the rules for their conduct during the trial.
Something may have happened in the courtroom. When a
judge declares a mistrial, a new trial must then be held.

However, some judges in the South have been just as racist
as their neighbors. They have not always protected the rights
of black defendants or those who are members of other minority groups. The story of the 1919 trials in Phillips County shows
us what then happens.

Moore v. Dempsey. Frank Moore was one of the Negroes
found guilty in the Arkansas trials. He and others turned to the
N.A.A.C.P. for help. Appeals were made, and the case reached
the United States Supreme Court. The decision in *Moore v.
Dempsey* was the first success by the N.A.A.C.P. as it worked to
gain full rights for black Americans tried in Southern courts.

Oliver Wendell Holmes was one of the great justices in the
history of the Supreme Court. He believed that all people
should have the same rights in a courtroom. In this case, all but
two of the other justices agreed with him. Here are some of the
things Holmes described in the decision he wrote for the
Court.

— The white lawyer who came to town to help Moore and the
  others was arrested himself on a charge of murder. He was
  kept in jail for a month. In this way Moore lost his right to
  have a lawyer of his own choice.
— The governor of Arkansas had set up a Committee of Seven
  to help settle the problems in Phillips County. These men
  had helped the mobs in the streets instead of working for
  justice.

Justice Oliver Wendell
Holmes believed in a fair
trial for all citizens.

— The Committee and the mobs whipped and tortured Negro witnesses until they agreed to give evidence against the defendants.

— The judge in Phillips County appointed a lawyer for Moore and the other defendants. This lawyer never met with the defendants. He did nothing to defend them. He did not even call any witnesses.

— The jury trial lasted 45 minutes. Negroes were barred from serving on the jury. The jury found all of the defendants guilty in five minutes.

— A mob raged in the streets before and during the trial. These men loudly threatened to lynch the defendants and to punish any member of the jury who did not vote "guilty." A fair trial was impossible with this mob ready to explode at any moment.

The Supreme Court ruled that Moore and the others had not had a fair trial. A new trial was ordered.

The case of *Moore v. Dempsey* showed the whole country how unfair some trials really were. In this case, at least, the defendants were saved from an unfair conviction. But one court decision could not change the way all cases were tried. No person could be sure of a fair trial in any place where mobs could freely gather and take action. Lynch law remained powerful—often more powerful than judges and courts.

Unfair trials continued in much of the country. In one way or another, Negroes were still barred from juries. Many men who served on juries were racists who would always decide against a black defendant. Mobs in the South still lynched blacks. Few Negroes had enough money to hire good lawyers. Few white lawyers were willing to defend a Negro. The N.A.A.C.P. and other defense groups could not provide lawyers for all the defendants who might need help.

A First Step. The 79 people found guilty in Phillips County were later freed. From 1923 on, the Supreme Court would decide in favor of defendants who had been denied their rights. If a case came to the Supreme Court, the defendant would be given a new trial if he had not been permitted to have a lawyer, if he had received an unfair trial because of mobs roaming the streets or if witnesses had been forced to testify untruthfully. Yet very few cases in which trials had been unfair ever reach the highest courts.

The *Moore v. Dempsey* case had spelled out the problem. It had not solved it. Congress still refused to pass a law to punish lynch mobs. It still refused to pass laws to give all minorities the right to serve on juries, to vote and in other ways to escape from unequal laws. Only a small first step had been taken. There was so much still to be done.

I. WHAT ARE THE FACTS?

Write a short answer to each question.

1. What was the occupation of most black people in Phillips County, Arkansas, in 1919?

2. What reason did the white mobs give for attacking the black farmers?

3. How many people were reported killed during the attacks in Phillips County?

4. Why did the N.A.A.C.P. enter the case?

5. Who was Frank Moore?

6. Who appointed the Committee of Seven in Phillips County?

7. What order did the Supreme Court give to Arkansas in the *Moore v. Dempsey* decision?

8. State one fact to show that the decision in *Moore v. Dempsey* did not really bring equal justice to all black people in the South.

9. What did Congress do about lynch mobs after the *Moore v. Dempsey* decision?

10. Why weren't Southern juries impartial in cases in which Negroes were defendants?

II. SHOW YOUR UNDERSTANDING.

Define each of these terms.

1. sharecropper
2. farmers' union
3. public trial
4. due process of law
5. court-appointed lawyer
6. forced testimony
7. impartial jury
8. mistrial

III. THINKING IT THROUGH!

Discuss.

1. Why do you think any person would ever act as his own lawyer when he has not been trained to be a lawyer?

2. What responsibility does a judge have in a trial? How can he help a defendant get a fair trial? How much is he to blame when a defendant does not receive a fair trial?

3. Explain why you agree or disagree with this statement: All black citizens of the United State benefited from the Supreme Court's decision in the *Moore v. Dempsey* case.

4. Explain why you agree or disagree with this statement: Congress should always pass laws to help carry out the ideas in Supreme Court decisions.

Can a City or State Require Separate Schools for Black Children?

10 In 1849 Sarah C. Roberts was five years old. Sarah, a free Negro child, lived with her family in Boston. Her father tried to register her in the nearest school. He was told to take her to a more distant school, one for black children only. Mr. Roberts had come to Boston because Massachusetts was a free state. Its constitution said, "All men, without distinction of color or race, are equal before the law." Didn't his daughter have the right to go to the same school as the white children of the neighborhood? He decided to sue the city of Boston.

• • • •

In 1954 the parents of black children all over the country wanted an end to segregated schools. A group of lawyers, led by Thurgood Marshall of the N.A.A.C.P., had brought four cases to the Supreme Court on appeal. Each case tried to end a state law that permitted or required separate public schools for black students. The four states were Kansas, South Carolina, Virginia and Delaware. Didn't these states deny a right promised to all Americans by the Fourteenth Amendment—equal protection of the laws? The states answered that they were giving black children "separate but equal" education.

Did Sarah Roberts have the right to go to the same school as the white children of her neighborhood?

The Court's decision came on May 17, 1954. It was written by Chief Justice Earl Warren; all nine justices agreed. When Justice Warren read his decision, he began a great series of changes in American life. For the first time since the Plessy case of 1896, the Court was ready to give up the idea of "separate but equal"!

What Are Segregation and Integration?

How Did Segregated Schools Harm Black Children?

Why Was the Brown v. Board of Education Decision So Important?

How Did the White Leaders of the South Oppose This Decision?

What Has Happened to Segregated Education in the South Since 1954?

Charles Sumner, the great lawyer and abolitionist, argued for equal rights in education. How long has it taken for his arguments to be accepted?

Segregation in the North. In 1849 Northern laws and customs treated free Negroes differently from other Americans. The cities practiced segregation. This means keeping one group of people apart from other groups in housing and other ways. It also meant that black children had to attend separate schools. The black citizens of Boston objected to this. Again and again they asked Boston's Board of Education for integration, the opposite of segregation. When schools are integrated, white and black children attend the same classes and receive the same education. This would have been equal treatment, as the constitution of Massachusetts promised. The school committee refused.

Sumner Attacks Segregated Education. When Sarah Roberts' father sued, he had one of the great lawyers of American history on his side. Charles Sumner was a leader among those working to end slavery in the United States. Here are Sumner's words when he presented his case before the Supreme Court of Massachusetts:

. . . The Constitution of Massachusetts says *all men, without distinction of color or race, are equal before the law.* The state's Bill of Rights says 'all men are *born* free and equal.' No person can have rights that all his fellow citizens do not enjoy equally.

This is the right of every person who breathes upon this soil, whatever his condition may be, whoever his parents may be. He may be poor, weak, humble, black. He may be of any religion, nationality or race. Before our Constitution all these differences disappear. He is not poor, or weak, or humble, or black. He is not of any race, religion or nationality. He is a MAN—the equal of all his fellowmen.

Separating children in the public schools of Boston on account of color or race robs them of their equality. It means *the black and white are not equal before the law.* . . .

Who can say that this does not harm the black children? It makes them more separate from the rest of the people of Boston. The school is the little world in which the child is trained for the larger world of life. All classes of people should meet in the school. There they can begin the equal life which our Constitution and laws promise to all.

The whites are also injured by this separation. They are taught to think of another group of human beings as a separate and lower class. They are later unable to erase this idea from their minds. Their characters are hurt by this, and they become less fit for the duties of citizenship.

These words were spoken in 1849! Charles Sumner had expressed a complete argument against segregated schools. His ideas remained alive, even though little was done to end segregated education in many states for another 100 years.

A Defense of Segregated Schools. The Chief Justice of Massachusetts, Lemuel Shaw, gave his decision in the case of *Sarah C. Roberts v. The City of Boston.* Here is part of what he said:

. . . All persons in Massachusetts are equal before the law. This does not mean they should be treated the same. It only means that they are equally entitled to protection under the laws. Colored persons must have equal rights. The question is, do separate schools for colored children take away these rights?

The laws of Massachusetts do not order how schools should be organized. These things are decided by the school committee of each town. The Boston School Committee has decided that it is best to have separate schools for colored and white children.

It is said that these separate schools lead to poor treatment for Negroes. This prejudice is not created by law and probably cannot be changed by law.

Justice Shaw had ruled that segregated schools were permitted in Massachusetts. But this was not the end of the question. In 1855, six years after the Roberts case, a new state law ended segregated schools anywhere in Massachusetts. Yet it was 1954 before the United States Supreme Court decided, in *Brown v. Board of Education,* that segregated public schools were not permitted by the Constitution. Its reasons for this decision were almost the same as those first offered by Charles Sumner!

A Different Supreme Court. By 1950 the Supreme Court had come to believe that the United States government should more fully protect the rights of all citizens. In that year the Court ended segregated dining cars on trains. It gave black students the right to admission and fair treatment in graduate schools. Yet such decisions did not bring great changes in the everyday lives of minority-group members. Civil rights groups saw that they had to make a direct attack on a part of Jim Crow that hurt all black people every day. The N.A.A.C.P. led this attack. Its lawyers agreed to represent black citizens whose children were being forced to attend segregated public schools. If young people could be treated equally in their schools, whatever their race, then a key idea of Jim Crow would be destroyed. Children who grow up as students together can learn to live integrated lives. Black children, who had for so long received poorer education than white children, could then begin to receive an equal—a better—education.

The School Segregation Cases. The first case came from Kansas. Negro parents in Topeka asked the Supreme Court to declare the state's 1949 law permitting segregated schools in its cities unconstitutional. The white officials of Topeka's school system had decided to keep their elementary schools segregated. The district federal court had agreed that doing this hurt black students, but ruled that the two groups of schools were otherwise equal.

The second case came from South Carolina. That state's laws required segregation of schools. Black parents in Clarendon County sued to have this law declared unconstitutional. Again a federal district court ruled against the demand for an end to segregated schools. All it would do was order the state to make the Negro schools equal in quality to the white schools.

The third case came from Prince Edward County, Virginia. The parents of some black high school pupils sued to have their children admitted to a white high school. The state's constitution and laws required segregated schools. Again the federal district court followed the "separate but equal" rule of the Plessy decision. It ordered that Negro schools in the county be improved.

The fourth case came from New Castle County, Delaware. The parents of Negro children attacked the parts of the state constitution and laws that required separate public schools. Delaware's Supreme Court ruled that the schools for black children were of poor quality. They were too crowded, and students often had to travel too far to get to them. For these and other reasons it ordered that black students be admitted to white schools. This time it was the white school officials who appealed to the United States Supreme Court!

The Court Considers the Cases. In each case a group of black citizens had charged that the Plessy rule denied their right to equal protection of the laws under the Fourteenth Amendment. The judges in the state courts and federal district courts had answered that the Plessy rule was the law of the land. The justices of the Supreme Court listened to the arguments. Could segregated schools ever be "equal"? Thurgood Marshall and his fellow lawyers said they could not. If this were true, then black children were not receiving equal protection of the laws. The Fourteenth Amendment was meant to remove all differences in the way laws treated citizens. The Plessy rule, made in a transportation case rather than an education case, had been used to permit all kinds of segregation. How could the Court continue to say that this was proper?

Justice Warren's Decision. The Supreme Court considered the cases for two years. At the end of that time, all nine justices agreed on all the points in the cases. Justice Warren explained the new answers the justices had found to six questions. These answers remind us of the points raised by Charles Sumner 100 years earlier!

1. *How important is education?*
   "Today, education is perhaps the most important function of state and local governments. . . . It is required in the performance of our most basic public responsibilities, even service in the armed forces. It is the very foundation of good citizenship."

Former Chief Justice Earl Warren (center) and associate justices of the Supreme Court. In 1967 Thurgood Marshall (upper right) became the first Negro to be appointed to the Court.

2. *How does education shape a child's life?*

"In these days, it is doubtful that any child may reasonably be expected to succeed in life if he is denied the opportunity of an education."

3. *Why should the Supreme Court be concerned with education?*

"[Education] is a right which must be made available to all on equal terms."

4. *Can separate but equal schools give such equal education?*

[We believe that] segregation of children in public schools solely on the basis of race, even though [the schools] may be equal, deprive[s] the children of the minority group of equal educational opportunities."

5. *Should separate schools be permitted any longer?*

"To separate [children in grade and high school] from others of similar age and qualifications solely because of their race generates a feeling of inferiority as to their status in the community that may affect their hearts and minds in a way unlikely ever to be undone. . . .

We conclude that in the field of public education the doctrine of "separate but equal" has no place . . . we hold that the plaintiffs and others similarly situated . . . have been . . . deprived of the equal protection of the laws guaranteed by the Fourteenth Amendment."

6. *What should be done to end segregated schools?*
  "We have now announced that such segregation is a denial of the equal protection of the laws."

The Court then ordered the states in the cases to prepare plans to end the separate schooling of black and white children. These plans would be reviewed by the Court.

This was one of the most important decisions in the history of the Supreme Court. It had decided all four cases as a group. The first of these had been begun by Oliver Brown of Topeka, Kansas, who wanted his daughter to attend a white school. His case was the first mentioned by Justice Warren. Therefore, the decision became known as the Brown Decision of 1954 (*Brown v. Board of Education of Topeka*).

Jim Crow Under Attack? The Court had given the states time to prepare their answers to its ruling. In 1955 it ordered these states to begin integrating their schools. This meant that black and white children would have to be admitted to the same schools. White people in the South had never believed this could happen. Since Reconstruction they had believed they could make whatever decisions they wished about how black people would be treated. Now they were being told that the power of the United States government could be used to make them end one of the most important parts of Jim Crow!

Let's look at some of the ways Jim Crow had hurt black Americans. The white people of the South had worked out ways to keep whites and blacks separate in one way after another. Blacks and whites could not sit together on a train, in a bus, in a theater or in a school. At the same time, black people had the worst seats on trains and buses, had to use the balconies of theaters when they were admitted at all and went to poorer schools. Blacks and whites could not use the same hospitals. They had separate public toilets and water fountains. They had different public parks. They even had to use different entrances to many public places! In all these ways, white Southerners forced a feeling of inferiority upon black Americans.

Negroes might have regained their rights if they had been able to vote freely and hold public office. But the same white men who ruled Southern towns were in charge of the tests given to new voters. They saw to it that few black citizens ever passed these tests. Blacks were also kept from voting by the use of terror. Often fear kept them away even when they had every legal right to vote. There were some parts of the South where black people were a majority. In such areas white political leaders changed district lines so that the black districts were broken up. With so little voting power, few Negroes ever held public office.

Trials might have been fairer if black citizens had served on more juries. However, white judges controlled the lists of voters who were used on juries. They kept Negroes off these lists, and therefore off juries. We saw in *Moore v. Dempsey* how far white people would go to prevent black workers from joining or forming unions. In most of the South black workers were kept out of white-controlled unions. This meant that they had to work at lower pay without the protections that came with being union members.

The white leaders of the South used Jim Crow laws to prevent black people from sharing in the improvement of life that came as the nation developed. "White supremacy" meant that white people alone would gain from any economic growth in the South. Integrated schools would weaken white supremacy. They might lead to many other forms of equality.

Why were private schools such as this one in Liberty, Mississippi, set up throughout the South after the Supreme Court ruled that public schools must be integrated?

Southern politicians quickly attacked the Supreme Court after the Brown Decision. They announced that they would fight any plan to integrate their schools. Whites in all the Southern states set up groups to carry on this fight. Many called themselves White Citizens Councils. These councils quickly planned ways to prevent integration in the public schools.

Refusing to Obey the Supreme Court. In 1955 the Supreme Court told the South to integrate schools "with all deliberate speed." Each state has one or more federal courts. These courts were given the task of carrying out the Brown Decision. But most of the judges of these courts were Southerners who believed in Jim Crow. They became part of the Southern fight against the Supreme Court's orders.

The Southern members of Congress made their own plans. On March 12, 1956, 101 of them signed a statement they called a "Declaration of Constitutional Principles." It has become known as the Southern Manifesto. The men who signed this statement asked their states to refuse to obey the Supreme Court's order. They also promised to block it in every possible legal way. Here are the chief ideas they presented to the country:

— The Supreme Court does not have the power to order an end to segregated schools.
— Only a state, and not the federal government, can decide whether or not schools should be segregated.
— The "separate but equal" rule of the Plessy case has become part of the life of the people of many states. To change this rule now would deny parents the right to decide how their children should be educated.
— The states are correct in deciding to oppose the Court's order "by all lawful means."

The men who signed the statement promised to try to have the Brown Decision changed. They would also prevent the government from using force as it tried to carry out the decision.

A Challenge to the Nation. The United States now faced a challenge that brought back memories of the Civil War. One part of the country was refusing to obey the Constitution. It was saying that it did not have to accept the decisions of the

President Eisenhower sent soldiers to guard black students at Central High School in Little Rock, Arkansas. Was he right to do so?

Supreme Court. Black Americans faced a serious problem as well. What should they do when Southern states refused to obey the law of the land? How could they gain the right that the Supreme Court had told them was theirs—the right to an integrated education? And if segregation was wrong in schools, wasn't it just as wrong in every other part of their lives? How could they end it in other areas?

The chief question was this: Would the government stand behind the Supreme Court's decision? Dwight D. Eisenhower was then President. He never made a public statement favoring the Brown Decision. He did not believe the power of the government should be used to force changes in the way people lived. He believed change had to begin in the minds of men.

The minds of most white men in the South were not ready for change. Civil rights groups had to go to court again. A case in Arkansas in 1957 led to events that shocked the whole country. Central High School in Little Rock was ordered to admit black students who applied. Nine boys and girls were accepted by the city board of education. Governor Orvil Faubus of Arkansas then ordered the state's National Guard to keep them out! For three weeks white mobs roamed the streets of Little Rock. They refused to obey the law. President Eisenhower had to send soldiers of the United States Army to enforce the law. These soldiers remained at the school to keep peace for the rest of the school year. Eight of the nine students finished the school year.

By 1956 about 125 black students were attending "white" colleges in the South. Yet the state universities of Alabama, South Carolina, Georgia, Mississippi and Florida refused to make this change. In February, 1956, a federal judge ordered the University of Alabama to admit its first black student, a girl named Autherine Lucey. Riots followed. In the end Miss Lucey was forced to leave.

Mississippi held out until 1962. Then a court case led to an order to the state university to admit a young black veteran named James Meredith. Mississippi's Governor Barnett himself prevented James Meredith from registering. President Kennedy then sent 320 United States marshals to the university, and soldiers to help them. An all-night riot followed. Thousands of men from other parts of Mississippi joined students in an attack on the marshals. Two people were killed; 375 were hurt. The Army had to be used to keep order. Meredith remained and graduated—with United States marshals at his side day and night.

Mob rule could not hold back federal court orders. The leaders of the South turned to other steps. They passed laws that again barred integrated schools. They closed their public schools and gave state money to private schools set up for whites only. Southern federal judges allowed cases that attacked these steps to drag for years. In some parts of the South these judges accepted plans to integrate schools one grade a year. This could mean twelve or more years before an entire school system was integrated!

Federal marshals protected James Meredith at the University of Mississippi until he graduated! Here he is shown being driven to class.

Meanwhile the federal government began to spend more money to help the country's schools. Some of the laws granting this money stated that it could be given only to integrated school systems. Many southern school districts, even when they needed the money, refused it rather than end segregation.

Most Southern schools remained segregated. In the 1960's foreign affairs began to become the most important concern of the federal government. The United States and Russia came close to war. Cuba became a threat to the safety of the United States. The country became deeply involved in a war in Vietnam. Presidents found that they needed the support of Congress. Southern members of Congress were among the strongest supporters of war-like moves by the country. The Presidents wanted their support for the war in Vietnam. Some people began to say that the government was more interested in the war halfway around the world than in improving the rights of minorities at home. By 1969 only a few hundred of the thousands of schools in the South had been integrated.

Then, in 1969 and 1970, the Supreme Court made decisions in cases from several Southern states. These states had asked for more time to change their school systems. President Nixon was willing to give them this time. But the Court would not permit further delay, even though federal judges in the South had ruled that it was proper.

The Court had a new Chief Justice in 1969—Warren Earl Burger. He and all the other justices agreed to orders that promised a quick end to segregation. The order to Mississippi, for example, was clear and simple:

— Mississippi schools must be integrated immediately.
— No person is to be kept out of any school because of race or color.
— The federal court in Mississippi must make the carrying out of this order its most pressing business.

An End to Segregated Schools? The events of 1970 seemed to mean an end to segregated Southern schools. One school district after another agreed to integrate its schools. Some of them had to plan to bus students from one neighborhood to another to do this. President Nixon believed such busing was wrong. New cases came before the courts on this question. However, by 1971 much of the Southern refusal to integrate schools had ended. At the same time hundreds of all-white private schools had been opened. By this means parents of white students were able to keep their children from an integrated school life. However, most Southern white parents could not afford the cost of such schools. For most white and black children in the South, 100 years of segregated schooling seemed to be coming to an end.

I. WHAT ARE THE FACTS?

Write the letter of the choice that best completes each statement.

1. Charles Sumner believed that (a) black children should be educated in separate schools, (b) black and white children should attend the same schools, (c) a board of education should have the power to decide where black children should be educated.

2. In the case *Sarah C. Roberts v. the City of Boston*, the court decided that (a) segregated schools could continue, (b) segregated schools should be ended, (c) it had no power to rule on school questions.

3. The Supreme Court did little against Jim Crow laws between 1896 and 1954 because it was following the rule it had made in the case of (a) *Moore v. Dempsey*, (b) *Plessy v. Ferguson*, (c) *Dred Scott v. Sandford*.

4. In 1954, Thurgood Marshall was chief lawyer for (a) the N.A.A.C.P., (b) the Justice Department, (c) the State of New York.

5. The Warren decision in the Brown case was agreed to by (a) five of the nine justices, (b) seven of the nine justices, (c) all of the justices.

6. In the Brown decision, the Supreme Court ruled that (a) all Jim Crow laws are unconstitutional, (b) states have no power to make rules for local school systems, (c) education must be available to all on equal terms.

7. The Court held that segregated schools must be ended because they (a) gave poor education to all children, (b) denied equal protection of the laws, (c) did not permit parents to decide how their children should be educated.

8. A chief goal of the White Citizens Councils has been to (a) bring

about peaceful segregation of Southern schools, (b) oppose all integration of Southern schools, (c) form new political parties.

9. The Southern Manifesto told the country that Southern states would (a) obey the law and accept the Brown Decision, (b) oppose the Brown Decision, (c) secede unless the Supreme Court reversed the Brown Decision.

10. President Eisenhower (a) gave full support to the Brown Decision, (b) refused to accept the Brown Decision, (c) enforced the Brown Decision when Southern mobs used violence to block it.

11. A chief cause of the troubles in Little Rock, Arkansas, was the refusal of (a) white teachers to teach black students, (b) black students to attend Central High School, (c) the governor of Arkansas to obey a federal court order.

12. Autherine Lucey was admitted and then forced to leave the University of (a) Alabama, (b) Mississippi, (c) Georgia.

13. President Kennedy had to use federal marshals and soldiers to help James Meredith remain at the University of (a) Alabama, (b) Mississippi, (c) Georgia.

14. One reason for the failure of most Southern schools to integrate since 1954 has been that (a) no President has accepted the Brown Decision as the law of the land, (b) Presidents have not fully enforced the Brown Decision and the Supreme Court orders that followed it, (c) Presidents do not have the power to enforce a Supreme Court decision.

15. In 1969 and 1970 the Supreme Court ordered Southern school districts to (a) integrate their schools at once, (b) spend more money on schools for black students, (c) make plans to integrate schools one grade at a time.

16. In the years since 1954, integrated education has been begun in (a) no school districts in the South, (b) only a few school districts in the South, (c) most school districts in the South.

II. UNDERSTANDING THE FACTS.

Answer each question in a sentence or two.

1. What is the difference between discrimination and segregation?

2. How is freedom different from equality?

3. How can segregated schools for black children harm white children?

4. Why is it fair to have schools for one sex and not fair to have schools for one race?

5. Why did President Eisenhower send troops to Little Rock, even though he believed the power of the federal government should not be used to carry out the Brown Decision?

III. WHAT DO THEY MEAN?

Explain each of these words or phrases.

1. segregated public schools
2. integrated public schools
3. equal educational opportunities
4. a feeling of inferiority
5. unanimous
6. with all deliberate speed
7. by all lawful means
8. manifesto

IV. THINKING IT THROUGH!

Discuss.

1. Explain why you agree or disagree with Charles Sumner's statement that: "No person can have rights that all his fellow citizens do not enjoy equally."

2. Would all-black communities mean an end to inequality? Explain.

3. What problems might you face if you were the first black student in an all-white school or the first white student in an all-black school?

4. Why do you agree or disagree with the statement that minority-group children educated in segregated schools must develop a feeling of inferiority?

5. How true do you find this statement by Justice Earl Warren?

"In these days, it is doubtful that any child may reasonably be expected to succeed in life if he is denied the opportunity of an education."

Why Do Schools in Northern Cities Remain Segregated?

11 Metropolitan High School is a make-believe school in a crowded, older area of a large American city. By 1970 the residents of this area were almost entirely black. Many of its buildings are in poor condition. Apartments are small and crowded. Metropolitan is a segregated school, even though the Brown Decision and the laws of the state and city in which it is located have tried to end segregated schools.

A school in New York City's Harlem. Why does its location make it actually a segregated school?

Schools in most large cities receive their students from the blocks of apartments nearby. So many people are crowded together in these blocks that schools must be built only a few blocks apart. New York City has about 1,000 schools. Most of them are crowded. They are called "neighborhood schools." Often they are really segregated schools. Why have the large cities of the country been unable to end segregated schools?

Why Have Schools in the Large Cities Remained Segregated?

What Has Been Done to Try to End Such Segregation?

Why Has "Community Control" Become a New Goal of Big City Minority Groups?

Segregated Neighborhoods. Housing discrimination has been found in most of the United States since the Civil War. For more than 100 years, the larger cities have suffered most of all. Minority-group members have been refused housing except in neighborhoods where others of their group already live. These "segregated" neighborhoods—or *ghettos*—are often the cities' worst slums. The ghettoes that remain today are filled chiefly by non-whites—blacks, Puerto Ricans, Chinese, Japanese, Filipinos, Indians and Mexican-Americans. In the big cities, it is the blacks, Puerto Ricans and Mexican-Americans who most often find they must live in the slums.

De Jure and De Facto Segregation. The term *de jure* ("by law") means something required or permitted by law. *De jure* segregation in housing has been ended by Supreme Court decisions and by the Fair Housing Law of 1968. But housing is still segregated in every large city in the country. This is because of *de facto* segregation.

The term *de facto* ("in fact") describes something that exists even though it is not required by law. Negroes, Puerto Ricans and Mexican-Americans are among our poorest people. They cannot afford to live in new, expensive housing. They have had to live in the cheaper apartments found in old buildings in the slums. This has created *de facto* segregation.

Many cities have built large new buildings to provide homes for poorer people. These buildings are usually built in groups called "public housing projects." Since most of the poorer people in the cities are members of minority groups, *de facto* segregation has appeared in public housing too.

Slum Housing. The population of the country's large cities has grown greatly since the 1940's. The cities need a million or more new homes and apartments each year just to keep up with their needs. Builders make more money from expensive homes than they do from those needed by the poor. The cities do not have enough money to build the amount of public housing people need. Some help has come from the federal government. For example, one block on 114th Street in New York City's Harlem was repaired and rebuilt at a cost of millions of dollars. But the amounts spent by the national government have been small. A 1968 law promised much more such help, but many years may pass before it brings any real changes to the slums. Meanwhile, *de facto* segregation grows greater each year.

Usually it is non-whites who are forced to live in ghetto slums. What effect does this have on their children?

School Integration in the North. The story of segregated "neighborhood schools" in the North can best be understood by examining New York State. New York has done more than most other states to help its minority-group citizens. It was the first state to set up a Commission on Human Rights. It has done more to protect workers than most other states. Its courts have tried hard to give equal justice to all.

New York State took steps to weaken school segregation shortly after the Brown Decision of 1954. Most of the schools in its cities and large towns were neighborhood schools. This meant that they were segregated wherever minority-group citizens lived in one neighborhood. This was *de facto* segregation. Problems were found in the small towns as well as in the cities. These were the same towns and cities in which housing discrimination against members of minority groups had forced them to live in only a few neighborhoods.

The State Commissioner of Education, Dr. James Allen, ordered many towns to take steps to integrate their schools. This was easy to do in a small town that might have only a few schools. Children would not have to travel far to get to one school rather than another. School buses are used in most small towns. These buses could bring black children to schools that had always been "white" and white children to schools that had always been "black." Dr. Allen and the state government believed it should take little time to end the separate schools that were found all over the state.

They were wrong. Some white parents did not want their children to attend school with black or Spanish-speaking children. They gave many reasons for their objections. Minority school children did not read as well as the white children. Mixing them could mean that the white children would not learn as much. Negro children, they said, were less well behaved. They might fight with or otherwise harm white boys and girls. Children should not have to travel from their own neighborhood to go to school. Parents should have the right to decide which children will be the classmates of their own children. The one reason they did not give was often the true reason: many parents were prejudiced against members of minority groups. They did not want their children to grow up as part of an integrated world.

Local school boards and groups of parents went to court to fight the orders of the State Commissioner of Education. Most of these cases were settled by agreements that led to some integration, with the promise of more integration to come. Some of them failed to bring the changes the state ordered.

An important case came in Rochester in 1963. The Board of Education of that city moved the fifth and sixth grades of an all-white school to the building of a school 2½ miles away. Most of the students already in the new building were black. The parents of the white children went to court to block the plan. They kept their children out of school for most of the school year. They acted in a way similar to white parents in some parts of the South—keeping their children out of an integrated school while they fought their case in court. The Rochester Board of Education was trying to end *de facto* segregation in both schools. A state court agreed that it was proper to bus the children from one school to another so that both schools could be integrated.

A second important case came in 1964. The towns of Long Island were chiefly white. Black and Puerto Rican families lived in segregated parts of these towns. This meant that their children went to *de facto* segregated schools. In 1964 the State Commissioner of Education ordered Hempstead, one of the largest towns on Long Island, to take steps to end its segregated schools. He told the town to stop sending all children to neighborhood schools. It was to assign boys and girls to schools so that all schools would be integrated. Hempstead refused and went to court. The court ruled against Hempstead. It had to do as the Commissioner had ordered.

The changes have come slowly in New York State. They are even slower in other states in the North. They are slowest of all in the very large cities. Again and again groups of white parents go to court to prevent or delay school integration. In some cities it has become clear that real integration may be impossible.

Open Enrollment in New York City. There are enough schools in New York City so that it would seem possible to end *de facto* segregation in all of them. The city's government really tried to do this. But travel is slow in the city. Buses must move through heavy traffic. They can need an hour or more to pick up several groups of children in one neighborhood and deliver them to a school in another neighborhood. Black and white

One way to end *de facto* segregation is by busing students to other schools. Here white students are bused to a formerly all-black school. Does this seem to you to be a good way to solve the problem?

parents often feel that it is wrong to expect young children to spend hours traveling to and from school, even though such travel can mean better integrated schools. New York City had to permit each parent to make this decision for his own children. The plan was called *open enrollment*. A parent of a child in a *de facto* segregated school could agree to have his child go to a school in another neighborhood. Thousands of children did travel to new schools in this way. However, most parents preferred to have their children attend a school within walking distance, even though it remained segregated. By 1960 the open enrollment plan had brought some integrated education to many schools that had been chiefly white.

The federal government gave special help to these schools. They received more teachers, after-school programs, free lunch programs and extra money for books and supplies. But a new and unexpected problem quickly appeared. It was one to which the city could offer no solution. The parents of many of the white children in these open-enrollment schools moved away. They were replaced by minority groups. One open-enrollment school after another became a new *de facto* segregated school.

Open enrollment had failed to make many schools truly integrated.

Growing Minority-Group Neighborhoods. Minority-group neighborhoods in large cities are so large that dozens of schools in each of them have become all-black, all-Puerto-Rican or all Mexican-American. There seemed to be no way to integrate them. In 1970 more than half the students in New York City's public schools were Negro or Spanish-speaking. In Manhattan, the center of the city, more than three-fourths of the students were black or Puerto Rican. How could their schools be integrated when there were so few white children—most of them living in other neighborhoods?

Other cities have had the same problem. Most of the students in Washington, D.C., are black. So are those in Newark, South Chicago and other cities or large parts of cities. Many white children do not attend the public schools. Instead, they are in private or church-operated schools where most students are white.

The Anti-Busing Law. The final blow to plans for integration in the big cities of the North came from the state legislatures. They passed new laws—later declared unconstitutional—that weakened or blocked these plans. The law passed by the New York State legislature in 1969 seemed to set this new pattern. It stated two new rules. The first seemed to promise integrated schools. The second made them impossible!

1. No person shall be refused admission into any public school in the state of New York on account of race, creed, color or national origin.
2. . . . no student shall be assigned [to] any school on account of race, creed, color or national origin, or for the purpose of achieving equality in attendance . . . or reduced attendance, at any school, of persons of one or more . . . races, creeds, colors or national origins. . . . Nothing contained in this section shall prevent the assignment of a pupil in the manner requested by his parent. . . ."

This has become known as the "anti-busing" law. It meant that most children in New York State would continue to attend their neighborhood schools. A white parent could refuse to permit his child to be sent to another school to help integrate it. Black or Puerto Rican parents could still ask that their children be part of an "open enrollment" plan. In 1970 a federal court ruled that the anti-busing law was unconstitutional. The case was then appealed to the United States Supreme Court. Until the court rules, the law continues in force.*

Decentralization. What can be done to improve the education of minority-group children? The federal government has supplied hundreds of millions of dollars to the country's schools each year. This money is used to bring about better education. Children of minority groups receive special services. Their classes are smaller. Their schools buy more books and supplies. Their teachers receive extra training. But there is a great distance between a community and the Board of Education that runs a large city's schools. Sometimes those in charge do not really understand the needs of the children of a given neighborhood. A school system that is run by a part of a city's government is said to be *centralized*. The central group makes all the decisions about the schools of every neighborhood in the city. People began to ask for *decentralization*. This would mean that the people of each community would make the decisions about how their schools should be run.

New York City decentralized its school system in 1970. The city was divided into thirty "communities." Each of these elected its own community school board. The new boards received great power over the schools in their districts.

Other cities waited to see what success community control of schools might have. This new way to run a large city's school system might work out well. The new chief goal would be to improve all schools. Integration would become less important.

Perhaps the most important part of community control will be the greater interest of parents in their children's schools. New York City hoped its minority-group parents would learn more about their schools and help make needed changes. This might become the answer to the lasting problems of *de facto* segregated schools.

*In May 1971, the United States Supreme Court held that anti-busing laws were unconstitutional. This means that the 1970s would see an end to local efforts to prevent school integration through busing.

I. WHAT ARE THE FACTS?

Answer each question in a sentence or two.

1. What is a "neighborhood school"?

2. What is *de facto* segregation?

3. What does the term *de jure* mean?

4. What is *open enrollment?*

5. What is *decentralization?*

6. How did the New York courts rule when towns such as Hempstead tried to keep their schools segregated?

7. How did the New York anti-busing law weaken efforts to integrate the state's schools?

8. What is a "community school board"?

II. WHAT ARE THE PROBLEMS?

Explain the problem or problems that result from each of these situations.

1. Most students in each big-city ghetto are members of the same minority group.

2. Large cities have not been able to end segregation in most of their schools.

3. Small towns do not want their schools to be integrated.

III. THINKING IT THROUGH!

Discuss.

1. White people have been moving away from neighborhoods whose schools are being integrated. Minority-group families also move out of these neighborhoods when their incomes rise. How does such "moving away" weaken plans to integrate big city schools?

2. Most big-city teachers and principals are white. Parents in segregated school districts have asked for more minority-group teachers and principals. For what reasons would you favor or oppose this change?

3. What changes have been made in your community to improve the education of minority-group children? Which have been most successful? Why? Which have not been successful? Why?

Unit Three

MEXICAN-AMERICANS

Most Mexican-Americans live in the Southwest, an almost
forgotten minority. Americans in other parts of the country
know little about them. This unit tells their story and
describes the problems they have known since the United
States took half of Mexico in 1848. The Mexicans living in
that conquered land were part of the first great culture of
North America. They soon lost most of their contact with it.
They lost their own land. Most became poor farmers and
workers. They were treated poorly by the Americans who took
control throughout the Southwest. Mexican-Americans were
denied equality under the laws and in their daily lives. Today
they suffer the results of more than a hundred years of unequal
treatment. Most have had little education; without it they
cannot improve their lives. They have little power in local or
state governments. Yet new movements have appeared
through which they are working for a better future. They hope
to regain some of the land stolen from them. They have set up
unions to better their lives as farm workers. They are taking
steps to rebuild their old culture. They add their voices to
others crying for equality and justice. At last, they hope, they
will be heard.

Who Are the Mexican-Americans?

1 More than five million Americans are of Mexican ancestry. Many call themselves Chicanos, from the last part of the word *Mejicano*. Others resent this name; they prefer to be called Mexicans or Mexican-Americans. Most speak of their people as *La Raza*—The Race. This minority is at least five times larger than that of the American Indians. Mexican-Americans are a suffering minority, a people who live in the Southwest but gain very little from the business and wealth of that area. Yet they are proud. They know that they keep an old culture alive—one that is really the mixture of many cultures.

They too are a mixture. Their ancestors were Aztecs, Toltecs and members of other great Indian tribes. These ancestors later married and mixed with Spaniards and others who were not Indians. Mexican-American roots go back more than 10,000 years, to a time when white Europeans were just learning how to farm and build villages. The first contact with Europeans came after the year 1500. The Aztecs, a powerful Indian tribe, then ruled central and southern Mexico. They had conquered the more civilized tribes of Mexico. These Mexican Indians knew how to work with copper, tin, bronze and other metals. They were master farmers who grew corn, beans, tomatoes, potatoes, cotton and other crops. They had developed skill in medicine, astronomy and mathematics. Long before the Europeans arrived, these Indians had built pyramids 25 stories high and almost 700 feet square at their base.

Then, in 1519, Hernando Cortez and a small army of about 550 Spaniards came to Mexico. Their weapons —guns and cannon—made it easy for them to conquer the Aztecs. Cortez tricked and then killed the emperor of the Aztecs. He made himself ruler of the great Aztec empire. Mexico was ruled by Spain for 300 years. Spain permitted the people of different races to marry. A new people developed—*La Raza*. When the United States took half of Mexico in 1848, part of *La Raza* became a conquered people living in a conquered land!

Why Did the United States Go to War With Mexico?

What Changes Were Made After the Mexican War?

How Did These Changes Affect the Mexican-Americans?

With the capture of Montezuma, Cortez made himself ruler of the Aztec empire. How was he able to conquer such a great civilization?

The Meaning of Manifest Destiny. John L. O'Sullivan was the editor of a newspaper of the 1840's called *The United States Magazine and Democratic Review.* He tried to get the country to believe that it had to keep moving west. He said it should take all of the land between the Atlantic and the Pacific. His idea was shared by many leaders in Washington. The land west of the Mississippi might hold great riches. It might become the home of millions of farmers, miners and cattlemen. Pushing for more land in the West soon became almost a religion. People began to speak of the nation's *destiny* —something that had to happen, as if God had planned it would happen. Anything that is *manifest* is so clear that it is plain to everyone. O'Sullivan told his readers it was the "manifest destiny" of the United States to take all the land between the oceans.

161

The United States stretched from the Atlantic to the Mississippi when the country gained its freedom from England. Then in 1803 it added the Louisiana Purchase. In 1819 it added Florida. In 1835 it did not yet have the Pacific Coast and the area we call the Southwest—from Texas through California.

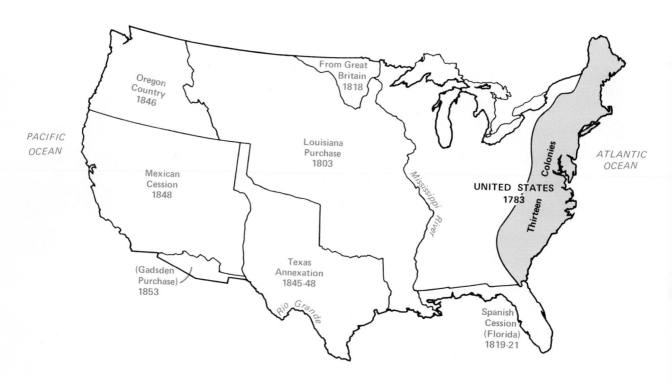

THE GROWTH OF THE UNITED STATES. What were the ways in which this nation gained its land?

Changes in Mexico. A few thousand Spaniards took over Mexico in the 1500's. They ruled millions of Indians. The men from Spain knew that they would have to make these people more like Spaniards if they were to keep control over them. They used their armies to force Indians to become Christians. Once many of the Indians were Roman Catholics, the churches could be used to help control them. Then the Spaniards took steps to make the Indians accept Spanish culture. They destroyed the fine schools and libraries Indians had developed over hundreds of years. Their "book-burning" was so complete that today we have remaining only about fifty written Aztec works! Spanish-speaking schools were begun, and Indian children near the many churches attended them. Spanish religious plays replaced the entertainments the Indians loved. Printing presses were brought from Europe, and Spanish plays, histories and religious books were soon spread through Mexico. Few people realize that the first literature, theater, music and history written in the Americas came from Mexico!

The Indians had no choice. They had to accept much of Spanish culture. But they also kept much of their own. Mexican music became part Spanish and part Indian. Mexican dances became a mixture of Spanish and Indian forms. Each province soon had its special dances and music, each different because different Indian tribes lived in each area. Indian styles of clothing, weaving and pottery mixed with those of Spain to make a "Mexican" style. Spaniards learned the best ways to farm Mexican land from the Indians, as well as better ways to build with clay and stone.

The Spaniards divided the land of Mexico in a new way. When the Indians had owned all the land, it had belonged to the tribes. The Spaniards gave large "land grants" to men from Spain, and other land grants to Indian villages. Few people lived in the northern half of Mexico, the land north of the Rio Grande River. Few people lived in California, even though its fishing and farmland were good. Texas, with good farmland and grazing land, was almost empty. New Mexico, where it was believed important gold mines would be found, was held by Indian tribes who had never been conquered.

The Spanish rulers of Mexico, beginning even before 1600, tried to settle their northern provinces. Priests often led the way, setting up little towns built around churches, called missions. There was a string of these along the coast of California, and more than 25 in the area we now call New Mexico and Arizona. Men from Mexico who brought settlers into the new lands were given land grants, sometimes of fifty square miles or more. Each village begun in the northern half of Mexico also received a large land grant. This land belonged to the whole village, not to one person.

Mexico also offered land to people from the United States who were willing to move into the new lands. Large estates called *ranchos* were given to Americans who moved into California and became citizens of Mexico. Other groups moved into Texas and New Mexico. They had to promise to become Mexi-

Large estates called *ranchos* were given to Americans who moved to California and became Mexican citizens.

can citizens and Roman Catholics, but this law was never really enforced. In the 1820's there were settlements of people from the United States scattered from Texas to California. The first large settlement in Texas was begun by Stephen Austin in December, 1821.

Texas Breaks Away from Mexico. Most of the settlers from the United States came from the South. They brought their black slaves with them, for Spain permitted slavery in Mexico. Then, from 1800 to 1821, most of Spain's colonies in the Americas gained their freedom. Spain was weakened by the wars that tore Europe between 1792 and 1815. It could no longer raise and support the large armies needed to crush the many independence movements in its American colonies. A revolution in Mexico in 1821 was soon successful. The people of Mexico set up a new government, the Republic of Mexico. For three years the different political groups in Mexico struggled for control. It was 1824 before Mexico's new republic had really organized itself and written a constitution.

Mexican laws gave large amounts of land to settlers, and as much as 100 square miles to any man who brought enough settlers to begin a new town. Settlers poured in, bringing their slaves with them and then adding more slaves. However, these people had to obey Mexican laws. Mexican officials ruled Texas, aided by Mexican soldiers. Then the Mexican government passed a law that made the new settlers willing to use force to break away from Mexico. The new law ordered an end to slavery!

By 1830 there were about 5,000 Mexicans and 20,000 Americans in Texas. The Mexican government began to fear that the large number of settlers from the United States would try to gain independence from Mexico. It ordered a halt to new settlement by Americans. It freed all slaves. The Texans refused to obey either law. Mexico's government was weak. Its armies were busy keeping order in the provinces south of Texas. It was therefore unable to enforce its laws for several years.

By 1835 the Texans were ready to act. They declared themselves no longer part of Mexico. They set up a new government and raised an army. Many Texas Mexicans joined it. The American and Mexican Texans, led by Sam Houston, defeated the Mexican armies sent against them. It was a short war in which few people were killed. Its result was the loss of Texas and even greater weakness for the government of Mexico. Texas was free, but the Mexican government did not accept this "freedom." If and when it could, Mexico promised to regain control over Texas.

The war to free Texas from Mexican rule was led by Sam Houston. Why would Americans in Texas want to be free of Mexico?

Manifest Destiny Ideas in Washington. The Texans wanted their new "independent" country to become part of the United States. The leaders of Congress did not want to take this action. They realized it would mean taking control of land that was really still part of Mexico. Yet more and more Americans were accepting the ideas of Manifest Destiny. The United States would move west until it owned all the land between the oceans. President James Polk, who took office in 1845, quickly moved to get Congress to add Texas to the United States. He then tried to get Mexico to agree to sell the rest of its land north of the Rio Grande. Mexico refused, and Polk decided to take these lands through war.

The Mexican War. Early in 1846 President Polk sent an army to the Rio Grande. The border with Texas had never been clear. Texas said it was the Rio Grande River; the Mexicans replied that it was another river north of the Rio Grande. This meant that the American army was going into land claimed by Mexico. A Mexican army moved north. The commander of the American forces soon reported to President Polk that the Mexicans had fired at American soldiers on American soil. The President asked Congress to declare war against Mexico.

> . . . Mexico has passed the boundary of the United States, has invaded our territory and shed American blood upon American soil. . . . War exists . . . by act of Mexico itself.

The war that followed was won by the United States. Fighting lasted about a year, as American armies moved into Mexico City and across the lands north of the Rio Grande into California. Mexico had to agree to a peace treaty in 1848, the Treaty of Guadalupe Hidalgo (the Mexican town in which it was signed).

The treaty brought about what is known as the Mexican Cession. It ceded, or gave, the United States half of Mexico—land that today is California, Arizona, New Mexico, Texas, Utah, Nevada and parts of Wyoming and Colorado. Ulysses S. Grant, later President of the United States, was an officer in this war. He later called the Mexican War the "most unjust ever waged by a stronger against a weaker nation." Why had it happened? He believed the reason was "to acquire territory out of which slave states might be formed."

President James Polk carried on the Mexican War to gain Texas and other lands in the West. Why was the war later called the "most unjust ever waged by a stronger against a weaker nation"?

The Mexican-Americans. Between 60,000 and 100,000 Mexicans, and an unknown number of Indians who had accepted Mexican rule, lived in the lands gained by the United States in 1848. They had been ruled by Mexican officials; they would now be ruled by English-speaking officials of the United States. The Mexicans, who found themselves living under United States rule, were different from other Americans. They spoke a different language. They had a different culture. Most of them had lived far enough away from any government so that each town or village really ruled itself. Most of the settlements of the Southwest outside of Texas were filled with Mexican-Americans. How were their rights to be protected? What would be done with the lands they owned? The Treaty of Guadalupe Hidalgo made important promises on these subjects.

—Mexicans in the lands taken from Mexico "shall be free to continue where they now reside, or to remove at any time to the Mexican Republic . . ."
—". . . property of every kind, now belonging to Mexicans . . . shall be . . . respected." This meant property owned by the Mexican-Americans living in the new lands, and also by Mexicans in Mexico.

This set of promises must have pleased the new Mexican-Americans. At least their land would not be taken from them. Yet they remained uneasy. Settlers would now pour in from the United States. How would these people treat the Mexican settlers who had already built homes in the Southwest? United States officials would take charge of all government activities. How would they treat their country's new "citizens" who knew so little about United States government and customs? The Americans were slaveholders while the Mexicans were not. What changes would come when these slaveowners settled among free men? Most important was the fear no man could escape—would the United States keep its promises? Indians had had treaties making similar promises, and tribe after tribe had been forced to move. These problems must have seemed even greater to any Mexican-Americans who saw statements like the one below. It appeared in 1848 in an important Washington newspaper.

Have we not driven back the insolent enemy, who invaded

Texas and shed the blood of our citizens upon our own soil? Have we not pursued him into the heart of his own country, seized all his strongholds upon the coast, and occupied his capital?

. . . Now they are tamed as before. . . . Does anyone now believe that their spirit is not humble. . . ?

They will be stripped, too, of a large portion of this territory. They may be stripped of more . . . we can truly say that we have every reason to be proud of the war, and proud of the peace which it has obtained us.

I. WHAT ARE THE FACTS?

Answer each question in a sentence or two.

1. Why do most Mexican-Americans live in the Southwest?

2. What is the meaning of *Manifest Destiny?*

3. What races mixed to produce the Mexican-Americans?

4. Name some of the skills of the Aztec Indians.

5. How did the Spaniards change the culture of the Mexican Indians?

6. What is the meaning of *La Raza?*

7. What caused most of the Aztec culture to disappear?

8. What is a land grant?

9. What is a mission?

10. How did Spain lose control of Mexico?

11. How did Texas break away from Mexico?

12. Name the states made from the Mexican Cession.

13. What promises were made to Mexican Americans in the Treaty of Guadalupe Hidalgo?

14. How was slavery a cause of the war between Mexico and Texas? Between Mexico and the United States?

15. Where does the word *Chicano* come from?

II. UNDERSTANDING WHY.

Explain why each of the following happened.

1. Hernando Cortez and about 550 Spaniards were able to conquer the Aztec Empire.

2. Mexican culture today is both Spanish and Indian.

3. Americans who moved into Mexican land agreed to become Mexican citizens.

4. Mexico stopped American settlers from coming to Texas after 1830.

5. President Polk decided to go to war with Mexico.

III. THINKING IT THROUGH!

Discuss.

1. What proof is there that the Indians of Mexico had advanced civilization before 1500?

2. Why was Manifest Destiny so acceptable to most Americans?

IV. IN THE LIBRARY.

Many Americans were against the Mexican War. Find books in your library dealing with the war. Report to your class who some of these Americans were, and why they opposed the war.

How Did Mexican-Americans Become a Forgotten Minority?

2 In 1848 most Mexican-Americans in the new lands of the United States were farmers. They loved the land that fed them, and they tended it with care. These lines from a poem tell us of this Mexican-American love for the land:

> When he sees his crops
> Grow before his eyes
> It delights his heart.
> He comes alive, knowing
> The earth, his mother,
> Is going to feed him.

Almost all Mexican-Americans have lost their land. Some are migrant farmers, moving from place to place in search of a few weeks' work. Some live in towns in farming areas, where they find work with farmers near the town. Most have moved to the cities, where they live in Mexican-American neighborhoods called *barrios*. Almost a million people live in the *barrios* of Los Angeles. About 200,000 live in those of San Antonio, Texas; perhaps 100,000 live in Denver, Colorado. In all such cities most of them hold low-paying jobs and are among the poorest people. Some of the *barrios* are among the worst slums in the United States.

How Did the Mexican-Americans Lose Their Land?
What Problems Do They Face in the Southwest Today?

Who Rules in the Southwest? One of the reasons Mexican-Americans have become a "forgotten" minority is that most live in one part of the United States—the Southwest. Almost 2½ million live in California. They are that state's largest minority group. Yet they have almost no political power. Voting districts in California have been set up so that Mexican-Americans find it almost impossible to elect one of their number to office. Texas has almost two million Mexican-Americans. The number changes from day to day, for thousands move back and forth between Texas and Mexico almost daily. Except for a few local officials, the Mexican-Americans of Texas have no political power. They feel forgotten by their state government. Conditions are the same in the other states of the Southwest. In New Mexico one person in four is a Mexican-American. So are one in six in Arizona and one in eight in Colorado. In all these states, political power is firmly held by English-speaking whites. The Mexican-Americans call them Anglos.

Mexican-Americans have had little power since the United States took control of the Southwest. The first United States officials came there as conquerors. They ruled in ways that were designed to take away the rights and land of a conquered people. The story of New Mexico shows how the promises of the Treaty of Guadalupe Hidalgo were broken.

Losing the Land. New Mexico did not become a state until 1912. For more than sixty years it was a territory of the United States. This means it was ruled by Congress. Its governor was appointed. He set up a legislature whose decisions about laws had to be approved by Congress. The territorial legislature of New Mexico was controlled by Anglos, although some Mexican-Americans were in it. New Mexico became a territory in 1850. During the next ten years few settlers from the United States came in. First the United States Army had to build forts, get Indian tribes under control and open more roads. New Mexico was larger than any state except Texas and California!

Large-scale settlement did not really begin until after the Civil War. Indians were forced into reservations. Cattlemen moved into the more fertile areas. Railroads did not begin to cross New Mexico until after 1878. This meant that most of the land was open but hard to reach. In 1869 William A. Pike was Governor of the Territory of New Mexico. During the next two years the Mexican-Americans lost most of their land.

Perhaps half the land in New Mexico had been given to settlers from Mexico before the United States took the territory. There were more than 1,700 Spanish and Mexican land grants. Some were owned by villages; some were owned by men who had brought in groups of settlers from Mexico. Copies of the land grants, or proofs of ownership, were kept in Santa Fe, the capital of New Mexico. Governor Pike and a group of other officials and lawyers made plans to take the land away from those who held Mexican land grants. First they destroyed the ownership records in Santa Fe. Then they set up a land company. Two of its partners were Governor Pike and T. Rush Spencer, Surveyor General of New Mexico.

Governor Pike's group became known as the "Santa Fe Ring." Pike ordered all people who owned land or wanted to own land to file a claim, or "patent." These patents would take the place of the destroyed land-grant records. When two people filed claims for the same piece of land, the Surveyor General decided which one was the true owner. Spencer ruled in favor of Anglos against Mexican-Americans in most of these cases. Often, he ruled in favor of members of his own gang. The Mexican-Americans in New Mexico lost about four-fifths of their land in this way. The governor's land company received about 2,700 square miles of the best land in New Mexico—at no cost!

Almost any claim by an Anglo would be accepted. Some men stole land from villages by paying someone in the village to sign a piece of paper with an X. This mark was then accepted by the Surveyor General as proof of a legal sale. The land owned by the village would then become the property of the Anglo who had filed the new patent.

The final way to take land from Mexican-Americans was through Anglo-controlled banks. Bank loans in New Mexico at one time received twenty per cent interest *each month*. A man who borrowed $1,000 would have to pay back $3,400 after one year! Most Mexican-American farmers who borrowed from banks lost their land when they could not pay back the loans.

Mexican-Americans who had lost their land in such ways asked for help. In 1891 a special Court of Land Claims was set up in New Mexico. Its job was to hear cases about the true ownership of land. Thousands of cases were brought before this court. In most of them its judges ruled against the Mexican-Americans. Almost 95 per cent of the land they had lost and then asked to have returned was declared the property of the new Anglo owners for all time.

Land was stolen in similar ways all over the Southwest. Mexican-American land-grant records were destroyed in Texas, while the records of Anglos were not. In Colorado the land near villages, which Mexican-Americans had been using as village land, was taken away. In California the state government ordered all owners of land grants to have their rights approved in state courts. In most cases these courts refused to approve the grants.

Coming from Mexico. In the past 100 years, the number of Mexican-Americans has grown from about 100,000 to between five and six million! They have come from Mexico and have remained in the United States. It has never been possible to patrol closely the 1,600-mile border between the two countries. Each year as many as a million Mexicans enter the United States and try to remain as "illegal immigrants." That is, there have been years in which as many as a million have been found and returned to Mexico! A great number remain in the Southwest without being found by the immigration officials.

Mexico is a poorer country than the United States. Its people believe they have a better chance to make a living in the United States. Men come alone, or with their families. Most seek farm work. The Southwest has good farmland. Its farmers need help, chiefly in the planting and harvesting seasons. State governments do little to keep Mexican farm workers out. Until 1964 the United States permitted free movement of these farm workers, called *braceros*. Then it limited their number by requiring special permits. In 1968 the permit plan was also ended.

Until 1968 Mexican *braceros* worked on farms in the Southwest doing difficult "stoop labor." Why do you think the government stopped them from coming across the border?

Still, illegal immigration has remained high. Smugglers bring Mexican farmers north in harvest seasons. Many Anglo farmers, in great need of help, accept them even though they know they too are breaking the law. The *braceros* receive low pay. Still they believe they can save some money to bring back to Mexico after the harvest season has ended.

A strange work system has developed for these workers. They speak only Spanish and know little about how to act in the United States. Mexican-Americans who speak English become work contractors. They agree to provide a farmer with the workers he needs. He pays the contractors, who in turn pay the men. Few *braceros* save much, for they receive less money than American farmers for the same kinds of work.

Poverty in the Cities. Mexican-Americans do not have much farmland. Those who have remained in the hundreds of villages in the Southwest make a poor living from the small amounts of land they are able to farm. Most of them have moved to the cities, where they hold the lowest-paying jobs. They work in restaurants, as laborers, at low-paying factory jobs. They find it harder than Anglos to enter the professions or get better-paying jobs. One reason for this is that many Mexican-Americans still speak Spanish rather than English. Another is that they are poorly educated. A third reason is as important as all others. They suffer from discrimination by Anglos. Mexican-Americans—darker-skinned, often Indians, different in their ways of dressing and acting—are just beginning to break through the walls of prejudice.

It has been very difficult for Mexican-American children to receive an education. Most come to school speaking no English. The schools have made these boys and girls speak only English in school. This makes the first years of any child's education very hard. In some schools in the Southwest, boys and girls who speak Spanish instead of English are punished. Some have been beaten, others fined. Still others have been made to do extra work or stay after school. In 1968 thousands of high school students in Los Angeles went on strike to protest such treatment. In 1969 Los Angeles began to use textbooks written in Spanish for some of its Spanish-speaking students. Students were also allowed to speak Spanish. But in most of the Southwest, Mexican-American children must still try to learn in English, a language many of them are just beginning to use when they enter school.

Mexican-American parents have complained that their children learn only "Anglo" subjects. There is little taught about the culture and history of *La Raza*. California, for example, has special schools for the children of farm workers who move from harvest to harvest. These schools teach "American" subjects only. It is their goal to make these children more like Anglo-Americans. Mexican-American parents have been asking for an end to education that teaches that everything American is better than anything Mexican. Perhaps this can help us understand some of these facts:

— Most Mexican-American children never finish high school. More than half of them drop out.
— In some parts of the Southwest one child in five never goes to school at all.
— One child in seven in California is Mexican-American. In 1970 only one college student in 200 was Mexican-American!

Some local and state governments in the Southwest have tried to improve the education of Mexican-American children. However, poverty has brought special problems to those trying to improve the schools. Farm-working families move often. They go to wherever work can be found. A boy or girl may have to attend three or four different schools in a single year.

Housing. Most Mexican-Americans live in city neighborhoods called *barrios*. Most of these are slums that are worse than those

Mexican-American slums, called *barrios*, are among the worst in the nation. Why do you think Mexican-Americans find it difficult to improve their housing?

found in New York, Chicago, Philadelphia or Detroit. Many streets have no lights, no sewers and no mail service. People live crowded together in old buildings, and often in tin shacks. Health problems are greater here than in any other city slums. Mexican-Americans can do little to improve their housing. They are too poor. Next to American Indians, they are the poorest of all Americans. Those who work as farmers earn as little as $30 a week. Those who live in the cities are the first to lose their jobs. Very few Mexican-Americans belong to unions. They do not receive the same wages paid to Anglo workers doing the same work. In most parts of the Southwest, they receive as little as an employer wishes to pay them, or as little as men will accept.

No Voice in Government. Mexican-Americans have had almost no power in their city and state governments. Few have been elected mayor of a large city or governor of a state. As late as 1970 only four Mexican-Americans were in Congress. They were Senator Joseph Montoya of New Mexico and Congressmen Eduardo Roybal of California, Eligio de la Garza of Texas and Henry González of Texas. Today such men have given the problems of *La Raza* their first real hearing in the national government. They saw to it that Mexican-Americans were helped by the Office of Economic Opportunity (the War on Poverty program) and have asked for aid from groups like the Ford Foundation.

However, the great problems are still unsolved. Most Mexican-Americans are poor. They have little real education. They are farmers without land to farm. Their culture has not been accepted by the Anglos who rule them. They have not been able to form strong organizations that could carry on the fight for their rights.

Senator Joseph Montoya of New Mexico and Representative Henry Gonzáles of Texas were two of the four Mexican-American Congressmen in the early 1970's. Why do you think there have been so few?

A song is sung in the farm labor camps of the Southwest that tells us much about the hopelessness facing so many Mexican-Americans:

> To see myself alone
> Like a leaf in the wind;
> I would like to cry,
> I would like to die,
> In my misery.

I. WHAT ARE THE FACTS?

Write the letter of the choice that best completes each statement.

1. In 1848 most Mexican-Americans were (a) miners, (b) traders, (c) farmers.

2. A *barrio* is (a) a neighborhood, (b) an official, (c) an organization.

3. Most Mexican-Americans live in the (a) Rocky Mountain states, (b) Pacific Coast area, (c) Southwest.

4. The Santa Fe Ring was most interested in (a) railroads, (b) trading posts, (c) land.

5. The Surveyer General of New Mexico made final decisions about (a) land ownership, (b) service in the state militia, (c) the boundary between New Mexico and Mexico.

6. The Court of Land Claims made rulings that favored (a) Anglos, (b) Mexican-Americans, (c) owners of old land grants.

7. People who have left one country to settle in another are called (a) Chicanos, (b) immigrants, (c) migrant workers.

8. *Braceros* are (a) Mexican landowners, (b) work contractors, (c) farm workers from Mexico.

9. The language most Spanish-speaking children must use in the schools of the Southwest is (a) Spanish, (b) English, (c) whatever language their parents want them to use.

10. Mexican-Americans move often because they (a) search for good farms to buy, (b) are migrant workers, (c) make enough money to take long vacations.

II. CAUSES AND RESULTS.

Write the letter of the item in Column B that best completes each statement in Column A.

	Column A		*Column B*
1.	Many Mexican-American children are school dropouts because	a.	Mexico is a poorer country than the United States.
2.	Mexican-Americans live in *barrios* because	b.	they believe they are not taught subjects important to them.
3.	Mexicans try to move to the United States because	c.	they suffer from job discrimination.
4.	Few Mexican-Americans own land because	d.	their land was taken from them.
5.	Most Mexican-Americans hold low-paying jobs because	e.	they suffer from housing discrimination.

III. THINKING IT THROUGH!

Discuss.

1. Why are so few Mexican-Americans public officials?

2. Why would you oppose or favor the ending of the use of the words *Anglo* and *Chicano* to describe the two most important groups of people in the Southwest?

3. What kinds of discrimination have Mexican-Americans faced in the cities of the Southwest? Compare these to the kinds of discrimination faced by Indians and black Americans.

4. Why have Americans made all children learn the same subjects in the public schools?

5. Prepare a list of the changes you would favor in the way Mexican-Americans live. Explain why each item is on your list.

How Are Mexican-Americans Trying to Improve Their Lives?

3 There are between four and five million farm workers in the United States today. This is really a small number—one that grows smaller each year. The country was once filled with small farms. Most were between forty and 160 acres in size. Then, after 1920, the invention of many new farm machines changed the life of small farmers. Machines could do the work farmers had always done. They could prepare the land and plant the seeds. They could pick the crops and get them ready for market. Such machines cost more than a small farmer could afford. Slowly, small farmers sold their land or lost their leases on farmland. Dozens of small farms were combined into large ones that could buy and use the expensive machinery. Farming became a big business.

Between 1920 and 1950 millions of farmers and farm workers moved to the cities. Others who once worked on farms all year long found that the only work left was during the different crop harvests. They could get a few weeks' work at one large farm and then a few weeks' work at another when these farms were ready to harvest their crops. Such traveling farm workers are called migrant farmers. California has more of them than any other state—between 200,000 and 400,000 at a time.

Migrant farmers have had to accept whatever low pay was offered to them, for there often have been more workers than jobs. It was not until 1962 that a farm workers' union was begun in California. It has tried to protect and represent the poorest of all migrant workers—the grape pickers—most of whom are Mexican-Americans.

How Have the Grape Pickers Organized to Improve Their Lives?

What Are the Goals of Mexican-Americans Today?

What Is the Message of Reies Tijerina?

179

Cesar Chavez leads his United Farm Workers in picketing a Seattle, Washington, supermarket. What could he hope to gain through such actions?

Cesar Chavez. The best-known Mexican-American in the United States is the son of a migrant farmer. He and his family moved from job to job so often that he could not even finish the eighth grade. Yet he became the spokesman for millions of Mexican-Americans. He began and headed the union called the United Farm Workers Organizing Committee. When he started in 1962 with less than 300 members, it was called the National Farm Workers Association. Many of its members still call it by its old initials, N.F.W.A. The message of Cesar Chavez and his union is plain: "We are free men, and we demand justice."

With the late Senator Robert F. Kennedy at his side, Chavez breaks a 25-day fast for *La Causa*. Why would Senator Kennedy have been interested in this movement?

The town of Delano, California, is in the grape-growing part of that state. Cesar Chavez has made Delano the center of his drive. His goal is to improve the living and working conditions of all Mexican-American migrant farmers, or *campesinos*. In 1965 Chavez and his union began a strike. His grape pickers would not work unless they received a contract. The Spanish word for strike is *huelga*. *La Huelga* became a country-wide movement. People all over the United States who believed the grape pickers should have higher pay and better working conditions joined in a boycott. They refused to buy grapes. They picketed stores in which grapes were sold. They raised money to help the strikers. *La Huelga* became a drive to give equal rights to an important minority—the Mexican-Americans.

The strike went on and on. Cesar Chavez got important wine-grape growers to accept his union. But those who grew table grapes (grapes for eating) would not agree to a farm workers' union. They hired workers who were not in the union and tried to keep their farms going. However, the union did not give up. More than 20,000 migrant workers refused to work for almost five years. During that time all they received were small payments from their union—sometimes as little as $5 to $10 a month.

La Huelga became *La Causa*, the cause. Officials in the parts of the Southwest where the strike continued took action against the strikers. Many were arrested. In some places it became a crime to shout *huelga* in public! The more that was done to break the strike, the more the workers supported it. Mexican-Americans in the cities raised more money for the union. Other labor groups sent money. The boycott against grapes grew stronger.

It was April, 1970, before the union had its first real success with grape farmers. In that month two growers in California signed the country's first labor contract for table-grape pickers.

UFWOC
AFL-CIO

The black eagle, symbol of the United Farm Workers Organizing Committee. Housewives boycotted grapes that did not carry this stamp.

- The workers, who had been receiving about $1.65 an hour plus about 25¢ for each box of grapes picked, received about 10¢ an hour more, or a six per cent increase.
- The growers agreed to give the union 12¢ for each box of grapes picked. This money would be placed in funds to help the workers.
- The growers agreed to stop using dangerous sprays such as DDT.

By the end of 1972, almost all grapes, perhaps one fourth of the lettuce, and small amounts of other crops in California were being picked by union workers. Wages were slowly rising.

La Huelga goes on. Many more years may pass before the migrant workers—Mexican-Americans and others—have the protection that comes from unions. Most Mexican-Americans are Roman Catholics. Much of the work of getting the first agreements was done by a committee of five bishops of that church. Many church groups—Catholic and non-Catholic—have come to believe that justice for Mexican-Americans is part of their religious belief in the rights of all men. With such help, Chavez has been able to get other groups of farm workers to join his union. Among these have been many who are not Mexican-Americans.

Reies Tijerina. Another leading Mexican-American moves through the Southwest trying to gather his people behind a cause. His name is Reies Tijerina. The people of the little farming villages call him "The Tiger." Here are some of the messages he and his followers have spread.

> U.S.A. IS TRESPASSING IN NEW MEXICO!
> U.S.A. HAS NO TITLE FOR NEW MEXICO!
> ALL PIRATES GO HOME!
> ALL SPANISH AND INDIAN VILLAGES ARE
>   FREE FOREVER!
> LONG LIVE THE FREE VILLAGES OF NEW
>   MEXICO!

La Causa in the Villages. Reies Tijerina challenges the United States government, the states of the Southwest and the Anglos who own most of the land. He has built up an organization with thousands of followers. It is known as the *Alianza,* or Alliance. Tijerina tells his followers that the Treaty of Guadalupe Hidalgo was broken by the United States. He reminds them that the treaty promised all Mexican-Americans that they could keep their land. But the land was later taken from them. This was wrong. The land should still belong to those who first owned it. "It is never too late for justice," he says again and again.

The members of the *Alianza* try to gain national attention for their cause. One of their efforts was in 1967 at the town of Tierra Amarilla, New Mexico. A land grant of almost 600,000 acres once had its center in this town. In the 1880's the land was taken by an Anglo lawyer, Thomas B. Catron. He filed a

Reies Tijerina being taken to the New Mexico State Penitentiary after his arrest in 1967. Why do you think he chose armed attack as his way of aiding *La Causa?*

claim with the government of the territory and had it approved quickly. The villagers lost their land. In June, 1967, Tijerina led a move to take back the land. An armed group of *Alianza* members took control of the village courthouse. Two officers at the courthouse were wounded. Two thousand soldiers and police were sent to the town, where the *Alianza* members were arrested. A trial followed, and Tijerina told the jury:

> Yes, we are guilty of wanting our lands. We are guilty of believing in the Treaty of Guadalupe Hidalgo. . . . If I deserve to be punished for what I am doing for the poor people, then do it. But you cannot get rid of the land problem by putting Tijerina in jail.

The jury agreed that Tijerina was not guilty. Then, in 1969, he was arrested again after his followers had burned a National Forest signpost. He was accused of attacking two Forest Service

Rangers and was sent to a federal prison in Texas. His movement grows stronger, even though its offices have been bombed and most of its meetings have had to be held in secret. There is little hope that Mexican-Americans can ever regain their lost lands. People do not "return" lands after owning them for 100 years. Even Tijerina's followers understand this. Yet *Alianza* groups have been set up in most large Mexican-American communities. Tijerina, like Cesar Chavez, has awakened the members of this minority. Why should they remain a forgotten group? Perhaps by asking for the land they can make the country see the many problems facing them.

Community Self-Help. Mexican-Americans live chiefly in the cities of the Southwest. They also live in large *colonias* in rural areas. They did little to organize as a group until men like Chavez and Tijerina raised their calls for justice. Thousands of Mexican-Americans are members of the middle class. They own businesses or are doctors, lawyers and schoolteachers. They live as well as middle-class Anglos do. Until the 1950's these people seemed to be most concerned about getting along with the Anglos and making the best possible living for themselves. Today, however, they are active in community groups that try to improve the lives of all Mexican-Americans. The best known of these new organizations is the Community Service Organization in California. It has helped Mexican-Americans to work together in many ways.

The years ahead will see greater Mexican-American unity. Hundreds of organizations are already at work. Like other minority groups, they demand community control of their schools. They want an end to job discrimination. They want an equal chance to buy or rent a home in any neighborhood. They want equal treatment in the courts. They ask for the same kinds of public assistance (relief) that other groups receive. They have been trying to get more Mexican-Americans elected to public office. They have set up theaters and publishing houses to keep the culture of *La Raza* alive.

Rodolfo Gonzales, one of the new Mexican-American leaders, used to be a famous boxer. He left that road to riches and fame to work for his people. Gonzales is a writer and a poet. One of his statements describes the problems and goals of Mexican-Americans today. It is known as the "Plan of the *Barrio*."

. . . We lived together for over a century and never had to fence our lands. When the gringo came, the first thing he did was to fence land. We opened our houses and hearts to him and trained him to irrigated farming, ranching, stock raising, and mining. He listened carefully and moved quickly, and when we turned around, he had driven us out and kept us out. . . . Robbed of our land, our people were driven to the migrant labor fields and the cities. . . .

THEREFORE WE DEMAND HOUSING . . . (better housing in the *barrios*).

EDUCATION: We demand that our schools be built in the same communal fashion as our neighborhoods. . . . We demand a completely free education from kindergarten to college, with no fees, no lunch charge, no supplies charges, no tuition, no dues. . . . We demand that . . . Spanish be the first language and the textbooks be rewritten to emphasize the heritage and the contributions of the Mexican-American or Indio-Hispano in the building of the Southwest. We also demand the teaching of the contributions and history of other minorities which have also helped build this country. . . .

ECONOMIC OPPORTUNITIES: We demand that the businesses serving our community be owned by that community. . . . These industries would be co-ops with the profits staying in the community.

Other demands were in this statement. The Mexican-Americans want their land to be returned to them. They want all citizens to share in the wealth of the country. They want changes in the Homestead Act so that the natural resources of the country are divided among all its people. In March, 1969, Rodolfo Gonzales stated his hope for the future of all Mexican-Americans.

Brotherhood unites us, and love for our brothers makes us a people whose time has come.

I. WHAT ARE THE FACTS?

Answer each question in a sentence or two.

1. What organization is headed by Mexican-American leader Cesar Chavez?

2. What crop is picked by the migrant farmers Chavez represents?

3. What success has Cesar Chavez had in winning contracts for his followers?

4. What organization is headed by Reies Tijerina?

5. What is the chief goal of Tijerina and his followers?

6. What took place in Tierra Amarilla, New Mexico, in 1967?

7. What later happened to Tijerina?

8. What is the goal of the Community Service Organization?

9. Who was the author of the "Plan of the *Barrio*"?

10. What are the chief demands of the "Plan of the *Barrio*"?

II. WORDS TO KNOW.

Explain the meaning of each of these words or phrases important in the history of Mexican-Americans.

1. migrant worker
2. *campesino*
3. *La Huelga*
4. *La Causa*
5. *barrio*
6. *Alianza*
7. United Farm Workers Organizing Committee
8. "The Tiger"

III. THINKING IT THROUGH!

Discuss.

1. Reies Tijerina and his followers demand that the land once owned by Mexican-Americans be returned to them. What problems would result if an effort were made to carry out this demand? In what other ways could the needs of poor Mexican-Americans be met?

2. How are the problems of Mexican-Americans similar to or different from those of black Americans and Indians?

3. What changes would the state and national governments have to make to meet the demands in the "Plan of the *Barrio*"? Which of these changes could be made easily? Which would result in new problems? Why?

IV. A RESEARCH PROBLEM.

Senator Robert Kennedy supported Cesar Chavez and *La Huelga* before the Senator was killed in 1968. Check the file of *The New York Times* or any other important newspaper for the first half of 1968 to find out how he tried to help the grape-pickers. Report your findings to your class. Then discuss this question: Why should a Senator from New York feel so strongly about the problems of workers in California?

Photos by George Roos

Photos by Thomas Haar

Unit Four

CHINESE-AMERICANS AND JAPANESE-AMERICANS

Unit 4 describes the problems faced by two groups of
Americans from Asia—the Chinese and the Japanese. These
minorities have known great suffering and discrimination.
Yet each has contributed much to life in the United States.
The Chinese came here to be railroad workers, miners and
farmers. The Japanese were hard-working fishermen and
farmers. Both groups were soon hated by the Americans
among whom they lived. Both minorities were kept for a time
from entering the United States. Those already here were
denied their rights. Many could not become citizens or use the
courts. They did not receive equal protection of the laws. In
some areas they could not even own land! They suffered job
discrimination and had to work at the lowest-paying jobs.
The Japanese are the only minority group in American history
ever to be imprisoned without trial! This took place during
World War II, when a frightened United States imagined all
Japanese-Americans were Japanese spies. The Chinese were
the only minority to be hunted through city streets, often
beaten and sometimes killed. Yet, as the unit shows,
Japanese- and Chinese-Americans have managed to improve
their lives. They have been among the most loyal of all
our citizens.

How Did the Chinese Overcome a Century of Discrimination?

1 In 1862 Congress passed the Pacific Railway Act. It gave two railroad companies the right to build the country's first transcontinental, or coast-to-coast, railroad. The Union Pacific would lay tracks west from Omaha, Nebraska. The Central Pacific would move east from Sacramento, California. Each company would build as much track as it could until the two lines met.

The Central Pacific had the greater problems. Its track had to cross rocky, rolling land and high mountains. It could not get the men it needed. The work was hard; most of the building had to be done by hand. Work crews had to live far from any town or city for months at a time.

The railroad could not have been built without the help of those who came by the thousands from China. They were called *coolies* or *Chinee* by the people in this country. They worked harder and faster than any

The Central Pacific Railroad could not have been built without the thousands of Chinese laborers called *coolies*. Why would they have come from China in such numbers to do this backbreaking work?

railroad workers ever had before. The work was dangerous; perhaps 2,000 or more Chinese died in accidents. Charles Crocker, in charge of building the Central Pacific, was proud of his hard-working Chinese. They helped him build almost twice as many miles of track as he had hoped to complete.

> Wherever we put them, we found them good, and they worked themselves into our favor to such an extent that if we found we were in a hurry for a job of work, it was better to put Chinese on at once.

On a single day in 1869, Central Pacific crews laid more than ten miles of track in only twelve hours!

A few weeks later the two lines of track met. The work of building the railroad was over. Perhaps 20,000 Chinese were now out of work. Most returned to California. They found they were not wanted there. The life of Chinese in such cities as San Francisco and Los Angeles grew worse and worse. They could not find work. They had to live crowded together in ghettos. White Americans hated them. Finally, they were hit by riots and massacres.

The Chinese had come here to build a railroad and to make a better living than they could in China. They stayed to become a minority suffering from hatred they could not really understand.

Why Did the Chinese Come to the United States?
How Did the Chinese in California and the West Suffer?
How Did Immigration Laws Hurt the Chinese?
How Did the Chinese Overcome Most of Their Problems?

The Chinese-Americans. About 300,000 people in the United States are called Chinese. Most of them are citizens who were born in this country. Still, the way they look sets them apart. It makes them a minority group with special problems. Most Chinese-Americans live in three states: Hawaii, California and New York. One of them, Hiram L. Fong of Hawaii, is a member of the United States Senate. Like other Chinese in Hawaii,

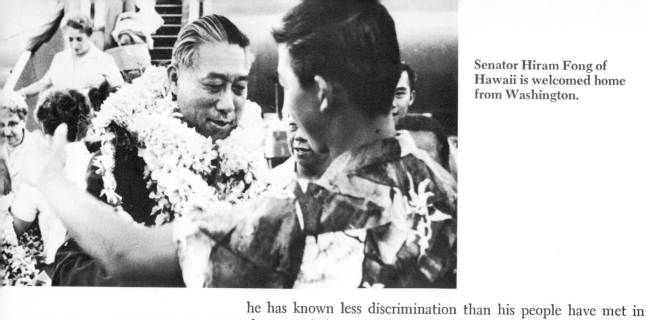

Senator Hiram Fong of Hawaii is welcomed home from Washington.

Architect I. M. Pei was chosen to design the John F. Kennedy Memorial Library.

he has known less discrimination than his people have met in the rest of the United States. He is one of the large number of Chinese-Americans who have become famous in this country—even while most others have been fighting prejudice.

The Chinese who came to the United States were part of the world's oldest civilization. Until about 1750, China was considered one of the most advanced nations in the world. Its culture has always valued educated men. Chinese who enter the professions seem to learn with great speed and success. Two Chinese-Americans, Dr. Tsung Dao Lee and Dr. Chen Ning Yang, have won the Nobel Prize for their work as scientists. Dr. Choh Hao Li developed one of the most important drugs for the treatment of arthritis. Dr. Ramman Chao is finding new ways to use light beams. Dr. Ju Chin Chu has been a leading space scientist. In other fields, I. M. Pei, a famous architect, was chosen to plan the John F. Kennedy Library in Boston. James Wong Howe became our best-known Hollywood cameraman. Keye Luke has been one of our busiest actors. Dong Kingman won world fame as a painter. Lin Yutang has written best-selling novels and books about China and the Chinese in the United States. Gerald Tsai is a leader in the world of finance. Men like these have made the Chinese-Americans one of the most successful minority groups in the United States.

The Chinese place the family names first and the given names last. In this chapter we are changing them to the American way of writing names. The Chinese would say Dr. Yang Chen Ning, or Dr. Chu Ju Chin.

192

Why the Chinese Came to the United States. In 1850 fewer than 800 Chinese lived in the United States, most of them in California. Like most of the Chinese who later joined them, they had been born in the province of Kwangtung in South China. Its chief city was the port of Canton, one of the few Chinese cities then open to trade with the rest of the world.

China, larger than the United States, was ruled by an emperor. "The emperor is all-powerful," the Chinese said, "but he is far away." Local military chiefs and small numbers of rich men ruled as they pleased in most of the country. They often ignored the emperor's laws and used their power to grow ever richer. Taxes were high. Farmers saw no way to escape their poverty.

The land near the city of Toishan, close to Canton, was one of China's poorest farming areas. In 1848 American ships arriving at Canton brought news that gold had been found in California. Soon thousands of poor farmers were speaking of *Gun San,* a land of golden mountains. Suppose a man left his home and family for a few years. He could become rich in this land of gold. Then he could return to China, buy land and share his wealth with his family!

Chinese law did not permit citizens to leave their country. However, the law was not enforced. Tens of thousands of Chinese came to Canton to board ships to the United States. In the form of Chinese spoken near Canton, the sounds *coo* and *lee* mean *bitter work.* The son of a Chinese farmer had no money and little education. He could make a living only by doing the hardest kinds of work. The word *coolie* came to mean a Chinese worker with no skills who could do only work that took great strength.

Chinese businessmen called "coolie traders" paid the cost of sending these workers to the United States. This was a loan, to be paid back at high interest. The traders sent along agents who received a worker's pay, kept a large part of it to repay the debt and then gave him the little that was left. Such agents might know enough English to deal with the Americans.

The coolie trade was active from 1850 to 1880. Because of a special treaty with China, perhaps 200,000 Chinese, almost all of them men, crossed the Pacific during those years. Most came to California. Thousands later returned to China with the money they had saved. The others remained in the United States, sending as much as they could to their families in China. Those who could sent for their families. Then, after

1880, the United States ended immigration from China. A law passed in 1882 made the Chinese the first national group to be kept out of the United States.

The "Different" Chinese. Most of the people in California in the 1860's and 1870's were men. They had come from the eastern states and Europe hoping to get rich quickly. They planned to send for their families or go back home to them. These men lived in towns that had grown rapidly. There were more men than housing, jobs or even food. Life was hard, and prices were high. Not all men could make a living. Some of them began to look for "scapegoats," people they could blame even though they had nothing to do with the problem. The Chinese, different in every way, were an easy target for their anger.

Men began to complain about the Chinese. The coolies were not Christians. Some men began to call them "savages" —the same word used to describe the hated Indians! The Chinese lived together. Few of them learned much English. They dressed as they had in China, in long robes or loose "pajamas." They shaved their heads except for the long braid called a *queue* that they wore hanging down their backs. The Chinese were different—in color, in religion, in dress, in language, even in food habits. It was soon said that they took away white men's jobs by taking lower pay for the same work.

Angry Californians blamed the Chinese for the bad times that came after the gold mines closed down and the railroad-building jobs disappeared. Each Chinese with a job was said to be taking bread from a white man's mouth. Most Chinese received the same pay any other men would get for the jobs they did. In some fields the Chinese found jobs and did them better than white men could. For example, many Chinese had been good farmers before they came to the United States. They were very much in demand by American farmers. Even at low pay, the Chinese seemed to get along better than white men did. They were willing to eat the simplest foods. They lived wherever they could find a bed and a roof, and they had no families to support.

Men without jobs formed mobs in California's towns and cities. They roamed the streets at night looking for Chinese to attack. When they found a Chinese man, they cut his queue, tore his clothing and beat him. The Chinese were robbed and cheated at every turn. They were frightened away from their jobs. Laws were passed to keep them from getting justice in

The Chinese were different in appearance and way of life. Why is it easy to blame problems on someone who is "different"?

the courts. In California no Indian, Negro or Chinese could speak in court against a white man. In 1871 the United States Supreme Court agreed that a state could pass a law to keep Chinese from ever becoming citizens! Most of California's Chinese moved to the cities where other Chinese already lived. There they bought guns, as other people did in the West, and learned how to use them. Still they remained peaceful, even when mobs seemed ready to murder them.

Riot in Los Angeles. The trouble they had feared came in 1871. A number of Chinese had been shot in a mining camp. Chinese in the cities were being beaten in the streets. Politicians began to call for laws to keep any more Chinese from entering California. Groups of Chinese even fought among themselves. In Los Angeles one of these fights among Chinese led to the closing off of Chinatown, the small Chinese ghetto. The police then moved in to bring peace. Many men followed to watch the Chinese being brought under control. One of these men was shot during a fight between the police and some frightened Chinese. When this man died, mobs gathered to attack the Chinese and punish them for everything people thought they had done.

The mob carried guns. Men gathered on rooftops while others forced the Chinese out into the streets. P. S. Dorney was present during this raid on Chinatown. He later described what he had seen.

[The Chinese] were shot in their hiding places or hunted from room to room out into the open courtyard, where death from the bullets of those on the roof was certain . . . A chorus of yells telegraphed the fact to the surrounding mob, and the yells were answered by a hoarse roar of savage satisfaction.

. . . Men were dragged forth . . . and hurled headlong from a raised sidewalk to the ground. To the necks of some of the most helpless the mob fastened ropes and, with a whoop and a hurrah, rushed down Los Angeles Street to the hanging place. . . . A boy was thus led to the place of slaughter. The little fellow was not yet above twelve years of age. He had been but a month in the country and knew not a word of English. . . . He was hanged.

. . . It was midnight, and a body of men appointed by the sheriff cut down the dead—twenty-three in number. Nearly all had been dragged through the streets at the end of a rope, and all were found shot and stabbed as well as hanged.

Anti-Chinese riots became common after 1871. This one took place in Denver, Colorado. How could it have been prevented?

Eight of the men who took part in this riot were tried and found guilty. They were sent to jail for from two to eight years. However, all eight were freed within a year.

The Chinese Exclusion Act. American workers were forming unions by the 1870's. Union leaders led a fight to keep any more Chinese from entering the United States. These leaders claimed Chinese workers kept wages low. They would not join unions. Now they were beginning to bring their friends and families from China. The Burlingame Treaty of 1868 between China and the United States allowed the people of each country to go freely to the other. But by 1877 the white people of California seemed united in their hatred of the Chinese. Mobs were led by Dennis Kearney, himself an immigrant from Ireland. They were urged on by his repeated cry, "The Chinese must go!" He said:

> We declare that the Chinaman must leave our shores. We declare that white men, and women, and boys, and girls, cannot live as the people of the great republic should and compete with the single Chinese coolie in the labor market. We declare

196

that we cannot hope to drive the Chinaman away by working cheaper than he does. None but an enemy would expect it of us; none but an idiot could hope for success; none but a . . . coward and slave would make the effort. To an American, death is preferable to life on a par with the Chinaman.

The treaty with China was changed in 1880. From then on the United States could "suspend" Chinese immigration. In 1882 Congress passed a law later known as the Chinese Exclusion Act. *Exclusion* means "keeping out." The law barred the Chinese for ten years. It was followed by other laws that continued the exclusion and even made it hard for a visitor from China to enter the United States!

The Exclusion Act did not end the attacks against the Chinese. One of the worst took place in Rock Springs, Wyoming, in 1885. About 500 Chinese coal miners worked near this town. They were attacked by a mob of white workers, most of whom were foreign-born themselves. Twenty-eight Chinese were killed and fifteen wounded. Most of the remaining Chinese left the town. Such attacks drove the Chinese out of the Rocky Mountain states. They have never returned. In 1960 Wyoming had fewer than 200 Chinese-Americans, Colorado about 700 and Utah only 600.

The Exclusion Act did not keep all Chinese out. Each year a few thousand could enter—chiefly members of the families of Chinese who already lived here. A greater number returned to China each year and remained there. Between 1882 and 1924 the Chinese population in the United States stayed under 100,000. Life was too hard. Most of those who lived here were men. In fifteen states, laws prevented them from marrying white or black Americans. Chinese families were few.

Changes Since 1924. A new immigration law passed in 1924 kept out all Chinese, even the wives or children of Chinese already living here! This law was unchanged until 1943. China was then an ally of the United States in World War II. Congress ended the Chinese Exclusion laws and also permitted Chinese in the United States to become citizens. It allowed 105 Chinese a year to enter as immigrants. Other laws added about 50,000 more Chinese by 1965. Some were the brides of Americans who had served in the armed forces. Others were doctors, scientists and other skilled people the United States needed, with their families.

Another large group of Chinese has come to the United States. A Communist government has ruled China since 1949. Hundreds of thousands of Chinese escaped to the English-owned island of Hong Kong, south of Canton. A special law passed in 1962 admitted 15,000 of them to the United States. Since new immigration laws were passed in 1965, it has become easier for Chinese to enter. Today as many as 20,000 a year are able to join the Chinese already here. More than 17,000 did so in the first year of the new immigration rules. Most of these were women and children. At one time there were 28 Chinese men in the United States for each Chinese woman. Today the numbers are almost equal. This means that at last we have tens of thousands of Chinese families instead of only single men.

Perhaps 500,000 Chinese have come to the United States since the 1850's. Those who remained here, and their children, are today's Chinese-Americans. They have worked out ways to get by, and then to succeed, even though they have been faced with great discrimination.

Chinese-Americans Today. The first Chinese to come to the United States became miners, railroad workers and farmers. Except for some of the farmers, they had to give up these ways of making a living. They had to settle in the cities and find other jobs. A few bought and sold goods they traded with Chinese businessmen in other parts of the world. Some were skilled tailors who entered the clothing industry. But tens of thousands of other Chinese could not make a living because white people would not hire them.

What were these Chinese to do? They discovered that the large numbers of single white men in the West needed laundries. This was hard, hot work, all done by hand. The Chinese were used to the hardest kinds of work. They opened small laundries wherever they could. At one time, 7,500 Chinese worked in laundries in San Francisco alone. Laundry work has remained important to Chinese-Americans all over the United States. Today from 40,000 to 50,000 of them make their living in this one industry. Many own small family laundries in which all the members of a family share the work. Others run large laundries that do part of the washing and ironing for the smaller neighborhood stores.

The second important Chinese business has been the restaurant. The Chinese are among the world's finest cooks. Peo-

Chinese laundries such as this one have become a part of American life. In what other fields are large numbers of Chinese found?

ple in their country learned long ago how to make the simplest foods taste good. Chinese-Americans in the West soon found that Americans enjoyed Chinese-style cooking. Chinese restaurants were quick successes. They have spread all over the United States. Most of these restaurants are family businesses. Often the owners, cooks and waiters are related. Many rich Chinese owe their fortunes to the restaurants they and their families have owned. Today perhaps one Chinese-American in four or five still makes his living in or because of a Chinese restaurant.

> The words *chop suey* mean "small pieces of different kinds of food." Chop suey is one of the most popular Chinese dishes in America. However, this dish and others found in most Chinese-American restaurants are not examples of China's best cooking. They are more like the food of the poor people of that country, says Dr. Peter Ching, a Chinese scholar. Fine Chinese cooking is an art that cooks must study for many years to learn well. Dr. Ching feels that the love of carefully prepared foods, rich in flavor and appearance, is an important part of Chinese culture. It is a major contribution of the Chinese to this nation and the world.

Americans have had some strange notions about the Chinese. Years ago they thought all Chinese were ignorant people who could not even learn English. They did not understand that most Chinese did not plan to stay here and did not think it important to become more like Americans. As time passed, more and more Chinese did decide to become Americans. Yet discrimination and unfair laws pushed them together into Chinatowns.

The Chinese had to set up their own community rules and even their own unofficial governments. These groups were called *benevolent societies*. They are still important. The benevolent society of each city may have its own name, but all do the same kind of work. They are elected by the Chinese communities. They are given the power to settle differences between Chinese. Remember that the Chinese could not use the courts for many years. The "government" of a Chinatown makes rules for its people—rules that are followed because people understand that they need this government they have chosen to rule over them. One of the rules is that help is given to any Chinese who are in need. The Chinese are a proud people. They want their children to learn about China's great culture. Many Chinese-American children attend special schools for a few hours each week. There they learn Chinese language, literature and history.

Sometimes the "governments" of Chinatowns could not keep peace. Fights between groups of Chinese might lead to violence and even death. Americans who read about such events became more and more certain that the Chinese were strange and

Although discrimination against them has weakened, many Chinese-Americans in big cities still live together in neighborhoods called Chinatowns. Why do you think this is so?

different. When Chinese characters appeared in books or motion pictures, they were often shown as evil criminals. The spread of such false ideas made it hard for educated Chinese-Americans to find jobs. Until the 1940's they could not do the work for which they were best educated. In this way they were like the people of some other minorities. They had to work at jobs that did not use all their training and skill.

Still, Chinese-Americans have been proud and loyal citizens of the United States. Few of them have broken the laws. They protect the honor of their families. A wrong done by any Chinese disgraces his family and all his relatives. People in Asia call a loss of honor a "loss of face." No Chinese-American wants his family or relatives to "lose face." This helps explain why Chinese children do so well in school. Each success by a boy or girl honors the family as well as the student.

Great changes have come to the Chinese-Americans since 1945. Other Americans began to end discrimination based on race, color, religion or national origin. The Chinese were among the first to benefit. This may have been because so many of them were well educated. Today perhaps one in four makes his living in a profession or in a good job in some large business.

Large numbers of Chinese-Americans have left the Chinatowns. They now live in other parts of the cities, with non-Chinese as their neighbors. Their lives have changed greatly. At one time they were accepted only in Hawaii. Today they are rising to positions of honor all over the United States. One reason for this is that they are very active in their communities. Like other English-speaking Americans, they join in church activities and in the work of service groups. At the same time they try to keep their old culture alive. Few American minorities have suffered as much and then succeeded as well as the Chinese-Americans. Yet the memory of 100 years of "bitter work" and discrimination will always remain.

I. WHAT ARE THE FACTS?

Write the letter of the choice that best completes each statement.

1. A transcontinental railroad goes from (a) coast to coast, (b) continent to continent, (c) one state to the next state.

2. The word *coolie* came to mean a man from Asia who was (a) a farmer, (b) a skilled worker, (c) an unskilled worker.

3. The number of Chinese killed while working on the Central Pacific Railroad was (a) 2,000, (b) 10,000, (c) 100,000.

4. When we compare the numbers of American Indians, Mexican-Americans and Chinese-Americans, the smallest group is the (a) American Indians, (b) Mexican-Americans, (c) Chinese-Americans.

5. Hiram L. Fong was elected Senator from (a) California, (b) New York, (c) Hawaii.

6. Toishan is important in the history of Chinese-Americans because (a) it is the Chinese religion, (b) the largest number of Chinese immigrants came from Toishan, (c) it is the Chinese word for a community leader.

7. The Chinese were badly treated by the people of (a) Hawaii, (b) California, (c) Hong Kong.

8. The man who told people that "The Chinese must go!" was (a) Theodore Roosevelt, (b) P. S. Dorney, (c) Dennis Kearney.

9. An area from which the Chinese were driven was (a) Chicago, (b) New York, (c) the Rocky Mountain states.

10. The first exclusion act in the history of American immigration was passed in (a) 1848, (b) 1882, (c) 1924.

11. The first of these kinds of work in which Chinese were successful was (a) restaurants, (b) laundries, (c) railroad-building.

12. For many years, Chinese could not (a) own property, (b) work for white people, (c) become citizens.

13. The oldest of these cultures is that of (a) the United States, (b) Mexico, (c) China.

14. Today the number of Chinese-American women is (a) about one-tenth the number of men, (b) almost equal to the number of men, (c) much larger than the number of men.

15. The number of Chinese-Americans today is about (a) 100,000, (b) 300,000, (c) 500,000.

075027

II. WHAT MADE HIM FAMOUS?

Match the names in COLUMN A with the descriptions in COLUMN B. You may look back in the chapter.

COLUMN A	COLUMN B
1. Dr. Tsung Dao Lee	a. Leader in the world of finance.
2. Dr. Chen Ning Yang	b. Famous American painter.
3. I. M. Pei	c. Nobel Prize winner.
4. James Wong Howe	d. Planned John F. Kennedy Library.
5. Keye Luke	e. Wrote best-selling novels.
6. Dong Kingman	f. Well-known actor.
7. Dr. Choh Hao Li	g. Hollywood cameraman.
8. Dr. Ju Chin Chu	h. Leading space scientist.
9. Lin Yutang	i. Developed important drug for arthritis.
10. Gerald Tsai	j. Nobel Prize winner.

III. THINKING IT THROUGH!

Discuss.

1. Compare the reasons for Chinese immigration with the reasons for the immigration of the Mexicans.

2. Why do you think white Americans hated the Chinese for more than fifty years? Why does one group come to hate another?

3. How were the Chinese treated in California after 1869? Compare this with the treatment of black Americans in the South after the Civil War.

4. Compare the "coolie traders" with the Mexican-American work contractors discussed in Unit III. Why are immigrants who do not speak English often cheated and paid less than they should be paid?

5. How did the Chinese suffer from riots? What evidence can you offer to prove that riots are still an American problem?

IV. BUILD YOUR UNDERSTANDING.

We have seen that American Indians, Mexican-Americans, Chinese-Americans and other minority groups as well want to pass their cultures on to their children. Why do they insist on this instead of trying to be like the American majority in every possible way? Why would you defend or oppose them in this?

How Were Japanese-Americans Treated During World War II?

2 On December 7, 1941, a Japanese fleet attacked Pearl Harbor, the United States naval base in Hawaii. Three thousand Americans were killed or wounded. The United States Pacific fleet was destroyed. Most of the Air Force planes in Hawaii were wrecked on the ground. This "sneak attack" shocked the people of the United States. President Roosevelt called December 7 "a day that will live in infamy." On December 8 Congress declared war on Japan.

Japan attacked Pearl Harbor on December 7, 1941. Why did President Roosevelt call it "a day that will live in infamy"?

A feeling of panic spread across the United States. People said Japanese-Americans spying for Japan had guided the Japanese attack. Some said thousands of Japanese-Americans were spies planning a Japanese attack on the West Coast. People reported strange lights, radio messages and Japanese hiding near defense plants. One newspaperman wrote that the "Japanese in California . . . should be under guard to the last man and woman. . . ." General John DeWitt commanded the armed forces along the Pacific Coast. He reported to Washington that "The Japanese race is an enemy race." He asked that all Japanese-Americans be locked up. How else could he defend against an attack that might come at any time?

On February 19, 1942, President Roosevelt gave the Army power to move "any and all persons" from military areas. A month later Congress passed a law to support this order. By the end of 1942, 112,000 Japanese-Americans were in special camps. Most of these people were American citizens—born in the United States. This was the only time in our country's history that large numbers of its citizens were jailed without trial and kept in jail! Germany and Italy were also enemies of the United States in World War II. German-Americans and Italian-Americans were not treated as the Japanese-Americans were.

When Did the Japanese Come to the United States?
How Did They Lose Their Rights and Property in 1942?
How Has Their Life Changed Since World War II?

Settling in the United States. Until little more than 100 years ago, Japan was a country of farmers without much contact with the rest of the world. In 1868, however, its emperor began to move his country into modern ways. Factories, railroads and new industries grew rapidly. A strong army was trained. By 1895 Japan was strong enough to win a war against China. A quiet land had changed; it had become a war machine, ready to fight to gain power over much of Asia.

Many Japanese feared the changes in their country. Taxes rose. Soldiers ruled the land. Some people made plans to leave. A second war came in 1904. This time the Japanese defeated Russia. Thousands of peaceful Japanese decided they could not remain in a warlike country. They left for the United States. Most came to Hawaii and California. In 1906 1,000

Japanese a month entered California. They soon learned that they were not welcome.

The people of California had worked to end immigration from China. Now they saw a new danger of the same kind. The same warnings were made and believed. Those poor people from Asia would work at low wages. They would drive white people out of good neighborhoods. They were non-Christians who would not follow American ways.

The Gentlemen's Agreement. In 1906 there were 93 Japanese children in San Francisco schools. The white people of that city still discriminated against Asians. The Board of Education ordered Asian boys and girls to attend a segregated school that would have no white students. The Japanese government viewed this action as an attack on its honor. Japanese newspapers spoke of war to punish this loss of face. President Theodore Roosevelt understood that war with Japan was a real possibility. Why should the United States fight a war because of the prejudice of the people of San Francisco? He asked the school board to give up its plan to segregate Japanese students. In return he promised to take steps to end immigration from Japan.

The Japanese government wanted above all to save face. It agreed to keep its people from coming to the United States if Congress did not pass a Japanese Exclusion Act. Roosevelt agreed. The agreement became known as the Gentlemen's Agreement. From 1908 on, immigration ended. However, Japanese coolies could still settle in Hawaii, which needed farm workers.

The Japanese had saved face. They could point to the words Roosevelt had used in a letter he wrote in 1905.

> I am utterly disgusted at the [ideas] which have begun to appear on the Pacific slope in favor of excluding the Japanese exactly as the Chinese are excluded. The California State Legislature and various bodies have acted in the worst possible taste and in the most offensive manner to Japan.

The Gentlemen's Agreement lasted until the 1924 immigration law barred all Japanese as it did all Chinese.

Success in the United States. More than 200,000 Japanese-Americans live in Hawaii. They are more than one-fourth of that state's population. Few of them suffer from discrimination. They have married people of other races. Their children have known little prejudice. Japanese-Americans are in all the professions in Hawaii. They are important in politics. They, like the Japanese-Americans in California, think of themselves as Americans, not as Japanese. Not one Japanese-American was found to be a spy for Japan during World War II, even though many of them were jailed as suspected spies. One of the best fighting units of the United States Army in Europe was made up of Japanese-Americans.

More than 100,000 other Japanese lived in California. Most became farmers. They bought land that Americans thought too poor to be farmed. They tended it with the great care and skill their people had given land for hundreds of years in Japan. They drained swamps. They built step-like terraces on rocky or hilly land. Often they brought soil for these terraces from the valleys below. They used irrigation to water land in dry areas. Japanese farmers were used to the hard work needed to make crops grow on poor land. By 1940 they had changed some of the worst land in the West to the finest farmland.

These farmers saved their money and bought or rented more land. Their children also became farmers. Many opened businesses in nearby towns. California's Japanese-Americans became a well-to-do minority. They owned more than $400 million worth of land, buildings and businesses. Their children, like their parents, believed in education. Many went to college. Each Japanese-American family tried to become part of the life of the town in which it lived.

The Nisei. There were more than 110,000 Japanese-Americans in the West Coast states in 1941. About 75,000 of them had been born in the United States. The Japanese use the word *Nisei* to describe their American-born children. Until 1898 state laws in the West had barred the Nisei from citizenship. In that year the United States Supreme Court decided the case of *United States v. Wong Kim Ark*. It held that the children of immigrants were citizens, for any person born in the United States and governed by its laws was a citizen under the Fourteenth Amendment.

The Nisei had special problems. Their parents were content to remain apart from white Americans. The Nisei went to American schools and wanted to take part in the same activities other children enjoyed. They met discrimination. Some of them

Japanese-Americans were among our best farmers. Why do you think they were able to grow such fine crops on what was often poor land?

went to Japan to complete their educations. After 1937 Japan refused to allow any more Nisei to do so. Young Nisei decided to avoid the problems Chinese were finding in the cities. Most of them remained farmers or settled in small towns.

Soon after the first Japanese farmers showed that they could succeed on almost any land, white farmers in California began to plan to get back the land they had sold them. A state law barred any person who could not become a citizen from owning land. This meant anyone born in Asia. In 1923 the United States Supreme Court agreed that the state had the power to pass such a law! Japanese farmers had to transfer their land to their American-born children, or to friends or relatives who were citizens. California then passed a law to prevent any Japanese from selling his land. It was 1948 before the United States Supreme Court ruled, in the case *Oyama v. California*, that a state could not pass such a law. It would be taking away property rights without due process.

Hate the Japanese! The coming of the war brought a sudden wave of hatred of Japan and the Japanese. It grew worse when stories of torture and death camps reached the United States. The Japanese had given wounded prisoners little or no medical care; many had died. Other prisoners had been beaten or starved to death. Men had been shot after surrendering. Newspapers, magazines and then motion pictures began to picture all Japanese as monsters. Each enemy citizen was just as evil as the generals who ordered soldiers to kill prisoners. In the words of General DeWitt, "A Jap's a Jap, and that's all there is to it." Japanese-Americans could only watch and wait for the trouble ahead. When Congress passed a law to remove them from the West Coast, they knew the worst had come.

In the Concentration Camps. By April 1, 1942, the Army was ready to remove all Japanese-Americans from California, Oregon and Washington. All those born in Japan, or whose families had come from Japan, had to report to centers. From there the Army moved them to camps in other states. This meant that more than 75,000 American citizens, and 37,000 Japanese-born older people, were placed in jail without trial! They could take with them only what they could carry. One or two suitcases had to hold the possessions from forty years or more of life in the United States.

A Japanese-American family reporting to a "relocation center" in 1942. How do you think they felt? What probably happened to their home and the rest of their belongings?

Their bank accounts had been frozen by government order on December 8, 1941. No Japanese-American could take his money out of a bank. It was 1967 before the $4 million frozen by this order was returned to its owners! To raise some cash, they had to sell what they could. White Americans took advantage of this. They offered a few hundred dollars for a car; a few thousand for a store and everything in it; a tenth of its value for a home. Japanese fishermen lost their boats. Most could not sell everything they owned. Farms, homes, even clothing, were lost forever. In some towns local governments took everything the Japanese left and sold or gave it to white Americans.

What is a concentration camp? It is a place where a large number of prisoners are kept behind barbed wire fences. They are guarded by armed soldiers, with bayonets on their guns, who have orders to kill anyone trying to escape. The world was

In this camp for Japanese-Americans in Colorado, a space 20 by 25 feet was allowed for each family. What would life be like in such a place?

shocked when the Germans put millions of people in camps as part of its drive to kill Jews and others. Americans held meetings to protest this terrible loss of freedom and life. Yet there was little protest when the Japanese-Americans were made prisoners.

The Supreme Court Agrees. Did the United States government have the power under the Constitution to take away the freedom of these American citizens? The question came before the Supreme Court. First it decided that the Army did have the power to limit the right of people to move freely near a defense area. In December, 1944, it decided the case *Korematsu v. United States.* This was a challenge to the removal plan. Some Americans were reminded of the Indian Removal plan of a hundred years earlier. Yet the Court ruled that it could not prevent the government from taking steps to remove those believed to be enemies during wartime. Justice Murphy dissented. He reminded the country that it was guilty of a racist attack on Japanese-Americans. During the Civil War the Court had ruled that no person could lose his right to a trial so long as the courts could still operate. The courts in California and the other states were still open. Why hadn't each suspected spy been charged in a proper trial?

Justice Roberts also dissented. He said that the removal of the Japanese-Americans was wrong. It was a case of

> . . . convicting a citizen as a punishment for not submitting to imprisonment in a concentration camp, based on his ancestry, and solely because of his ancestry, without evidence or inquiry concerning his loyalty . . . toward the United States. . . . Constitutional rights have been violated. . . . [Korematsu] is a native of the United States of Japanese ancestry who . . . is a loyal citizen of the nation.

The Court ruled in another case that the Nisei could not be held in camps unless each one was charged with and found guilty of breaking a law. It had in part accepted Justice Murphy's argument. This freed the American-born prisoners. About 35,000 of them had left the camps by the summer of 1944. But their Japanese-born parents had to remain in the camps until the end of the war. Many of these were old people. At least half of the Nisei stayed in the camps to care for their parents. Those Japanese-Americans who wished to do so were allowed to join the armed forces. More than 30,000 Nisei became soldiers. They were proving their loyalty to the United States even though their families had been jailed without due process! They were placed in two segregated Army groups—the 100th Infantry Battalion and the 442nd Regimental Combat Team. The 442nd became the best fighting force in the United States Army. It and its members received more decorations than any other unit in United States history. Sixty per cent of its members were killed or wounded in the fighting in

Although their families remained prisoners in their own land, Japanese-American soldiers fought heroically for their country. What do you think made them such outstanding soldiers?

Europe! This was the greatest loss suffered by any group in the Army.

The American people learned little about life in the camps. There were few reports in the newspapers. It was never known, for example, that the people in those camps tried to help the United States win the war. One camp set up a factory to make nets for hiding battle cannon from the enemy. The nets were well made and useful. However, the Army soon refused to use them, or any other products made by Japanese-Americans.

The highest award a soldier can win in a war is the Congressional Medal of Honor. Again and again some Japanese-American parent in a prison camp was visited by an Army officer delivering a Medal of Honor. This part of the story of some of our honored heroes was not known to the American people.

Below: Famous professor and college president S. I. Hayakawa. Bottom: Sejii Ozawa has conducted our greatest symphony orchestras, one of the youngest men to have done so.

After the War. Japanese-Americans were released from the prison camps at the end of the war. They found that the white people of California did not want them to return. Groups had been organized to keep them out. One of these, the Japanese Exclusion League, had branches all over the state. Rich white farmers had taken many of the Japanese farms. Their group, the Associated Farmers, wanted to keep these farms and had the help of the state legislature. Japanese-Americans had owned 5,135 farms in California before the war. Most of them were lost forever, as was most of the other property that had been left behind.

More than 1,000 Japanese-Americans had been fishermen before the war. California passed a special law in 1945 to keep them from returning to their old trade. Torao Takahashi, one of these fishermen, sued for his right to make a living. His case, *Takahashi v. California Fish and Game Commission*, came to the Supreme Court. It decided in his favor—an important decision to protect the rights of people who were not citizens. Here are some of the ideas found in the Court's decision.

— Takahashi had a license to fish in ocean waters from 1915 to 1942. During the war, he had been taken out of the state by the Army. Now he has returned. He meets all the requirements for a fishing license.
— All persons within the United States have the same right in every state and territory to the full and equal benefit of the laws. This includes the right to obtain a license from a state.
— The California law under which Takahashi was denied a license is directed only against the Japanese. This makes it a discriminatory law, one more example of the anti-Japanese fever found in California.

At last due process was again being enforced. Almost two-thirds of the Japanese-Americans returned to the West Coast. They began again. Many settled in the cities. Others started new farms. They began cases to get back their lost property.

In 1948 Congress agreed to pay for some of it. It gave Japanese-Americans less than ten cents for each dollar they had lost. This was the only admission by Congress that it had done any wrong to the Japanese-Americans during the war.

Large numbers of Nisei were helped by the laws against discrimination passed in the 1950's. Like the Chinese, they were well trained and educated. They moved to cities in other parts of the United States. By 1970 more than 20,000 had come to Chicago. Thousands more went to such large cities as New York, Philadelphia and Detroit. More than 5,000 Nisei settled in Texas, which had made all members of the 442nd honorary citizens of Texas after the war. Many Nisei found jobs with the United States offices of Japanese companies. Others became leaders in the professions. They became doctors, lawyers and college professors. S. I. Hayakawa, born in Canada but long famous as a college professor in the United States, became president of a college. Minoru Yamasaki gained fame as one of our country's leading architects. Isamu Noguchi became a great sculptor whose work is in many American museums. Sejii Ozawa conducted the New York Philharmonic and other leading orchestras. Japanese-Americans have found their greatest success in Hawaii. They hold important posts in that state's government. They have been state attorney generals and superintendents of education. One of Hawaii's two Senators is Daniel K. Inouye. Its two Representatives in Congress are Spark M. Matsunaga and Patsy Takamoto Mink.

The Japanese-American Citizens League. The children of the Japanese farmers who came to the United States to find peace and democracy have learned how hard it can be for a minority to gain these goals. Still, they are not bitter. Less than 5,000 Japanese returned to Japan after their years in the prison camps. All the others remained here. Here is part of the statement of beliefs of the Japanese-American Citizens League, their largest organization in the United States.

> I am proud that I am an American citizen of Japanese ancestry, for my very background makes me appreciate more fully the wonderful advantages of this nation. I believe in her institutions, ideals and traditions. . . . She has granted me liberties and opportunities such as no individual enjoys in this world today. She has given me an education . . . [the right to vote]. . . . She has permitted me to build a home, to earn a livelihood,

Below: Hawaiian Senator Daniel Inouye. Bottom: Congressional Representative Patsy Mink.

to worship, think, speak and act as I please—as a free man equal to every other man.

Although some individuals may discriminate against me, I shall never become bitter or lose faith. . . . Because I believe in America, and I trust that she believes in me . . . I pledge myself to honor her at all times and all places; to support her Constitution; to obey her laws; to respect her flag; to defend her against all enemies. . . .

I. WHAT ARE THE FACTS?

Answer each question in a sentence or two.

1. Explain the phrase "a day that will live in infamy."

2. In what states did most Japanese-American live in 1941?

3. Why had the Japanese settled in these states?

4. What problem affecting Japanese-Americans developed in San Francisco in 1906?

5. How did the Gentlemen's Agreement end Japanese immigration?

6. How did Japanese-Americans become a well-to-do minority?

7. How were Japanese-Americans helped by the decision of the United States Supreme Court in *United States v. Wong Kim Ark*?

8. Why did General DeWitt want to remove Japanese-Americans from the West Coast?

9. What is a concentration camp?

10. How did the United States Supreme Court rule in the case that challenged the power of the government to remove Japanese-Americans to concentration camps?

11. How did Nisei soldiers gain fame during World War II?

12. How did California try to prevent Japanese-American fishermen from making a living after World War II?

13. What happened to the property owned by Japanese-Americans in 1942?

14. To what cities in the East have Japanese-Americans moved?

15. How have Japanese-Americans benefited from trade with Japan?

II. WHAT DOES HE DO?

Match each name in COLUMN A with his occupation in COLUMN B.

COLUMN A

1. S. I. Hayakawa
2. Minoru Yamasaki
3. Sejii Ozawa
4. Daniel K. Inouye
5. Spark M. Matsunaga

COLUMN B

a. Representative in Congress
b. Senator from Hawaii
c. Conductor of symphony orchestras
d. Leading architect
e. California college president

III. THINKING IT THROUGH!

Discuss.

1. Why do you think not a single Japanese-American became a spy for Japan during World War II?

2. Why do you agree or disagree with the statement that any minority group might one day find itself in concentration camps as the Japanese-Americans were?

3. Why did most Americans hate all Japanese during World War II?

4. Ask older people you know these questions and report on their answers:
a) What were your feelings toward Japanese-Americans during World War II?
b) How much did you know about the camps for Japanese-Americans?

IV. A RESEARCH PROBLEM.

You can find the answers to these questions in an encyclopedia. Your librarian can help you find the articles you will have to read.

1. Compare concentration camps in Germany during World War II with those for Japanese-Americans in this country.

2. How were Indian reservations similar to or different from concentration camps?

3. How did concentration-camp life compare with that of a slave on a plantation?

Harvey M. Stein

Unit Five

CATHOLIC AMERICANS

American Catholics were a small religious minority for most of our country's history. Their numbers have grown until today they are about one-fourth of all Americans. This unit traces their change from a suffering minority to a strong group that has provided the United States with important leaders. At one time the rights of Catholics were limited. Their right to worship was challenged. Their daily lives were full of danger. American Protestants viewed them as enemies. Groups such as the Ku Klux Klan made Catholics their special targets. In 1928 Alfred E. Smith became the first Catholic to run for President. He lost after a campaign in which he was attacked for his religion more than for his political ideas. But by 1960 Americans had changed their views. John F. Kennedy, a Catholic, was elected President. This time the campaign was not marked by religious prejudice. The years since 1960 have seen a continuing improvement in the position of Catholic Americans. Today, with all religious groups moving closer together, Catholics are freer to make their full contribution to American life.

Why Have American Protestants Discriminated Against Catholics?

1 The French and Indian War was the last of several conflicts between the French and English for control of North America. This was a bitter war. The French and their Indian allies attacked along the frontier. The colonies called out their militia to defend against such attacks. In Pennsylvania a special law in 1757 ordered all men between seventeen and fifty-five to serve in the militia when called upon. Quakers, who opposed all wars, were excused. Roman Catholics were barred! No Catholic or suspected Catholic could be a soldier. They had to hand in all their guns and ammunition. Their homes could be searched to make certain they did this.

There were only a few thousand Catholics in the colonies. Other colonists did not trust them. France was a Catholic country that made all its people support that religion. England was a Protestant country. It had broken away from Catholic control and had fought long wars to remain independent. Pennsylvania Catholics in 1757 were meeting a special kind of discrimination. They were losing one of their rights as citizens—the right to help defend your country. At the same time, the new law made them pay a special tax to help support the militia that barred them!

Why Were Protestants and Catholics Often Bitter Enemies?

Why Did So Few Catholics Come to the Colonies?

Why Did Large Numbers of Catholics Later Come to the United States?

What Special Problems Did They Face?

Are the Catholics a Minority? The largest religious group in the United States today is the Roman Catholics. They are more often called Catholics. In 1970 the United States had about fifty million Catholics. Their religious leader is Pope Paul VI, who lives in Rome. He is the head of the Catholic Church, which numbers about 600 million people throughout

The Vatican in Rome is the home of the Pope, head of the Roman Catholic Church. How can one man "rule" 600 million people in countries all over the world?

the world. The Catholic Church has always been run like a kingdom. The pope is its elected ruler. His religious subjects are 600 million people around the world. He "rules" them through his appointed princes, called cardinals. Each cardinal represents the pope in one part of the world. When a pope dies, the cardinals elect a new pope.

In 1970 the United States had nine cardinals. Below them were archbishops (who rule archdioceses) and bishops (who rule dioceses). Each bishop was in charge of the churches and other Catholic institutions in his district, or diocese. Each church was led by one or more priests. The area served by a church is called a parish. The United States in 1970 had more than 18,000 parishes. More than 250,000 Catholic men and women in the country were priests and nuns. All had decided to spend their lives serving their religion. Eleven million students attended Catholic schools and colleges. The Roman Catholic Church is the richest and most powerful single religious group the United States has ever known. Yet for most of their history in this country, Catholics have been a poor minority suffering from great discrimination.

Religious Groups in the United States		
Protestants—65%	Catholics—25%	Jews—3%
In No Religious Group—5-7%		

Catholics and Protestants. The Roman Catholic Church had been the only religious power in most of Europe for 1,000 years. Then, after 1500, millions of Christians broke away from Catholicism. They set up national churches that refused to accept the rule of the pope. The new churches were called Protestant. They began as a protest against Roman Catholicism. Protestant churches were alike in several ways. Members prayed in their national language instead of in Latin. They used Bibles in that language too. They felt free to make changes in their ways of worshiping. Protestant churches were often run in a very democratic way. Members of the churches made their own rules and elected their own officials. There was no outside control.

France and Spain remained Catholic. They were among the most powerful countries in the world. They fought religious wars against the Germans, English and others who broke away from the Catholic Church. Catholics and Protestants became enemies in country after country. Each group punished the other, taking away rights and even killing one another. Europe was torn by religious differences for about 200 years. They were still sharp when the English began their colonies in North America.

All the English colonies except Maryland were settled by Protestants. Many of these settlers had suffered in Catholic countries. They had learned to fear Catholics. They often hated them. Many Catholics had been driven out of England; those who remained were persecuted. English rulers did not want Catholics to settle in their colonies. The test of a Catholic was to make him take the Oath of Supremacy. He would have to swear that the King of England was his ruler in all matters, religious as well as non-religious. No Catholic could take this oath. The oath became required in most of the colonies.

Lord Baltimore was one of the few Catholics in England who was able to keep his wealth and power. He became the proprietor of Maryland. Most of those who settled there were Protestants. In 1649 that colony passed a Toleration Act. It permitted all Christians to worship freely. Five years later the people of the colony turned against their Catholic officials. The Toleration Act was ended. Catholics could still settle in Maryland, but their rights were limited. In Maryland, as in other colonies, they lost the right to vote unless they first took the Oath of Supremacy.

The Catholics knew they were not welcome in most of the

The leader of the movement known as the Protestant Reformation was Martin Luther, a German priest.

colonies. By the 1770's there were only a few thousand of them among the colonists. Samuel Adams, a leader of the American Revolution, observed that Catholics were being denied full rights. He wrote in 1772:

— Catholics believed that the pope had the power to force out the head of a government.
— Catholics in many lands had punished and even killed those who would not accept their religion.
— Catholics were not prepared to live in a democratic country, for they believed their pope's power could never be challenged.

Protestant Americans feared and hated Catholics. Many were certain they would never permit Catholics to be part of their new country. Then, during the Revolution, Catholic France became the ally of the new United States. American leaders began to soften their anti-Catholic feelings. Later, when they wrote the Constitution, they decided that their new government would have to permit religious freedom for all. The First Amendment to the Constitution made this clear.

Congress shall make no law respecting an establishment of religion, or prohibiting the free exercise thereof . . .

This meant that no religion can be supported by the United States government. It also means that any person can follow the religion he chooses. The Second Amendment tried to prevent the problem that had appeared in Pennsylvania in 1757. Congress could not take away any person's right to serve in his state militia.

Equal Rights for Catholics. State constitutions also gave all people the right to worship freely. More Catholics began to come from Europe. Priests came too. They set up churches and parishes. In 1791 they had their first bishop. He was Father John Carroll of Baltimore. The pope has the power to appoint all bishops. He had often sent Italians to rule over Catholics in other lands. This time he named an American priest who had been chosen by other American priests. Today, all American cardinals and most other high church officials in the United States are Americans.

Some states tried to keep Catholics out of public office. It

In 1533 King Henry VIII of England broke away from the pope and set up the Church of England.

was 1806 before New York ended an oath for officeholders that had been designed to bar Catholics.

One of the rights gained by Catholics was the protection of the practice called confession. A Catholic confesses his sins to a priest with the understanding that his words will always remain secret. In 1813 a Father Kohlmann heard a confession by a thief. He later returned what the thief had stolen to its owner. A judge asked the priest for the name of the thief. The priest refused. The matter came to court. It was decided that no priest could be made to tell what he had learned in a confession. The Constitution guaranteed freedom of religion. To force a priest to break the rules of his religion would be to interfere in that religion. This ruling remains part of American law today.

American Protestant churches rule themselves. In 1831 members of a Catholic church in Philadelphia demanded this right. Archbishop Kenrick of that city ordered the church's activities suspended. He made it clear that the pope, through his appointed officials, would alone rule this or any other Catholic church. Since then no American Catholic group has ever tried to take control of a church from its priests. However, since the second Vatican Council, 1963–1965, many changes have been made to give members of the Catholic Church a much larger voice in its government.

By the 1830's there were about 300,000 Catholics in the United States. They had set up eleven dioceses, each with its own bishop.

The Irish Catholics. Ireland was an English colony until 1922. For centuries Irish Catholics had suffered under Protestant England's rule. English landlords owned the best farmland in Ireland; they taxed their Irish tenants heavily. These farmers grew poorer and poorer. Many of them made plans to settle in the United States. Poor crops after 1840 left millions of Irish starving. They fled their country faster than almost any other group in the world's history. Most who left came to the United States. About five million in all have become Americans—the largest number between 1850 and 1890.

These Irish were Catholics. They were poor farmers without the skills to make a living in cities. They had received little education in Ireland, since it was controlled by the English. As they came without money, few could afford to move to the farmland open to them in the West. Most remained in cities such as Boston, New York and Philadelphia. There they had to take the lowest paying jobs. They became ditch diggers, servants and construction workers. Their labor built important canals and roads. Thousands took jobs with railroad companies. The Irish did most of the work of building the Union Pacific and other railroads after 1850, just as the Chinese had been the workers on the Central Pacific.

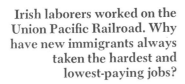

Irish laborers worked on the Union Pacific Railroad. Why have new immigrants always taken the hardest and lowest-paying jobs?

The Irish met great discrimination. They were Catholics in Protestant cities. Compared with Protestant Americans, the Irish were fun-loving and lively. Other Americans began to speak of the "wild Irish." They said these newcomers drank heavily and were quick to fight. Such charges were usually false. Still, the Irish had learned to "stick together" in their fight against persecution. They built their churches and centered their lives around them. Soon they had become voting citizens. Cities such as Boston became Irish centers of political power.

An anti-Catholic movement appeared in much of the country in the 1850's. It became known as the Nativists, or the American Party. (People called this group the Know-Nothings.) A Nativist was someone who wanted to end immigration, especially that of Catholics. Nativists also wanted to limit the rights of those who came here from other countries. Such groups have appeared many times in American history. The Ku Klux Klan has been nativist. It has opposed Catholics, Jews and foreigners of all kinds as well as blacks. In the 1890's the American Protective Association, an anti-Catholic nativist group, had about a million followers.

In 1835 Samuel F. B. Morse (inventor of the telegraph) wrote attacks against the Roman Catholics. His ideas remained the nativist belief for the next hundred years.

— Catholics do not believe in democracy.
— The Catholic Church in Europe supports kings and works to end democracy there and in the United States.
— Europeans who hate democracy pay the cost of spreading the Catholic faith in America.
— Roman Catholic priests tell their followers how to vote.
— Politicians seeking votes follow the orders of Catholic priests.
— Secret Catholic groups are building armies to take control of the United States.
— We should not permit immigrants to become voting citizens. Only those born in the United States should ever have the right to vote.

Nativist groups sometimes used violence against Catholics. In 1844 riots hit Philadelphia. The churches and homes of Irish immigrants were attacked. Shots were fired. Two churches were burned. In city after city, signs appeared at Protestant-owned businesses—NO IRISH NEED APPLY.

A Nativist riot against Catholics in Philadelphia in 1844. Here the rioters, in tall beaver hats, are attacking the state militia sent to quiet them. How does this appear different from the anti-Chinese riot on page 196?

Italian immigrants at Ellis Island in New York City. Why do you think so many immigrants came to this country from other lands?

Other Catholics Arrive. The Irish were the first great masses of poor people in the cities. Other Catholic groups later joined them. They were hoping to make a better living. Some came to find religious freedom. Many came from Germany. This group was better educated than the Irish. Many had skilled trades; some had money. They had less trouble fitting into American life. Almost 700,000 came from France. Perhaps half a million came from Poland. Five million came from Italy. Large numbers came from Austria. Most of these immigrants came between 1880 and 1920. They settled chiefly in the cities. Since 1945 about two million more Catholics have joined them, the largest number from Mexico and Puerto Rico. Hundreds of thousands came from Cuba to escape Fidel Castro.

Most of the Catholic immigrants were poor. They took the lowest-paying jobs—the only ones they could find. By 1920 more than 20 million Catholics lived in the United States. They had become a majority in some cities but were a minority in most of the places where they settled. They had set up 100 dioceses; 25,000 priests served their churches. By 1940 there were 35 million Catholics. By 1970 there were 50 million. They have been the most rapidly growing religious group in the United States.

Discrimination Against Catholics. The chief goal of the discrimination against Catholics seemed to be to keep them from holding any kind of power within the country. This discrimination took many forms.

225

Social Discrimination. White Protestants often refused to mix with their Catholic neighbors. Catholic students were not admitted to colleges. This made Catholics ever more determined to build their own colleges. When it was decided that religion could not be taught in the public schools, Catholics set up their own parochial schools. This further separated young Catholics from other Americans. Catholics formed their own organizations of every kind. Irish-American, Polish-American and Italian-American organizations sprang up in every large city. In the parts of the country where groups like the KKK were strong, Catholics had no other organizations they could join. In such areas Catholics became more and more separate from other Americans. Irish, Italians and Poles became the target of unkind humor for their accents, religion and customs.

Economic Discrimination. Newly arrived Catholics found that they could not get good jobs. Large companies refused to hire or train them. This kept these immigrants poor. Many landlords would not rent to Catholics. This kept many of them in city slums. Catholic workers remained in the building trades. They became important in lower-paying civil service jobs. In city after city they became sanitation men, policemen and firemen. Some entered growing industries, such as clothing and printing. Few were able to become professionals.

Educational Discrimination. In Europe the Catholic Church had controlled most of the education, even in schools supported, like American schools, by state funds. Priests were teachers and the heads of schools. Their religion taught that the Church should educate Catholic children. Catholics tried to build their own schools in each of their American parishes. These schools did not receive public tax money. Catholics had to pay regular taxes for the public schools and then raise the money for their own schools. Catholics feel harmed by the American belief that religious schools should not receive aid from a state or local government. They say their schools offer high quality education and also help relieve the growing burden on crowded public school

systems. Other Americans reply that giving aid to any religious school would be supporting that religion. This, they argue, is not permitted by the First Amendment.

A classroom in a Catholic school. Do you think the government should help support religious and private schools?

Political Discrimination. Catholic voters soon became a strong group in the cities. They became active in politics and by the 1870's controlled important city governments. Most of them became Democrats. The Nativist parties of the 1850's later joined the Republicans. The issue of slavery became more important than nativist beliefs. The position of many Catholics on the slavery issue was unclear. Since the Democrats at that time were controlled by the South, many Americans charged that Catholics supported the South and slavery. It became impossible for any Catholic to be elected in any area except the big cities. Voters charged the Democrats with being the party of Catholics and Civil War. It was not until after 1900 that Catholics had weakened this prejudice.

227

I. WHAT ARE THE FACTS?

Write the letter of the choice that best completes each statement.

1. Quakers did not fight in the French and Indian War because they (a) were excused for religious reasons, (b) would have supported the French against the English, (c) could not afford the cost of buying guns.

2. The highest position in the Catholic Church is held by the (a) bishop, (b) cardinal, (c) pope.

3. The smallest of the following is the (a) parish, (b) diocese, (c) archdiocese.

4. During the American Revolution, France (a) helped England, (b) helped the United States, (c) took no sides.

5. The courts of the United States have (a) forced priests to reveal the information they learn from confessions, (b) protected the right of priests to keep confessions secret, (c) made priests reveal the facts of a confession only when a crime can be solved in that way.

6. A nativist opposes giving equal rights to (a) all races, (b) immigrants, (c) the poor.

7. A large number of Roman Catholics came to the United States from (a) Greece, (b) Italy, (c) England.

8. The largest number of Americans are (a) Catholics, (b) Protestants, (c) Jews.

9. The purpose of the Oath of Supremacy was to (a) keep Catholics out of the colonies, (b) weaken slavery, (c) make the English army stronger.

10. The Maryland Toleration Act gave religious freedom to (a) Catholics only, (b) Protestants only, (c) all Christians.

II. EXPLAINING WHY.

Explain why each of these events occurred.

1. France and Spain fought wars against Protestant countries.

2. Most of the people in the colonies were Protestants.

3. Samuel Adams believed the rights of Catholics should be limited.

4. No religion can receive government support in the United States.

5. Millions of people left Ireland to settle in the United States.

6. Nativists wanted to prevent immigrants from becoming voters.

7. Many businesses refused to hire Irish Catholics.

8. American Catholics have built a complete school system.

III. THINKING IT THROUGH!

Discuss.

1. Class committees may present the facts about these recent examples of religious conflict:
   a) Hindus and Muslims in India
   b) Catholics and Protestants in Northern Ireland
   c) Christians, Muslims and Jews in the Middle East
Then discuss these questions:
   a) Why does one religious group hate another in the examples you have examined?
   b) What changes would each group have to accept before peace between the groups could be reached?
   c) Why do we not have great religious conflict in the United States?

2. What charges did non-Catholics make against Catholics in the 1800's? Why?

3. What does one group gain when it discriminates against another group? What does it lose?

Why Has Discrimination Against Catholics Weakened?

2 Alfred E. Smith of New York was a successful political leader. He had been a poor boy in a New York City slum. He slowly rose in the politics of his city and state. In 1922 he became governor. For the next six years he made New York one of the best-governed states in the country. In 1928 his party, the Democrats, chose him as its candidate for President. With all his talent in government, he never had a chance to win. Al Smith was a Catholic. The 1928 campaign became an attack and defense of the Catholic Church instead of a contest between Smith and the Republican, Herbert Hoover. Hoover won easily. An old "rule" of American politics had been proved true. The people would never choose a Catholic as President.

Al Smith campaigned for the Presidency in 1928 but was unable to overcome religious prejudice. Why do you think John F. Kennedy was successful in 1960 in spite of his religion?

The "rule" was tested again in 1960. Another Catholic, John F. Kennedy, was the Democratic candidate for President. The question of his religion seemed important at first. But Kennedy was able to convince the voters that religion should not be the reason for their choice of President. His victory seemed greatly to weaken political discrimination against Catholics. The problems of the country had changed. So had much of the discrimination against its largest minority.

Why Was Al Smith Defeated in 1928?
How Did John F. Kennedy Weaken Anti-Catholic Voting?
Why Have Anti-Catholic Feelings Weakened Since 1960?

Catholics in American Politics. Until about 1900 most Catholics were poor. They were workers rather than members of the middle class or owners of industry. Catholics did much to begin the country's unions. They worked for higher pay and better working conditions. For more than a hundred years most Catholics voted for the Democrats. They helped make the Democrats the party that most often spoke for working people.

Most Catholics live in our larger cities. They have often gained power in city and state governments. In Boston, New York, Chicago, Detroit, Buffalo and other places, candidates supported by Catholic voters won control. This was a way for Catholics to improve their lives. The United States had given them greater rights than they had ever known in Europe. The people of such countries as Ireland, Italy and Poland had never had the rights guaranteed by the United States Constitution. These rights could be used to fight discrimination.

Catholics in the cities remained closely united. Families gave part of their income to their churches. They built their lives around the work of these churches. They set up many organizations and used them to improve their lives. Catholics cared for one another. The Church did for its members many of the things governments do today. It helped the poor. It helped young people in trouble. It arranged for medical aid for the sick. Each church developed a large program of social activities.

Church officials believed they should guide Catholics in many ways. As part of this, the pope gave statements of the Church's views on problems he felt important to Catholics. As a result, non-Catholics often said that Catholics did not think for themselves. This charge was also directed against Catholic politicians.

The Campaign of 1928. The Democratic candidate for President, Al Smith, was widely attacked for his religion. In 1927 an open letter to him appeared in the *Atlantic Monthly*, a leading magazine. It gave four reasons for opposing a Catholic candidate:

— The Catholic religion holds that the Church is higher than any government when there is a difference between them on a religious matter.
— The Church alone decides what matters are religious.
— All religions are equal under our Constitution. The pope has said that they are not equal, and that it is "unlawful to place the various forms of divine worship on the same footing as the true religion."
— One pope had stated that "To [the Catholic Church] the only begotten Son of God entrusted all the truths which He had taught in order that it might keep and guard them and with lawful authority explain them, and at the same time He commanded all nations to hear the voice of the [Roman Catholic] Church as if it were His own. . . . "

In the South, the Ku Klux Klan led the attack against Smith. The KKK argued that all Catholics were part of a plot to take control of the United States. One of its charges was that if elected, Smith would move the pope from Rome to Washington. He would then use his power as President to make all Americans Catholics! Smith answered the attack in his speeches:

I . . . declare that I do not wish any member of my faith in any part of the United States to vote for me on any religious grounds. I want them to vote for me only when in their hearts and consciences they become convinced that my election will promote the best interests of our country. . . .
The absolute separation of State and Church is part of the

fundamental basis of our Constitution. I believe in that separation. . . .

I will take the office as President of the United States with absolutely no obligation except to devote myself to the best interests of this country and to promote the prosperity, the welfare and happiness of all the people.

Herbert Hoover won the election by six million votes. For the first time since Reconstruction, his Republican Party won in five states in the South. The attack against a Catholic candidate for President had succeeded.

Changes by 1960. It was 1960 before another Catholic ran for President. The world had seen great changes since 1928. A terrible depression had caused suffering to most Americans. The New Deal had brought laws that changed every person's life. Unions had grown stronger. People had gained some protection against unemployment and poverty. Anti-discrimination and civil rights laws had begun to be part of the country's life. The United States had fought a second world war. The atomic age had begun; it had brought the fear of atomic war. For fifteen years the United States and Russia had carried on a "cold war" in which each country viewed the other as its greatest enemy.

In the years since 1928 the power of the United States government had grown greater and greater. The President would be facing world as well as national problems. He would act with more power than any President had ever held before.

Herbert Hoover won the 1928 election by six million votes. Was this a true measure of his popularity?

233

Richard M. Nixon, the Republican candidate in 1960, and John F. Kennedy, the Democrat, agreed on many issues. The contest between them turned mainly on other questions: Which one would the voters prefer as a person? Which one could best be trusted with the great power of the Presidency? Which had the better judgment?

The Campaign of 1960. The questions of 1928 appeared at once. Could a Catholic be trusted to be President? Would he do what the country needed, or what the leaders of his church wanted? On September 12, 1960, Kennedy met with a group of Protestant ministers in Houston, Texas. He spoke to them of his religion, and of how it would not affect his work as President.

John F. Kennedy assured Protestant ministers in Houston that his religion would not affect his work as President. Was he believed?

I believe in an America where the separation of church and state is absolute—where no Catholic [church official] would tell the President, should he be a Catholic, how to act, and no Protestant minister would tell his parishioners for whom to vote; where no church school is granted any public funds or political preference; and where no man is denied public office merely because his religion differs from the President who might appoint him or the people who might elect him. . . .

. . . I believe in an America where religious intolerance will someday end; where all men and churches are treated as equal; where every man has the same right to attend or not attend the church of his choice. . . .

. . . I believe in a President whose views on religion are his own private affair. . . .

Less Discrimination. John F. Kennedy lived up to these beliefs during the almost three years he was President. Whatever his successes and failures while in office, his religion seemed to play no part in them. This more or less ended attacks against Catholics running for public office in most of the country. Other forms of discrimination against Catholics have also grown weaker. They are more easily admitted to colleges. Fewer Catholics are barred from jobs because of their religion. Non-Catholics and Catholics mix far more than in the past. In many states, public money provides services and lunches for children in religious schools. Here are some of the reasons that have been offered to explain such changes:

— There is a great movement to bring all Christians closer together. It is called the Ecumenical Movement. Pope John XXIII led it from 1958 to 1963. It has continued since his death. Many Christians hope that all churches can be joined in some way. This has meant that each Christian group has been more willing to admit that other Christians are not evil for being different.
— Hate groups in most of the United States have less power today. New laws have forced most of them to act in secret. National leaders have worked together to end religious discrimination. Motion pictures and television programs reach most Americans today. They try to show all groups in fairer ways than in the past.
— Catholic leaders have often fought for equal rights for minority groups. Senator Robert F. Kennedy made the needs of minorities his special interest from 1965 until his death in 1968. Other Catholic politicians have done the same.
— Many well-known priests have also become involved. They joined the freedom marches. They have fought for community control. Such actions have brought Catholics closer to other groups in the cities.
— American Catholics are no longer as poor as they were fifty years ago. They have become important in their communi-

Pope John XXIII led the Ecumenical Movement until his death. Is a movement to bring all Christians closer together a good thing? Why?

235

ties. Hundreds of Catholics have been heroes in their country's wars. Catholics have become important in every profession and in the arts. It is no longer possible to picture all Catholics as alike. The old attacks on "the Catholic" just do not make sense.

— The groups who were anti-Catholic for so long now have new targets for their fear and hatred. They see a threat to white supremacy. Black Americans and other minorities demand equal rights and equal power. These minority groups may be Catholic, like the Mexican-Americans and the Puerto Ricans. However, they are thought of as racial or national minorities rather than as religious groups.

Catholic Success. President John F. Kennedy's book *A Nation of Immigrants* reminds us that the United States grew great largely because of the "abilities and ideas" of its immigrants. American Catholics began as a group with very limited rights. They were the target of unfair laws and widespread hatred. They have overcome most of the discrimination against them. Today they are so large a part of the country that they can no longer be thought of as a minority. Their achievements have been too numerous to list. Thousands have become leaders in every part of our country's life.

In government they are important at every level. They have been Senators, such as Robert F. Wagner of New York and Patrick McCarran of Nevada; Cabinet members, such as Roger B. Taney, James Mitchell and Anthony Celebrezze; Supreme Court Justices such as Sherman Minton. They have been union leaders such as John Mitchell, president of the United Mine Workers, and political leaders such as Paul O'Dwyer, New York mayors Fiorello La Guardia and Robert F. Wagner, Jr., and Democratic Party chairman Lawrence O'Brien. Many have been journalists and writers—Heywood Broun, Bob Considine and George Jean Nathan among them. In music, Arturo Toscanini and Pierre Monteux were great conductors; Enrico Caruso was one of our greatest opera stars. Broadway composer and star George M. Cohan gave America some of its best-loved songs.

Baseball's "Babe" Ruth was a Catholic; so was football's great Knute Rockne. Enrico Fermi won a Nobel Prize in physics and did much to aid America's atomic research. Tom Dooley was a doctor to the poor in Asia and founded MEDICO, an organization to continue that work. Clare Boothe Luce has been

Top left: The great conductor Arturo Toscanini. Right: One of the greatest opera stars of all time, Enrico Caruso. *Bottom* left: Babe Ruth, record-setting baseball player. Middle: Nobel Prize-winning physicist Enrico Fermi. Right: Clare Booth Luce, actress, author and diplomat.

not only a playwright and author, but also a Congresswoman and American ambassador to Italy. Mrs. Jacqueline Grennan Wexler is an educator and college president.

Science, government, literature, the arts, business, education —Catholics are important in all these fields. They are of every race. They have come from every part of the world. Discrimination against them has weakened; it has not ended. Still, as the country becomes less concerned with religious differences, Catholics, like other Americans, will be judged for what they do, not for their religious beliefs.

I. WHAT ARE THE FACTS?

Answer each question in a sentence or two.

1. What political party was supported by most Catholics?

2. How did the pope and the United States Constitution differ on the equality of religions?

3. In what year was Al Smith a candidate for President?

4. State two reasons given by the KKK for its attacks on Al Smith.

5. What is meant by "separation of church and state"?

6. What is meant by "religious intolerance"?

7. Why have hate groups in most of the United States grown weaker?

8. What effect did the election of John F. Kennedy as President have on discrimination against Catholics?

9. How did Robert Kennedy try to help minority groups?

10. Who began the Ecumenical Movement?

II. WORDS TO KNOW.

Use a dictionary or encyclopedia to explain the meaning of each of these words or phrases. How does each help you to understand the facts in this chapter?

1. papal infallibility

2. ecumenism

3. papal encyclicals

4. voting on religious grounds

5. political preference

III. THINKING IT THROUGH!

Discuss.

1. How separate are Catholics and non-Catholics in your community? Why? What changes would you suggest in the way religious groups in your community deal with each other?

2. How many religious groups are represented in your school? How do the students of each group get along? Why are young people often less concerned than adults about religious differences? Compare the importance of religious and racial differences in choosing your friends.

3. Do you feel a Jew or a black American will someday be able to be elected President as John Kennedy was? Why or why not?

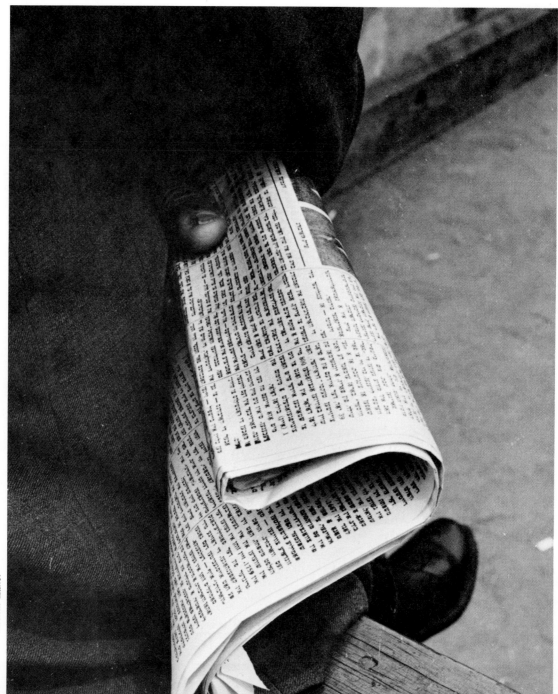

Arthur Laxer

Unit Six

JEWISH AMERICANS

Less than three per cent of all Americans are Jews. Unit 6
is about this religious minority in the United States. Jews first
came to America over 300 years ago in search of religious
freedom. It was not until the 1870's that they began to find it.
Until that time, state and local laws had often denied them
equal rights. Most of the Jews who came to the United States
were from eastern Europe. They came chiefly between 1880
and 1920. Most of these Jewish immigrants were poor. They
worked for low wages in the large cities in which most of them
settled. They struggled to help their children become well
educated. Today most American Jews have improved their
lives; some remain low-paid workers. Hatred and discrimination have harmed them greatly along the way. This unit
describes how they have been the special target of many hate
groups. It explains what hate groups try to do and why they
behave as they do. Attacks against Jews have brought many
Americans together to fight all forms of religious prejudice.
Yet American Jews still face problems of prejudice, often a
mirror of attacks against Jews in other parts of the world.

Should Asser Levy Be a Citizen?

1 A refugee is a person who flees one country to seek safety in another. Jews have been refugees for 2,000 years. The first Jews to settle in the Dutch colony of New Amsterdam (later named New York) arrived in 1654. They had lived in a city in Brazil but had left when Portugal captured it. If they had remained, they would have been forced to become Roman Catholics.

There were 23 people in the group. They were led by Asser Levy van Swellem, a butcher. Peter Stuyvesant, the governor of New Amsterdam, wanted to make the Jews leave. The Dutch West India Company in Holland ordered him to permit them to remain:

> . . . These people may travel and trade . . . and live and remain there, provided the poor among them shall not become a burden to the company or to the community, but shall be supported by their own nation.

The Jews could remain. Yet Stuyvesant refused to give them the rights enjoyed by other people in New Amsterdam. Asser Levy and others had to win one right at a time during the next ten years. Each time,

Governor Peter Stuyvesant wanted to make Asser Levy and his group leave New Amsterdam. Why wouldn't he have wanted them to stay?

Levy went to court against the governor. He then appealed the governor's decisions to Holland. The Jews slowly became citizens. They won the right to serve as soldiers. They gained the right to own their own homes. They were permitted to set up businesses. They were given the right to trade with other Dutch settlements along the Hudson River.

They kept these rights when England took the colony in 1664. Soon others were added. They opened their first cemetery. They became landowners. They built their first house of worship, or *synagogue*. In 1665 Asser Levy showed that he believed all religious groups should share their rights. He helped raise the money to build the city's first Lutheran church. In a few years Levy had helped the Jews move toward equality. In most of the rest of the world, Jews could not become citizens of the countries in which they lived. But they would be citizens of the colonies that later became the United States!

Why Have Jews Settled in the United States?
What Problems Did They Face?
How Did They Overcome These Problems?

A History of Discrimination. Christianity became the official religion of the Roman Empire in 325. The Romans had often punished peoples who did not accept Rome's rules. Four years later the first laws directed against Jews appeared. The Jews were charged with great crimes. They refused to become Christians. They were said to have killed Jesus Christ. They were blamed for the troubles in Christian countries. A scapegoat is someone who is blamed for the problems people face—even when he had nothing to do with these problems. Jews became the scapegoats of cruel rulers who held complete power over their people. Hatred of Jews was matched by laws that took away their rights.

From the year 329 on, Jews in Europe suffered great discrimination. Here are some of the problems they faced. The rulers of the countries in which they lived tried to force them to give up their religion and become Christians. Those who

Behind the walls of ghettos, Jews lived cut-off from the life of medieval cities. What meaning does the word *ghetto* have today?

remained Jews often found that Christians would not become their friends. Jews were not permitted to marry Christians. In some parts of Europe, Jews were barred from the streets at certain hours or on certain days. They always had to fear that their synagogues or their holy writings might be burned. They could not vote or hold public office.

Christian religious leaders accepted discrimination against the Jews. Some of them even led the attacks against Jews. One pope explained that "The Jews, like Cain, are doomed to wander the earth as fugitives and vagabonds. . . ." Many popes tried to protect the Jews from violence, even while they attacked them in public statements. Most Jews had to live in segregated neighborhoods. In some cities they had to live in walled communities called *ghettos*. There they tried to survive.

Each Jewish community elected a committee to make the rules needed to keep the group safe and to carry on its religion. Charity—helping those in need—was a most important activity. It was given to Jews and non-Jews—to members of the community and to strangers. The community collected its own taxes and paid them to the rulers of the city or country. It made rules for daily living: how to do business, what wages to pay, what prices to charge and how to live with one's neighbors. Each Jewish community had its own judges and courts. Jews obeyed them even though their only real power came from the willingness of the people to accept their decisions.

Education was an important goal of each family and each community. It was needed if a person was to survive—as a religious Jew who was the target of discrimination. All Jews had to read the Jewish Bible, the Old Testament. All boys had to attend schools run by the community. This meant that Jews could read and write (in Hebrew, and sometimes in other languages as well) at a time when only rich non-Jews had much education. Many Jews became important in Europe because of their education, even in countries where all other Jews had to remain in the ghettos.

Protestants became important in Europe after 1500. They too treated Jews harshly. Martin Luther, a founder of Protestantism, once ordered that the Jews be driven out of Germany. He demanded that "all their cash and jewels and silver and gold" be taken. He told his followers that "their synagogues or schools be set on fire, that their houses be broken up and destroyed. . . ." Mobs attacked the ghettos. Thousands of Jews were killed. They were driven out of some German cities. Jews were the only non-Christians in most of Europe. Again and again they were made to suffer.

Jews in the Colonies. A small number of Jews came to North America, most fleeing from Spain and Portugal. About 2,500 of them lived in the English colonies in the 1770's. Wherever they settled they had to struggle to gain the rights other people already had. Only in South Carolina did they find real freedom. The other colonies refused equal rights to Jews just as they did to Catholics. Even after the United States was formed, some states refused to give Jews equal rights. They did not gain the right to vote in North Carolina until 1868. They could not hold public office in Maryland until 1826 and in New Jersey until 1835. In New Hampshire, Jews and Catholics did not gain this right until 1876. Synagogues paid special taxes in Connecticut until 1843. Jews therefore settled in those cities where they were most fairly treated.

Jews in Europe had been barred from most kinds of work. Some of them did become craftsmen—tailors, leather workers, butchers and metal workers. Some became traders. Jews in each country kept in touch with Jews in other lands. Some European trade routes were kept open chiefly by Jewish merchants during the years 500 to 1000. These Jews then sold the goods brought by such trade at fairs or in their ghetto stores. This experience in small business was useful in the colonies. Most of the Jews in the colonies before 1700 were in some kind of trade or business, once they had won the right to do so. Like Asser Levy, they soon saw that they could not be better off in the New World than they had been in Europe unless they could first gain the rights given to other citizens. The coming of the Constitution in 1789 helped Jews as it did other religious groups.

The small number of Jews in the colonies had helped during the American Revolution. They had raised money for the army. They had served in the armed forces. Jewish merchants had sent supplies to Washington and other generals. Haym Solomon of Philadelphia raised money for Washington again and again. In 1783, two years after the war had ended, a group of Pennsylvania Jews asked for equal rights. They explained that they had earned them:

The Jews of Pennsylvania . . . have served . . . in the Continental army; some went out in the militia to fight the common

Haym Solomon of Philadelphia raised money for George Washington again and again.

enemy; all . . . have cheerfully contributed to the support of the militia, and of the government of this state; . . . they pay taxes; they have [given] as much as their circumstances would admit of. . . .

When the Constitutional Convention met in 1787, Jonas Phillips of Philadelphia asked it to add religious equality to the rights it would provide in the new Constitution.

Jews in the New Country. Some Americans wanted to prevent Jews from gaining equal rights. But there were very few Jews in the United States. As late as 1820 there were only about 5,000 Jews in the country. Most were in six cities—New York, Newport, Savannah, Philadelphia, Charleston and Richmond.

The United States was the first country in modern times to give Jews equal rights. Except for some limits to their rights in a few states, they were citizens equal to other citizens. George Washington wrote to several Jewish groups in 1789 and 1790. His letters contained his thoughts on the equal treatment of all religious groups:

May the children of the Stock of Abraham, who dwell in this land, continue to merit and enjoy the good will of the other inhabitants. . . .
The liberal sentiment toward each other which marks every political and religious denomination (group) of men in this country stands unrivaled in the history of nations. . . .

246

. . . the government of the United States, which gives to bigotry no sanction [approval], to persecution no assistance, requires only that those who live under its protection should not demean [lower] themselves as good citizens. . . .

Escape from Europe. In 1815 most of Europe was ruled by kings. They gave few rights to their people. During the next sixty years these people slowly gained more power over their governments. They sometimes won them only through revolutions. When a revolution failed, the people who had supported it often had to flee. The United States was ready to accept any immigrant who wished to come. Millions of people left Europe to settle in the United States. A large number came from Germany. Among them were more than 200,000 Jews.

The German Jews had come to find freedom, and also to make a better living. Most of them settled in the cities along the Atlantic coast. There they built strong communities. Many began businesses. Some began the clothing industry in cities such as New York. Others opened the first department stores in large cities. Some of the best-known department stores in the United States were begun by German Jewish families before 1860. Other Jews set out for the West. They opened stores in every state from Maine to California. A few became farmers. Others became peddlers on the frontier, moving with wagon and goods from one lonely farm to the next. A number of these peddlers went unarmed into Indian country, where they traded the goods they carried for furs.

By 1859 American Jews had built synagogues all over the country. Most Christians accepted them. These Jews presented no problems to a city or town, for they still remembered the rule—to take care of your own poor. In 1859 American Jews set up a national group to bring together the work being done by the many Jewish communities. It was called the Board of Delegates of American Israelites. Its many member groups began to build hospitals. These were open to all, Jews and non-Jews, although the costs of building and running them were paid only by Jewish communities.

Jews had many problems during the Civil War. Feelings against them appeared all over the country. North and South, they were blamed for the many problems that came with the war. They were accused of causing high prices. It was said that they caused the food and clothing shortages that developed. Judah Benjamin, a leader of the Confederacy, was a Jew. The charge was made all over the North that Jews favored slavery. At times it seemed that Jews might even lose their rights as citizens. In December, 1862, General Ulysses S. Grant ordered all Jews in Tennessee to leave at once. President Lincoln made Grant cancel his order before the Jews had been forced to leave.

The Great Migration. By 1870 much of Europe had become more democratic. Jews in France, England and Germany had gained greater rights, even though discrimination against them had not ended. About five million Jews lived in territory ruled by Russia and Austria. Many of those under Austrian rule remained terribly poor. Those under Russian rule were the target of attacks often planned by the government. They were *scapegoats*—those blamed by the government for whatever problems the country or its people faced. Wandering mobs, acting with government help or approval, would attack Jews, killing, burning and driving whole communities out of their homes. More than half of the Jews living in lands ruled by Russia and Austria fled to other countries.

At first these Jews went to Germany, France and England. But these countries could not hold the millions who wanted to leave Eastern Europe. They began to come to the United States after 1880. Their goal was clear. It was stated by a Jewish American poet, Moses Schreiber, in 1876:

> Unto these coasts
> Migrated hosts
> Jew and Gentile . . .
> Braved the sea
> To be here free.

A Jewish woman poet, Emma Lazarus, wrote the poem that is carved on the base of the Statue of Liberty. It is called "The New Colossus," and its lines have offered hope and a new beginning to millions of immigrant Americans:

> . . . "Give me your tired, your poor,
> Your huddled masses yearning to breathe free,
> The wretched refuse of your teeming shore.
> Send these, the homeless, tempest-tossed to me;
> I lift my lamp beside the golden door!"

There were about 300,000 Jews in the United States in 1880. Most had lived here for some time. They were largely members of the middle class. More than two million other Jews joined them in the next forty years. Almost all of them entered the United States through the port of New York. Most of them remained there; many later moved on to other cities. These new Jews were very poor. They had no money and few skills. Some came speaking the language of their country. More often they spoke only Yiddish, a language similar to early German that Jews had used for hundreds of years. They spoke no English and most knew little about life in the United States.

Life on New York's Lower East Side. Left: Inside a tenement dwelling. What kind of beds did the smaller children have? Right: A typical street. The Lower East Side soon became the most crowded slum in the United States.

The middle-class Jews already in the United States did much to help the newcomers. They found that they also had to feed and clothe many of them. They set up kitchens to provide free food. They found housing. The newly arrived Jews moved into the East Side of Manhattan. It soon became the most crowded slum in the United States. The immigrants came at a time

Jews entered the growing clothing industry in great numbers. Why were the places in which they had to work often called "sweat shops"?

when the clothing industry was growing rapidly. They entered this industry in large numbers. Families worked in tiny shops, at home and in factories. They received low wages and suffered terrible working conditions. Cities in those days did not help their poor people. There was no public assistance. Many immigrants starved or grew ill from lack of food.

The Jews taxed themselves heavily. Every synagogue and community raised money to help the immigrants. In 1884 the Hebrew Sheltering and Immigrant Aid Society was formed. In 1893 the National Council of Jewish Women began its work. These two groups became the bridge to a new life for the endless stream of Jewish immigrants.

New York became the world's largest center of Jewish population. Today two-fifths of the fewer than six million Jews in the United States live in or near that city. They became the workers in its largest industry—clothing. They set up many small businesses to serve that industry. Some became important in department stores and in trade and service industries. The city was growing rapidly. These businesses grew with it.

Jewish neighborhoods developed in the cities just as Greek, Italian, Polish, Puerto Rican and Norwegian neighborhoods have developed. Immigrant Jews felt safer living together. They kept their religion alive. They spoke Yiddish. They read Hebrew and Yiddish newspapers and magazines. Signs on stores were in Yiddish and Hebrew. They set up hundreds of self-help groups. Among these were burial societies, social groups for people from the same European city or country, literary societies, insurance societies and, perhaps most important, strong labor unions. In the clothing industry there were soon four important unions headed by immigrant Jews. From 1900 on these unions led the country in giving members better wages, better working conditions and special services. Jewish and Irish labor leaders worked together in 1881 to begin the American Federation of Labor. Samuel Gompers, its first president, was an immigrant Jew.

> Sidney Hillman, head of a clothing union, was a trusted assistant to President Roosevelt during World War II. David Dubinsky and Alex Rose helped form and lead New York State's Liberal Party. These union leaders worked with civil rights leaders to make their state the national leader in fair treatment of minorities.

Becoming Americans. By 1920 there were about 3½ million Jews in the United States. New immigration laws then ended the great migration. Since 1920 an average of fewer than 15,000 Jews have entered the United States each year. More than 85 per cent of American Jews today live in or near large cities. More than 75 per cent of them are American-born. They no longer suffer in the way described by an immigrant poet sixty years ago:

> Oh, here in the shop the machines roar so wildly
> That oft, unawares that I am, or have been,
> I sink and am lost in the terrible tumult;
> And void is my soul . . . I am but a machine.

Most American Jews were poor in 1920. Almost one million remain poor today. Most of the others are in the middle class. The change was caused chiefly by the drive among Jewish families to educate their children. For the first time they were in a country where children received a free public education. It became the goal of every family to give each child as much of that education as possible. This goal was shared by Italians and other immigrants in cities like New York.

Even free education often meant great sacrifices for parents. Fathers and mothers worked long hours—six or seven days a week—to provide for the family so that the children could remain in school. Many became ill from such hard work. Some died while still young. Yet it was of the highest importance to them that the children be educated. Here are some of the results today:

— Almost four-fifths of all college-age Jewish boys and girls are in college.
— More than half of all working American Jews are in professions or in business.
— Jews are less than three per cent of the country's population. They are a much larger part of the country's college graduates.

This drive toward education has made it possible for American Jews to make a very large contribution to their country's life. They have become important in motion pictures, theater and television, as writers and musicians and in medical science. They have risen in civil service positions. They have become leaders in the field of electronics. Many are public school and college teachers.

American Jews have been members of the Senate and House of Representatives, governors of states and mayors of cities, winners of Nobel Prizes, Supreme Court justices, members of the President's cabinet, war heroes and leaders of many national organizations. Yet their successes have come while they suffered a long and lasting discrimination. We will find out about that discrimination in the next chapter.

I. WHAT ARE THE FACTS?

Write the letter of the choice that best completes each statement.

1. Asser Levy and Peter Stuyvesant did not agree on the question of (a) special rights for Jews only, (b) equal rights for Jews, (c) the right of Jews to use the courts.

2. A European *ghetto* was a (a) walled city within a city where Jews had to live, (b) jail for Jews only, (c) police force that punished Jews.

3. In the 1800's Jews were sometimes denied equal rights by (a) the United States Constitution, (b) immigration laws, (c) state laws.

4. The small number of Jews in the colonies were most active in (a) trade, (b) clothing manufacture, (c) farming.

5. George Washington favored (a) equal treatment of all religions, (b) special laws to protect black Americans and other minorities, (c) greater rights for farmers.

6. During the Civil War, Jews were blamed for (a) starting the war, (b) high prices, (c) the ending of slavery.

7. The greatest immigration of Jews came (a) between 1800 and 1880, (b) between 1880 and 1920, (c) since 1920.

8. The city that became the world's largest center of Jewish population is (a) Jerusalem, (b) London, (c) New York.

9. Most American Jews today live in (a) farming areas, (b) small towns, (c) large cities.

10. American Jews have moved into the middle class chiefly because of their (a) freedom from discrimination, (b) ability to save, (c) high levels of education.

II. WHAT DO THEY MEAN?

Explain the meaning of each of these words or phrases.

1. refugee
2. synagogue
3. scapegoat
4. charity
5. Jewish Bible

6. religious equality
7. bigotry
8. migration
9. Yiddish
10. Israelites

III. UNDERSTANDING WHY.

Explain the meaning of each of these statements.

1. Jews have been refugees for 2,000 years.

2. Each religious group has its own cemetery.

3. Jews have always cared for their own poor.

4. Each immigrant group feels safer living together.

IV. THINKING IT THROUGH!

Discuss.

1. Christian leaders today agree that Jesus was killed by the Romans. For more than 1,600 years many Christians believed Jesus was killed by the Jews. How did this belief lead to discrimination against Jews?

2. Why has education been so important to the Jews? What lesson can some Americans learn from the Jews about the value of education?

3. Compare the treatment of Jews in Europe with the treatment of black Americans under Jim Crow laws. Give examples.

4. How does the history of Jews in Europe help explain why middle-class Jews did so much to help new Jewish immigrants?

What Is Anti-Semitism?

2 Only once in United States history has a Jew been lynched. The event showed the country that Jews could be the target of the most terrible hatred.

Leo M. Frank managed a pencil factory in Atlanta, Georgia, in 1913. He was a leader of that city's small Jewish community. American Jews were then being widely attacked. Newspapers, magazines and songs made fun of them. Theaters and movie houses presented "Jew comedies," in which Jews were always evil people. Even school textbooks attacked Jews and other minorities. Nativist groups were growing strong again; they hated Negroes, Catholics and Jews. Thomas Watson, later Senator from Georgia, printed many attacks on Jews in his weekly newspaper, *The Jeffersonian*.

On April 26, 1913, the body of a white Christian girl was found in the cellar of Leo Frank's factory. He was accused of attacking and then killing her. Watson's newspaper led demands that Frank be hanged—even before the case came to trial. Said Watson, "Lynch law is a good sign; it shows that a sense of justice yet lives among the people." Mobs began to bring terror to Atlanta's streets. A detective hired to help in Frank's defense was driven out of town for "selling out to the

Leo Frank, a Jew, was an innocent victim of "lynch law." What do you think would have happened to him if he had been a Christian? A black man?

255

Jews." Frank's lawyer was warned, "If they don't hang that Jew, we'll hang you."

Frank was found guilty, even though it was later shown that he was innocent. The governor of Georgia believed the trial had not been fair. He changed the death sentence to life imprisonment. Frank was sent to a prison farm. "Rise, people of Georgia!" called Watson. Another prisoner cut Frank's throat with a razor. On August 16, 1915, a mob of 25 men took Frank from his bed and hanged him. The *Marietta Journal* told its readers: "We regard the hanging of Leo M. Frank as an act of law-abiding citizens."

Why Has There Been Widespread Hatred of Jews in the United States?

How Has Such Hatred Harmed Jews and Other Minorities?

How Have Jews and Others Tried to End Such Hatred?

What Progress Have Jews Made Since 1900?

Anti-Semitism. A Semite is a person who speaks a language of one of the peoples called Semitic, whose roots lie in the Middle East. The best known of these languages are Hebrew and Arabic. The only Europeans who spoke a Semitic language were the Jews. The word "Semite" came to mean a Jew. In 1879 a German writer began to use the word "anti-Semitism" to describe his goal of taking away the rights of all Jews. The term has since been used to describe actions or beliefs designed to harm Jews as a group, or any person because he is a Jew. An anti-Semite is someone who wants discrimination against Jews.

Anti-Semites want to treat Jews much as black Americans have been treated under Jim Crow. The anti-Semite believes Jews are not as good as other people. He thinks they are crooks, Communists or "evil" in other ways. A five-year study of anti-Semitism among American Christians published in 1966 described some of the beliefs held by anti-Semites. They disliked Jews for many reasons. Some of them refused to have anything to do with Jews. They then charged that Jews wanted to keep themselves apart from Christians. Many anti-Semites believed it was proper for them to hate Jews. They thought any person who refused to become a Christian should be punished.

Any person who thinks hatred is proper stops looking for facts. He stops wondering whether the ideas he holds are correct. Hating becomes part of his life. We have seen this throughout American history. Black Americans, Indians, Americans from Asia, Puerto Ricans, Mexican-Americans, Catholics, Jews—all have suffered when other Americans made hatred part of their daily thoughts and actions. Very often, people who hate never even know members of the group they hate. The study found that anti-Semitism is strongest in those parts of the country where few Jews live. One-fourth of the anti-Semites did not know a single Jew well!

People who hate others often want to harm them. Anti-Semites practice every form of discrimination against Jews. They do not want to be friendly to them. They want to deny them the rights other citizens have. They try to keep them from getting good housing, good jobs, religious freedom and every other kind of equality.

Such ideas have been directed against Jews and other minorities many times in American history. We have seen earlier how they led to great problems for other minority groups. They have also harmed American Jews.

Governments and Anti-Semitism. Jews have suffered from anti-Semitism for almost 2,000 years. Conditions grew worst in the lands ruled by Russia after 1880. They were a chief reason for the great Jewish migration from Eastern Europe. Anti-Semitism became a government policy. The Russian people grew more and more open in their hatred for the Jews. Jewish children were beaten in the streets. Jews were barred from most schools. They could not vote, hold public office or become teachers. Russian Jews had to carry special passports. They were not permitted to enter or live in most cities. Their synagogues and cemeteries were destroyed again and again. In the 1880's the Russian government planned or approved attacks on Jews called *pogroms*. Thousands of Jews were killed in 215 pogroms in 1881. Such attacks continued until Russia became a Communist country in 1918. In recent years anti-Semitism has again appeared as a government policy in Russian-controlled countries.

Most countries in Europe have at one time or another also been anti-Semitic. Jews were driven out of one country after

Thousands of Jews in Russia were killed in attacks called *pogroms*. Why would the Russian government have encouraged such attacks to take place?

257

Supreme Court justice
Louis Brandeis.

New York Senator Jacob Javitz.

Former Supreme Court justice
and United Nations ambassador
Arthur Goldberg.

another. This happened in England, in France, in Spain, and in parts of Germany. Jews remaining in some German cities were forced to live in walled ghettos. The final blow was the killing of six million Jews by the Germans during World War II. This was one-third of the Jews in the world! This act of genocide left Jews everywhere with the fear that it might happen again in a country whose government and people became anti-Semitic.

Understanding and living with anti-Semitism has made most Jews support greater rights for all minorities. Jews who have gained important positions in government have worked hard to improve the rights of all people. Senators Herbert Lehman, Jacob Javits and Abraham Ribicoff worked for civil rights laws in the 1950's and 1960's. So have Jewish members of the House of Representatives. Justices Brandeis, Frankfurter, Cardozo, Goldberg and Fortas voted in the United States Supreme Court for decisions that improved the rights of black Americans and other minorities. Jewish governors and mayors have most often favored greater civil rights in their states and cities. In the United States as in other countries, this has often made Jews the target of people who want to limit the rights of minorities.

The Protocols of Zion. Jews in Europe had few rights. They had little or no power in any country. They were less than one-fiftieth of Europe's population. Still, a story came to be believed by millions of anti-Semites around the world. The charge was made and believed that the Jews had made a grand plan to take control of the whole world! The story was based on a false document called the *Protocols of Zion* ("Plans of the Jews"). It has also been called *Protocols of the Elders of Zion* and *Protocols of the Wise Men of Zion*.

In 1864 the French writer Maurice Joly wrote a book attacking Emperor Napoleon III of France. Joly described an imaginary plot by which Napoleon had made himself ruler of France. In 1868 another European, Hermann Goedsche, wrote a book that copied most of Joly's ideas. However, he changed the Emperor's "plot" to one by the world's Jewish leaders. Instead of France alone, his book said Jews wanted to gain control of the whole world.

Serge Nilus, a Russian writer, was a bitter anti-Semite. In 1905 he changed the story of the *Protocols of Zion* again. The Russian government used his story of a plot to excuse its discrimination against Jews. It spread the story of the *Protocols* around the world. By 1920 anti-Semites in many countries were using it. In 1921 the *London Times*, England's most important newspaper, traced the story of the *Protocols* back to the Joly book. It proved that the so-called Jewish plan was a false tale made up to excuse anti-Semitism.

Henry Ford and the *Protocols*. Henry Ford, one of the richest men in the world, used the *Protocols* to lead an attack against American Jews from 1920 to 1927. The story was changed so that it would deal with the United States. It was then printed in the *Dearborn Independent*, a national weekly newspaper owned by Ford. As many as 700,000 copies of each issue went all over the United States. Many were given away.

Through his newspaper, Henry Ford led an attack against Jews for years.

The story appeared at a time when hate groups were again strong. The Ku Klux Klan, the largest of these, had between one million and two million members. The KKK was strongest in the South, but it was also active in the rest of the country. Nativist feelings grew strong enough by 1924 to lead to the end of open immigration. A new immigration law made it hardest for immigrants to come from the parts of the world where Jews and Catholics lived—southern and eastern Europe.

Ford's publishing company also issued four books. Each told the same story. They invented a supposed plan by Jews to rule the world. They charged that Jews were enemies of the United States. Ford was trying to get other Americans to turn against one minority. Americans of many faiths joined to answer this attack. More than a hundred leading Christians signed a statement they called "The Peril of Racial Prejudice." Two ex-Presidents, Woodrow Wilson and William Howard Taft, were among the signers. So were Cardinal O'Connell of Boston and Cardinal Hayes of New York. The Federal Council of Churches, speaking for American Protestants, also attacked Ford's campaign. Still it did not end for seven years. Millions of Americans came to believe it. They began to act in anti-Semitic ways.

Aaron Sapiro was a Detroit lawyer and Jewish community leader. In 1927 Ford's newspaper attacked him as part of a group of "Jewish bankers who seek to control the food markets of the world." Sapiro sued Ford for a million dollars. The case was never decided in court. Ford soon closed down his newspaper. He made a public apology to all American Jews:

> I deem it to be my duty as an honorable man to make amends for the wrong done to Jews as fellowmen and brothers by asking their forgiveness for the harm that I have unintentionally committed . . . henceforth they may look to me for friendship and good will.

Although Ford stopped spending his millions on anti-Semitism, other men did not. Discrimination against Jews remained high in the 1920's and 1930's. Jewish businessmen lost Christian customers. Colleges barred Jewish students. Jewish children were attacked in the streets. Jews were prevented from buying homes in "Christian" neighborhoods. Social groups, hotels and big businesses kept Jews out. Much of this discrimination has continued until today, except where state laws prevent it. As late as 1959, a study showed that 1,500 companies in Chicago alone still refused to hire Jews or Catholics!

Continuing Anti-Semitism. The Nazis gained power in Germany in 1933. Their government became the most violently anti-Semitic in world history. Germany began to spend large amounts of money in country after country to support anti-Semitism. By 1941 the United States had 121 organizations that were openly anti-Semitic! They were in every part of the country. They used the mails to spread their attacks on Jews and other minorities. Millions of people accepted their ideas. The best-known of these groups was the German-American Bund. It and other Nazi-financed hate groups were ended by the government during World War II. But anti-Semitism remained even after the war. In 1948 there were still 45 openly anti-Semitic organizations in the country. They published seventy newspapers and six magazines.

Father Charles Coughlin was a Catholic priest whose national use of the radio brought him from ten to twenty million listeners a week during the 1930's. He tried to keep the *Protocols of Zion* alive. The hate groups who followed him, often called the Christian Front, had little effect on the American people. Jews, Catholics and Protestants joined to oppose Coughlin's ideas. Coughlin's bishop ordered him off the air in 1940. President Roosevelt, called a Jew by the Christian Front, answered that he would be proud to be a Jew. Wendell Willkie, Republican candidate for President in 1940, said that every anti-Semite was a possible traitor to America.

Anti-Semitism also remains a world problem today. Jews in

Communist countries remain second-class citizens. Most of the Jews in Arab countries have been forced to leave. Governments that receive aid from the Russians soon become more anti-Semitic. Some American political groups that want great changes in American life have also accepted anti-Semitism as part of their attack on the United States and its society.

New civil rights laws were passed in state after state beginning in 1945. The federal government had also passed such laws by 1958. The civil rights movement grew stronger after the Brown Decision of 1954. Anti-Semitic groups grew weaker; many of them died out. Still, many persons and small groups have remained actively anti-Semitic. In 1960 and 1961 the country saw a wave of "swastika incidents." The swastika ⴲ had been the sign used by the German Nazis. In hundreds of places all over the country, large swastikas were painted on synagogues, Jewish cemeteries and public buildings. Direct attacks on Jews have continued in many towns and cities. In 1968–1969 more than twenty synagogues in New York City were set on fire!

Roberta Savitsky cries bitterly as her father holds a priceless ancient scroll destroyed by fire. Vandals broke into the rabbi's Boston synagogue, burning and smashing its contents. What are the reasons for such an attack?

Fighting Anti-Semitism. Jews and other Americans have worked to weaken anti-Semitism and attacks on all minorities. Three national Jewish groups have been most active. B'nai Brith is a Jewish organization with more than 400,000 members. In 1913 it set up the Anti-Defamation League. Defamation is action against the reputation of any person or persons. Two other leading national Jewish groups are the American Jewish Committee (1906) and the American Jewish Congress (1918). These groups have become the most important spokesmen of American Jews. They have worked for fair treatment of all minorities.

Some Jews have formed self-defense organizations. The goal of such groups is to protect Jews who find themselves unsafe because of attacks by anti-Semites. In 1970 one of these groups, the Jewish Defense League, had more than 8,000 members. The older Jewish organizations oppose the League, saying that protection should be left to police and government.

Whether anti-Semitism ends will depend upon the actions of Christians who agree religious hatreds are wrong. Jewish and Christian leaders work together toward this goal in the National Council of Christians and Jews. Catholic leaders such as the late Cardinal Cushing of Boston teach that attacks on one religious

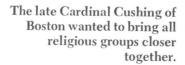

The late Cardinal Cushing of Boston wanted to bring all religious groups closer together.

group are a danger to all groups. The movement to bring all Christian churches closer together has also led to a weakening of religious hatreds. Yet the long history of anti-Semitism in the United States has not ended. It will remain a problem as long as some Americans feel that not all of our people should have equal rights and fair treatment.

Differences Among Jews. Most Americans do not realize that there are great religious differences among Jews. For most of their history, Jews had followed strict religious rules agreed to by their teachers, or rabbis, during the days of the Roman Empire. These rules had been set down in the books of the *Talmud*, the explanation of how Jews should conduct their lives and practice their religion. These rules were the same for Jews in every land.

However, Judaism—the religion of the Jews—has taken three paths in the United States. They are called Orthodox, Conservative and Reform.

There are about three million Orthodox Jews in the United States. In their synagogues men and women sit apart in separate sections. The men keep their heads covered. The chief language used in these synagogues is Hebrew. Orthodox Jews follow the religious practices used by Jews in Europe and other parts of the world for more than a thousand years.

There are more than a million Reform Jews in the United States. They have made great changes in their religious practices. Men and women sit together in their synagogues. The men do not cover their heads. The prayers have been greatly simplified; services are short. English is used more than Hebrew. Music is part of the service.

Conservative Jews stand somewhere between the other two groups. Men and women sit together in their synagogues. The men cover their heads. The prayer book is almost the same as the one used by Orthodox Jews, yet the service is more modern. There are about a million Conservative Jews in the United States.

The differences in religion among the Jews come chiefly from efforts to make their religion fit better into American life. One change was to use an English translation of the Old Testament. Another was to accept changes in the rules of life and religion found in the *Talmud*. Reform Jews have made more of these changes than the other groups. One Reform rabbi, Stephen Samuel Wise of New York's Free Synagogue, did much to make other Americans better understand Jews. He was the best-known American Jewish leader until his death in 1949.

Some Jewish Achievements. American Jews became important in the fields to which they were admitted. They had been doctors and scientists in Europe for hundreds of years. Second- and third-generation American Jews became leaders in medicine and science. Dr. Jonas Salk perfected the vaccine against polio. Albert Einstein, who fled Nazi Germany, was a leader in mathematics, physics and astronomy for almost thirty years.

Albert Einstein, his daughter (right) and his secretary take the oath of citizenship in 1940. How has America gained by offering a home to immigrants such as Einstein?

He was awarded the Nobel Prize in physics in 1921. Albert Michelson, who won the Nobel Prize in 1907, was the first to measure the speed of light. Emile Berliner designed the first helicopter. He also invented the phonograph record. Simon Flexner headed the most important research center in the country, the Rockefeller Institute of Medical Research. His brother Abraham was the first director of the Institute of Advanced Studies at Princeton. In the years 1959–1962, five American Jews won Nobel Prizes.

Jews were important leaders in the early days of motion pictures and television. They have remained important in the whole area of entertainment. Jewish writers have added greatly to American literature. Among the best known have been Saul Bellow, Norman Mailer and Bernard Malamud. Other American Jews have written important plays. They include Elmer Rice, George S. Kaufman, Lillian Hellman, Irwin Shaw, Sidney Kingsley and Arthur Miller. In the field of music, Irving Berlin became the country's best-known writer of popular songs. George Gershwin combined popular and serious music. Leonard Bernstein, Eugene Ormandy and William Steinberg led the country's most important symphony orchestras.

Jews have had little power in American industry. They have remained important in department stores, the clothing industry and the field of electronics. In the 1920's and 1930's anti-Semites charged that the country's banks were owned by Jews. There are only a handful of Jewish-owned banks in the United States. Until a few years ago, Jews were not often promoted in the banks that did hire them.

The more education a person has today, the better job he can hope to find. As members of minority groups improve their training, they find it easier to move from poverty to higher standards of living. Education is an important reason for the fact that most Jews today are in the middle class. This has made it possible for many of them to move to suburbs outside the cities. There they have sometimes found that they must again fight the battle against anti-Semitism.

Safe or in Danger? Is anti-Semitism ending in the United States? Jewish organizations reply that it is not. Synagogues are still being burned. Jews in some city neighborhoods are still being attacked. Many hate groups still pour out their attacks on Jews. Yet it is agreed that anti-Semitism is less of a danger than it was thirty or forty years ago. Today's laws make it harder for hate groups to do as they please.

Jews remain watchful. They work to fight anti-Semitism —and discrimination against all minorities—wherever it appears. David Edelstadt, a Jewish poet who died in 1892, believed in "a free and joyous world for all humanity." Jews today may remember these lines from one of Edelstadt's last poems:

> And even in my grave I'll hear
> My freedom's song, the battle's cue.
> And even there, I'll shed a tear
> For all the slaves, Christian or Jew.

I. WHAT ARE THE FACTS?

Write a short answer to each question.

1. What is the true meaning of the word *Semite*?

2. Define anti-Semitism.

3. How did one-third of the world's Jews die during World War II?

4. Why have American Jews favored greater civil rights for all?

5. What "plot" was described by the false *Protocols of Zion*?

6. How did Henry Ford spread the ideas in the *Protocols of Zion*?

7. How has the Talmud been important in Jewish history?

8. How are Orthodox, Conservative and Reform Judaism different?

9. What is a *swastika incident*?

10. What proof is there that anti-Semitism has not ended?

II. WHAT DID THEY DO?

Match each item in COLUMN A with the correct item in COLUMN B.

COLUMN A	COLUMN B
1. Jonas Salk	a. Justice of United States Supreme Court
2. Albert Einstein	b. Designed first helicopter
3. Albert Michelson	c. Nobel Prize-winner and leader of research in mathematics and physics
4. Emile Berliner	d. Well-known American songwriter
5. Leonard Bernstein	e. Symphony conductor
6. Norman Mailer	f. Measured speed of light
7. Arthur Goldberg	g. Developed vaccine against polio
8. Jacob Javits	h. Best-selling author
9. Irving Berlin	i. Member of United States Senate
10. Isaac Mayer Wise	j. Leader of American Reform Jews

III. THINKING IT THROUGH!

Discuss.

1. How does the case of Leo M. Frank help you to understand the state of civil rights in some parts of the United States in 1915?

2. Why does one group of people hate another group? How does such hatred start? How much harm can it do?

3. How has hatred affected each of these groups in American history?

a) Black Americans   e) Chinese-Americans
b) Puerto Ricans   f) Japanese-Americans
c) Italian-Americans   g) American Indians
d) Irish-Americans   h) Jewish Americans

4. Why did millions of people all over the world accept the ideas in the *Protocols of Zion*? What questions would you ask if you heard such a charge against any minority?

5. How have Jews fought anti-Semitism? How have other minority groups fought discrimination? How successful have they been?

Unit Seven

PUERTO RICAN AMERICANS

This unit tells the story of the Puerto Ricans, on their home island and later in the mainland cities of the United States. Puerto Ricans have known many of the problems faced by other newcomers to the United States. They did not speak English. Their culture was different. They followed a minority religion, set even more apart by their language differences. They did not have the skills they needed to make a living in the cities. Many became poor migrant workers; others took low paying jobs. They had to move into city slums. Yet even these troubles did not slow the flow of men, women and children to the North. Puerto Ricans soon began to find a place in the mainland communities. They set up self-help groups, learned the ways of the majority, yet managed to keep their own language and culture alive. Many remain poor, although large numbers are slowly moving out of poverty. Like other immigrant groups before them, Puerto Ricans are learning that they can find a place in American life through education and training. They still face many difficult problems. A small number believe these problems cannot be solved unless there are great changes in American society.

How Did the People of
Puerto Rico Become Americans?

1 By the 1890's American businesses had invested more than fifty million dollars in Cuba. Their trade with the Caribbean had grown to about 100 million dollars a year. The idea of Manifest Destiny had been the excuse for the growth of the United States toward the West. Now a new kind of Manifest Destiny thinking appeared. It was the idea that the United States should control the Caribbean Sea.

Cuba and Puerto Rico were colonies of Spain. Hundreds of Cuban and Puerto Rican leaders came to the United States to raise money and make plans to seek freedom for their countries. American political leaders began to demand war against Spain after 1895. In that year the Cubans began a revolution. The Spaniards crushed it harshly. For the next three years newspapers, politicians and finally millions of Americans came to favor war with Spain "to protect the people of the Spanish colonies."

The United States declared war against Spain in 1898. The stated goal was to free Cuba. It was a quick war. The fighting took place in Spain's colonies of Cuba, the Philippine Islands and Puerto Rico. At the war's end, Cuba was free. Puerto Rico, the Philippines and the Pacific Ocean island of Guam became the property of the United States. The flag of Spain came down in San Juan, capital of Puerto Rico. The flag of the United States took its place.

Who Were the People of Puerto Rico?

What Was Their Life Under Spanish Rule?

What Were the Goals of Puerto Rico's Leaders Before 1898?

What Changes in Puerto Rican Government Have Come Since 1898?

Ponce de Leon brought Spanish soldiers and settlers to Puerto Rico.

The People of Puerto Rico. The Indians who lived in the northern Caribbean were called the Arawaks. The tribe living in Puerto Rico when Columbus arrived there on November 19, 1493 (Puerto Rican Discovery Day) called themselves Tainos. They had named their island Boriquen, the "land of the brave men." The 30,000 or more Tainos had to be brave; they were under steady attack by the Carib Indians who raided north from Venezuela. The Tainos lived in small villages. Each was ruled by a chief called a *cacique*. One of these chiefs was chosen to rule over all of the Tainos. These Indians farmed their rich soil and took fish from the seas. They thought their many gods could control nature. They had a sharp sense of right and wrong—the chief god of most Tainos was a god of goodness.

The Spaniards did not really settle in Puerto Rico until 1508. In that year Ponce de Leon brought soldiers and Spanish settlers to the area near today's San Juan. The island's name became Puerto Rico ("rich port"). Soon the Spaniards set up a capital city they named San Juan Bautista (St. John the Baptist). The city of San Juan grew. It became the center of a ruling system designed to make Spanish officials and landowners rich. Priests and soldiers made the Indians accept Christianity. Thousands of Indians were made slaves. They were forced to work on farms or in mines. When the Indians tried to revolt, Spanish armor and guns defeated them. The Tainos began to leave the island rather than be slaves. They settled in other islands where they could remain free.

The Spanish government made new laws by 1544. From then on, Indians and Spaniards could live in peace. All Indian slavery was ended. Indians and Spaniards could marry. Men and women who had been slaves began to receive wages for their work.

Black slavery began in Puerto Rico soon after the Spaniards first settled there. By 1530 there were more than four black African slaves for each Spanish settler. Puerto Rico remained a slave center for 350 years. Over the years many slaves were freed or bought their freedom. Under Spain's laws they were then able to marry anyone they chose.

The number of Indians on the island grew smaller and smaller. There were only about 2,000 left in 1700. Many had left Puerto Rico to settle in other islands. Thousands had died during the years of slavery. European diseases had killed others. Most of the Indians who stayed had married non-Indians. They had become Puerto Ricans rather than Indians!

The Spaniards remained the rulers of the island. They owned the land and the businesses. A Spanish businessman might spend his whole life in Puerto Rico. He still thought of himself as a Spaniard who would one day return to Spain.

Living Under Spanish Rule. The people of Puerto Rico were ruled by officials sent from Spain. The governor had all the power of a king. He could make and change laws. He could punish people without trials. He could give people rights or take them away. He could set taxes and use his soldiers to collect them. For 400 years such governors also tried to make themselves rich during their years of power on the island.

Most Puerto Ricans remained poor. Sugar, coffee and tobacco grew well on the island. But Spanish laws permitted trade only on Spanish ships. Puerto Rican ships were kept by law from trading with other islands. However, English, Dutch and French pirates sailed the Caribbean. No ship was safe from them unless it was protected by warships. And there were better cargoes to be found in other Spanish colonies. Therefore, few Spanish ships bothered to come to Puerto Rico.

The only way to sell your crops was to smuggle them out of Puerto Rico. Smuggling soon became the way to do business. One Spanish official reported that everyone, from the governor to the owners of small fishing boats, was a busy smuggler. Slave ships were an important part of this smuggling, and made some Puerto Ricans rich.

The Beginnings of Self-Government. Puerto Ricans could enter Spain's armed forces. Some worked in the island's government. Richer Puerto Ricans sent their sons to Europe to be educated. By 1800 Spanish trading rules had been changed. The pirates were gone. Puerto Rico's products had made the island richer. It had 34 towns and 150,000 people. In 1810 Spain seemed to realize that the colony had grown important. Ramón Power, a Puerto Rican, became the island's first representative to the Cortes, Spain's legislature. A new Spanish constitution in 1812 made Puerto Rico a province (like a state in the United States) instead of a colony. Its people would be Spanish citizens. They would make many of their own laws. But then Spain was conquered by France. When it regained its own freedom a few years later, its king again treated Puerto Rico as a colony.

Spain's government changed many times during the 1800's. Slowly the elected Cortes gained more power. Its officials gave more rights to colonies. Puerto Rico was given more representatives in the Cortes. Its towns could elect many of their own officials. Political groups were begun on the island. There were many times when governors sent from Spain did not allow Puerto Ricans the rights of free speech and assembly. Still, each year seemed to see some growth in the people's rights.

Most Puerto Ricans agreed that slavery had to end. Abolitionist groups were set up. Their leaders soon found they could not work freely on the island. They moved to cities such as New York, Paris and Madrid. In 1873 their work led to success. Spain ended all slavery in Puerto Rico. At that time the island had about 50,000 slaves and an equal number of free Negroes.

The fight to end slavery had made many political leaders among the Puerto Ricans. Some of them became well known all over the world. Dr. Ramón Emeterio Betances led a growing movement for freedom from New York and cities in other countries. Eugenio María de Hostos became known as the "Citizen of America." He lived in country after country building support for freedom for Puerto Rico. Lola Rodríguez de Tió was a poetess. Her love of liberty led to her being forced out of Puerto Rico. She wrote the poem that became the words of Puerto Rico's national anthem—*La Borinqueña.*

Román Baldioroty de Castro began the first lasting political party working for self-government. Three men then became most important within Puerto Rico. Dr. José Celso Barbosa led a party that tried to gain greater rights from the United States. José de Diego led those who demanded full independence from Spain, and later from the United States. The third leader, perhaps the most important, was Luis Muñoz Rivera.

Luis Muñoz Rivera has been called "The George Washington of Puerto Rico." In 1897 he got the Spanish government to agree to permit Puerto Rico to rule itself. Self-rule began in 1898, just a few weeks before the Spanish-American War. It was ended quickly when the United States took Puerto Rico.

American Rule. There were about one million people in Puerto Rico in 1898. They spoke Spanish and had a culture much like that of Spain. The island was poor. Most people were poor farmers, or *jíbaros*. Only one person in five could read and write. One report tells us that there were only 600 teachers on the island! The only religion permitted had been that of Spain —the Catholic Church.

The United States Army ruled Puerto Rico for almost two years. Then Congress passed the Foraker Act in 1900. The law made Puerto Rico an American colony. It would be ruled by an American governor appointed by the President of the United States. Its people would not have a Bill of Rights; they would not be American citizens. They could elect part of their legislature, but this group would have no real power. Judges and most officials would be appointed by the President. The island could elect one representative to Congress. He could speak for Puerto Rico but could not vote.

Rule by the United States meant important changes for the Puerto Ricans. Many of these changes were for the good. Puerto Ricans paid no taxes to the United States. Any taxes that were collected could be used only in Puerto Rico. The United States opened many schools and hospitals. A university was begun. However, the new schools taught in English. Students had great problems learning in this "foreign" language. Freedom of religion came to Puerto Rico. Soon groups other than Catholics could worship freely. One part of the Foraker Act could have helped the *jíbaros*. No big business was permitted to own more than 500 acres of land. However, this part of the law was not really enforced.

All these changes did not mean real freedom. Some Puerto Ricans said even a fair court was unfair when strangers handed down justice in it. Luis Muñoz Rivera spent much of his time in the United States working for self-rule for his people. Just before he died in 1916, Congress agreed to end the Foraker Act. A new law, the Jones Act, came in 1917. It made Puerto Ricans citizens of the United States. It gave them some of the protections in the Bill of Rights. They gained the right to elect both parts of their legislature. However, the governor and most officials were still appointed by the President. The governor could still veto (refuse to allow) any law passed by the island's legislature.

Puerto Ricans made great use of the courts as they tried to gain more rights. Cases from Puerto Rico began to come to the United States Supreme Court. The Court held again and again that Congress could pass whatever laws it wished for Puerto Rico. It was a colony, not a state. The best-known case was decided in 1922—*Balzac v. Puerto Rico*. Jesús Balzac, editor of a Puerto Rican newspaper, was charged with libel (printing false information to harm another person). He asked for a jury trial. The Supreme Court ruled that he had no right to one:

— The Constitution does call for a trial by jury in criminal cases.
— However, it means trials in the states of the United States. The Constitution protects the people of a colony. The only way a Puerto Rican can get a jury trial is through a law passed in Puerto Rico and then approved by its governor.
— It is true that the people of Puerto Rico must receive "due process." However, due process in Puerto Rico does not have to be the same as due process in the United States.

Slow Changes. Puerto Rico remained a colony whose people had limited rights. The Great Depression of the 1930's made its people care less about politics than they had before. The main goal was to keep from starving. Some money was spent to help Puerto Ricans during these years, but it never seemed to be enough. Puerto Rico became known as "the poorhouse of the Caribbean." A few large American companies grew richer; most of the people of the island remained poor. It was 1940 before the Supreme Court ruled that no company could own more than 500 acres of land—a rule that had once been in the Foraker Act!

In 1940 a new political leader won the support of the people of Puerto Rico. He was Luis Muñoz Marín, son of Luis Muñoz Rivera. (In Spanish-speaking lands, the name of the mother is often added to the family name.) He had been

Luis Muñoz Marín became a leader of Puerto Rico in 1940. He worked for many years to gain greater rights for his people.

The Fortaleza, or Governor's Palace, in San Juan. Why was it many years before Puerto Ricans were permitted to elect their own governor?

educated in the United States. He knew his own country and the United States. He also knew what changes he could ask for and expect to receive. In 1946 one of these changes brought the island its first Puerto Rican governor, Jesús T. Piñero. Piñero supported Muñoz Marín's plans to gain greater self-government.

In 1947 President Truman signed a law that gave the people of Puerto Rico the right to elect their own governor. They chose Luis Muñoz Marín. A law passed in 1951 permitted the island to write its own constitution. A year later the new constitution replaced the Jones Act and other laws that had kept Puerto Rico a colony. Since then it has been a *commonwealth*. Puerto Ricans say they are a "free associated state" of the United States. July 25, 1952, was the beginning of the Commonwealth of Puerto Rico. This day is Constitution Day or Commonwealth Day in Puerto Rico.

As a commonwealth, Puerto Rico has its own bill of rights. It elects its own government and passes its own laws. In some ways it is like a state of the United States. It cannot pass any laws that are not allowed by the United States Constitution. It uses the same money and postal system that the United States uses. Its young men serve in the armed forces of the United States. The United States Supreme Court hears appeals from Puerto Rico just as it does from any of the states. Puerto Ricans are citizens of the United States.

Yet there are real differences between a commonwealth and a state. Puerto Ricans cannot vote for President or Vice-President.

They can move to any state. There they can gain this right to vote. While they are in Puerto Rico, they vote only for their island government and for the one non-voting representative Puerto Rico sends to Congress. Puerto Ricans do not pay taxes to the United States.

Puerto Rico could change from a commonwealth to a state if its people and the Congress voted for this change. However, in July, 1967, the people of the island who voted chose almost two to one to continue as a commonwealth.

I. WHAT ARE THE FACTS?

Write the letter of the choice that best completes each statement.

1. Puerto Rico is located in the (a) Atlantic Ocean, (b) Gulf of Mexico, (c) Caribbean Sea.

2. The country that ruled Puerto Rico for about 400 years was (a) Spain, (b) the United States, (c) France.

3. The United States took control of Puerto Rico in (a) 1776, (b) 1898, (c) 1947.

4. Boriquen is an old Indian name for the (a) Taino Indians, (b) earliest religion in Puerto Rico, (c) island of Puerto Rico.

5. The capital city of Puerto Rico is (a) San Juan, (b) Ponce, (c) Washington, D.C.

6. The last of these to end slavery was (a) England, (b) the United States, (c) Puerto Rico.

7. Puerto Rican trade was slow to develop because of the danger of (a) hurricanes, (b) pirates, (c) smuggling.

8. Puerto Ricans are citizens (a) only of Puerto Rico, (b) of Puerto Rico and the United States, (c) only of their own towns or cities.

9. A commonwealth is most like a (a) colony, (b) military base, (c) state.

10. Today the governor of Puerto Rico is (a) elected by the people of Puerto Rico, (b) appointed by Congress, (c) appointed by the President.

II. WHAT DO THEY MEAN?

Write the meaning of each of these words or phrases.

1. Tainos
2. San Juan Bautista
3. "Citizen of America"
4. *La Borinqueña*
5. *jíbaros*

6. "poorhouse of the Caribbean"
7. free associated state
8. Cortes
9. *cacique*
10. non-voting representative

III. WHAT DID THEY DO?

Match the names in COLUMN A with the statements of what they did in COLUMN B.

COLUMN A	COLUMN B
1. Dr. Ramón Emeterio Betances	a) The George Washington of Puerto Rico.
2. Lola Rodríguez de Tió	b) Author of *La Borinqueña.*
3. Román Baldioroty de Castro	c) Led movement for Puerto Rican freedom from New York and other cities.
4. Dr. José Celso Barbosa	d) First elected governor of Puerto Rico.
5. Luis Muñoz Rivera	e) Set up first Puerto Rican party seeking self-government.
6. Luis Muñoz Marín	f) Worked with Baldioroty de Castro's party to gain greater rights for Puerto Ricans.

IV. THINKING IT THROUGH!

Discuss.

1. Why did the United States try to control the Caribbean after 1898?

2. What explains the mixture of peoples in Puerto Rico?

3. In what ways were Spanish and American rule of Puerto Rico similar? In what ways were they different?

4. What advantages do Puerto Ricans gain so long as the island remains a commonwealth? What disadvantages do they suffer?

5. In class, prepare a list of ten facts about Puerto Rican history that all Americans should know. Compare your list with those of other members of the class. Explain why each fact on your list is important.

Why Have Puerto Ricans Moved to the Mainland Cities?

2 Herman Badillo is one of the best-known Puerto Ricans in the mainland United States. His life has been much like that of others who came to mainland cities. He was born in Caguas, a city in Puerto Rico. Life there was not easy. His family was poor. They decided to seek a better life in New York City. Once there, the boy faced the problems other Puerto Ricans knew. He lived in a poor neighborhood. He had to learn English. He had to accept American ways of living.

Congressman Herman Badillo talks to some of his supporters. Why is it important to minority groups to elect their members to public office?

Herman Badillo went to the public schools. At times it seemed he would have to drop out to make some money to help his family. Instead, he managed to stay in school with the help of part-time jobs. After he graduated from high school, he attended the City College of New York. His college years again saw him working part-time to pay expenses. He became one of the first Puerto Ricans to finish college in New York's school system.

He then decided to continue his studies, even while he held a full-time job. Evening classes made him an accountant, and later a lawyer as well. Meanwhile, he found time to be active in the city's Democratic Party. In 1965, after years of service to the city, he was elected President of the Borough of the Bronx. This was the highest elected post any Puerto Rican had ever gained in a mainland city. In 1969 Herman Badillo came close to being chosen his party's candidate for mayor of New York City. In 1970 he ran for Congress and was elected. He was the first Puerto Rican to be a voting member of the House of Representatives! At last Puerto Ricans on the mainland knew they had a voice in Congress. They hoped that Herman Badillo, who had worked and suffered like so many other Puerto Ricans, would now work to help solve their problems and those of other minorities.

Why Have 1½ Million Puerto Ricans Left Their Island?

Where Did They Settle?

How Did Operation Bootstrap Bring Many Puerto Ricans Back to Puerto Rico?

Why Have Most of Those Who Came to the Mainland Remained?

Problems in Puerto Rico. The people of Puerto Rico are very proud of the organization they call *Fomento,* a Spanish word meaning "to encourage." For years it was headed by Teodoro Moscoso, who later became an important official of the United States government. One of his successes was the building of the large modern tourist hotel that is today San Juan's Caribe Hilton. Thousands of tourists came to this hotel from the United States. Soon dozens of other hotels were built in and around San Juan and other cities. Since the 1950's up to a million Americans a year have chosen Puerto Rico as their vacation spot.

Air travel made this tourist traffic possible. Puerto Rico is only a few hours from any city in the eastern United States. Visitors report that the island has one of the best climates in the world. Its beaches are clean. Its forests, mountains, views of

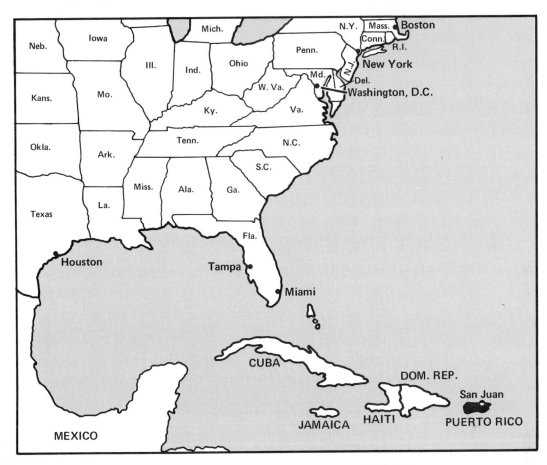

PUERTO RICO AND THE UNITED STATES

the sea and Spanish culture make any trip to Puerto Rico pleasant.

Most visitors see little of the many problems that have made about 1½ million Puerto Ricans leave their island to come to the United States. Most of these problems came from the great poverty that has troubled Puerto Rico since 1900. The number of people on the island doubled between 1900 and 1950. There was not enough work for all these people to make a living. The island had few industries. Farm workers worked for only about half of each year. Their wages were low.

What did poverty do to the people? Young men and women had little hope for a better life. They could not find places to live. Many built shacks on empty beaches. They lived without running water or electricity. They often were hungry. Malnutrition was a problem all over the island. There were not enough doctors. Most people had no money to pay for medical care. Children often were unable to go to school. Sometimes their

281

families could not buy them the clothing they needed. Sometimes their town or village just did not have enough classrooms. In 1940 only 31 of every 100 adults could read and write.

Coming to New York. There had been a Puerto Rican community in New York City since the 1860's, when Puerto Rican leaders had fled their island to avoid arrest. Those who came planned to stay only a short time. They hoped then to return to Puerto Rico. By 1920 7,000 Puerto Ricans lived in the city. Most of them were shipyard workers. They had found jobs and homes. They urged their families and friends to join them. By 1930 New York City had 45,000 people who had been born in Puerto Rico. Like Herman Badillo, they were young, hardworking and ambitious.

Few people came to New York from Puerto Rico during the 1930's. Times were bad. Tens of thousands of men in New York could not find work. Times were even worse in Puerto Rico. But why leave one place where you have nothing to go to another place where you know you will find nothing? In 1940 New York had about 70,000 Puerto Ricans. Several thousand of these had been born there.

The job picture in New York City improved during the 1940's. Workers with or without skills were needed in many industries. Puerto Rico remained a center of poverty. There just was not enough work for the ever-growing number of people. Those who could raise the $50 or less they needed for a plane trip to New York took the chance. They found people from their old home towns. They moved into the neighborhoods where these people lived. The part of New York City called East Harlem soon became a Puerto Rican center called *El Barrio*. By 1950 the city had 190,000 people who had been born in Puerto Rico. There were also about 60,000 of their children who had been born in New York.

This was one of the fastest immigrations the city had ever known. It continued during the 1950's. In 1952–1953 more than 58,000 people made the move from Puerto Rico to New York. The city became the largest center of Puerto Rican life in the world! Today it has about twice as many Puerto Ricans (and their children born in New York) as does San Juan. In 1970 New York City had about eight million people. One-ninth of these could call themselves Puerto Ricans.

The number of people coming from Puerto Rico became

more than New York City could find work for. Newly arrived families remained in New York for a while and then moved on to other cities. About 100,000 went to Chicago. Large Puerto Rican communities grew in Philadelphia, Boston, Newark and other cities. In 1970, 80,000 Puerto Ricans came to the mainland cities to escape hard times at home. By then more than 1½ million Puerto Ricans had settled in the United States. At least 25,000 Puerto Ricans still arrive in New York each year. Perhaps half of them later move to other cities.

Puerto Rico's Department of Labor has done much to help people who leave for the mainland. Its Migration Division has many offices in Puerto Rico and in the mainland cities. Puerto Ricans go to these offices for help in preparing for life in their new homes. They learn what problems they can expect to meet. They are taught some English. Joseph Monserrat headed the Migration Division offices in New York City for many years. He became one of the city's best known Puerto Ricans. In 1969–1970 he was President of the city's Board of Education. In that post he did much to improve the education of the city's Spanish-speaking children.

Joseph Monserrat is one of New York City's best-known Puerto Ricans.

There was a special reason for coming to New York rather than to other cities. In the 1940's and 1950's Vito Marcantonio was the Congressman from the district that included East Harlem. He set up offices to aid newly arrived Puerto Ricans in their search for jobs. New York leads the country in helping Puerto Ricans.

Back to Puerto Rico. About one-third of the Puerto Ricans who have moved to the mainland plan to return to Puerto Rico some day. Many of them do so. In this they are very different from other immigrants. A Swede or Italian who comes to the United States knows that he is making a lifetime decision. If he were later to return to his old country, he would have to begin again. The cost of returning is so great that all he can plan for is a visit or two during his lifetime. Puerto Ricans find it easy to move back and forth between the island and the mainland. The cost is low. They are American citizens. They do not need passports or permission to go or come back. In some years, more Puerto Ricans return to Puerto Rico than leave it.

A chief reason for returning is that life has become much better in Puerto Rico. During his years as governor, Luis Muñoz Marín took steps to build industry in the island. A great public housing program gave homes to tens of thousands of people. Schools were improved. Until 1948 Puerto Rican schools taught in English. Students who spoke only Spanish had the same problems Mexican-Americans have had. Muñoz Marín made Spanish the language of the schools, with English a second language. Today most Puerto Ricans read and write. Their vocational schools are among the best in the world. One of them, in San Juan, has 15,000 students! Many American companies have built plants in Puerto Rico. Trained Puerto Ricans can find better jobs than their parents, and at higher pay. Any Puerto Rican who comes to the mainland and learns a trade or finishes his education knows he can find work if he returns to the island.

The Puerto Rican government has had a plan to improve life on the island. Remember that businesses in Puerto Rico do not pay taxes to the United States government. The government of Puerto Rico promised that they would also pay no taxes in Puerto Rico for at least ten years. Puerto Rico was training workers for these factories. It added to its supply of electricity. It built better roads and improved its ports. It added large airports. Any company that built a plant in Puerto Rico knew it could not lose money because of high taxes, poor transportation or a shortage of workers.

In the first twenty years of the plan, more than 1,000 new factories and businesses were begun. As many as 100,000 new jobs appeared. The income of the workers in these businesses rose to more than five times what it had been in 1940. It remains lower than it might be in mainland United States. There is still great poverty in Puerto Rico. But it grows less each year.

Better times in Puerto Rico have also meant better health. One of the advantages of living in a mainland city is that hospital care is usually provided by city hospitals. Puerto Rico has built dozens of modern hospitals. Health services have improved. The growing University of Puerto Rico in San Juan contains a medical school where many of the doctors needed on the island are trained. Today, more than half of the people of Puerto Rico receive free medical care.

Hundreds of factories like this one have been built in Puerto Rico as part of "Operation Bootstrap." What does that name mean to you?

The Puerto Rican plan is known as Operation Bootstrap. The phrase "to pull yourself up by your own bootstraps" means to improve yourself without help from others. Operation Bootstrap has proved to the whole world that a people can do this. Thousands of visitors from the world's new countries study Puerto Rico's success. Then they return to their own countries to begin similar plans.

Remaining in the Cities. Most Puerto Ricans who have left the island return for short visits. Some go to visit their families or their home towns. They go to escape for a while from the colder climate of the mainland. They have roots in the island and also in the mainland cities. But they plan to remain in these cities, their new homes. There are many reasons for this. Most of those who left Puerto Rico were young. They married and have raised families in cities like New York and Chicago. Their children were born here. These boys and girls are now much like the children of other immigrant groups. They speak two languages. They know two cultures. They make plans and have hopes of success in the cities in which they live. Their parents have found jobs, made friends and joined in the life of the Puerto Rican communities.

Black Americans and immigrant groups have set up hundreds of organizations to handle all of the problems their people face. French-speaking, German-speaking, Italian-speaking, Greek-speaking—each minority group has its own newspapers, social clubs, churches and political organizations. So do the Puerto Ricans. They know that there is some group to which they can turn when they need help. In New York City

285

the many Puerto Rican organizations join to hold a great parade every spring. The Puerto Rican Day Parade brings hundreds of thousands of people together. Among these are officials of the Puerto Rican, city, state, and national governments.

Puerto Ricans have been important in the civil rights movement. Yet many of them have not been able to improve their lives. In 1970 two of every five Puerto Ricans in New York City still needed some kind of public assistance. In other cities the problem is the same. One cause of this was that Puerto Ricans, like black Americans, suffer from job discrimination. They too are among the last hired and the first fired. They too remain poor. They have tried to move out of the slums but cannot always afford to do so. As part of the civil rights movement, they have tried to end these problems.

Many Puerto Ricans have found work in industry. The clothing industry is the largest in New York. For fifty years most of its workers were Jewish and Italian immigrants. In the 1950's Puerto Ricans began to enter this industry. They have become the largest single group among its workers. Much the same has happened in the hospitals and in hundreds of small factories.

Thousands of Puerto Ricans have pulled themselves out of poverty. They have become doctors, lawyers, businessmen, policemen, teachers, firemen and political leaders in their cities. Like other minorities before them, many are finding a place in the life of the city. True, there are many problems. The next chapter will tell us more about them. But problems are easier to solve if one has a voice in making decisions about them.

I. WHAT ARE THE FACTS?

Answer each question in a sentence or two.

1. Describe the climate of Puerto Rico.

2. Who is Teodoro Moscoso?

3. How has air travel made Puerto Rico a tourist center?

4. There were one million people in Puerto Rico in 1900. How many lived there in 1950?

5. What mainland city became the most important Puerto Rican center?

6. Where is the section called *El Barrio?*

7. How many Puerto Ricans (and their children) now live on the mainland?

8. Name two important positions held by Joseph Monserrat; by Herman Badillo.

9. What is the goal of Operation Bootstrap?

10. Name three fields in which Puerto Ricans in the cities have found jobs.

II. UNDERSTANDING WHY.

Explain why each of these events took place.

1. Puerto Ricans moved to the mainland cities after 1945.

2. Puerto Ricans moved into neighborhoods where other Puerto Ricans already lived.

3. Many Puerto Ricans return to Puerto Rico.

4. Puerto Rico has more industries every year.

5. The health of the people of Puerto Rico has improved.

III. THINKING IT THROUGH!

Discuss.

1. Why has Operation Bootstrap been so successful?

2. How has the work of the Migration Division of the Puerto Rican Department of Labor made it easier for Puerto Ricans to succeed in the mainland cities?

3. Why do most Puerto Ricans on the mainland remain in the cities?

4. Why has Puerto Rico given its greatest attention to the improvement of education?

5. Why do Puerto Ricans continue to move to the mainland?

What Problems Have Puerto Ricans Faced in the Mainland Cities?

3 The union that today has the greatest number of Puerto Rican workers is the International Ladies' Garment Workers Union, or ILGWU. Its members make most of the women's clothing sold in the United States. In 1934 William D. Lopez of the Puerto Rican Federation of Labor spoke to the ILGWU's national meeting. He said that 100,000 women in Puerto Rico made their living sewing. They were paid much less than any workers on the mainland. Most of them did "piece work" at home; about one in six worked in a factory. There they received as little as $5 a week.

The ILGWU sent Rose Pesotta to Puerto Rico to see what could be done to help these women workers. She found many of them living in the worst poverty she had ever seen. One woman lived in an open shack. Her only furniture was a table and two home-made chairs. She slept on a sack of straw and cooked on an open fireplace. Yet this woman did fine embroidery work. She was paid only a penny or two for each garment she finished! Miss Pesotta helped the workers set up union groups. However, these were the days of the Great Depression. Times grew worse rather than better. The poverty of the workers did not end. As soon as they could, thousands left for New York City.

How Have Puerto Ricans Tried to Make a Living in Mainland Cities?

What Housing Problems Have They Faced?

How Has Language Been a Problem?

What Problems Have Their Children Had in the Public Schools?

Immigrants Face Special Problems. American Indians and some Mexican-Americans are the only Americans whose families did not begin as immigrants. An immigrant is a person who leaves his country to settle in a new country. Most immigrants have had to solve similar problems.

1) *Making a Living.* Most immigrants were poor in their old countries. They came here to make a better living for themselves and their children. Until 1890 new Americans could find free or cheap land. They could find jobs in the growing cities. They could fit into new industries. Often they took the place of other workers who had gained greater skill and moved on to better-paying jobs. Since 1900 most immigrants have remained in large cities, where jobs could be found.

2) *Learning English.* The immigrants knew they would be spending the rest of their lives in the United States. They had to learn English to get along with other Americans. Most of them learned it as quickly as they could. The largest amount of immigration came after the Civil War. It was greatest between 1880 and 1921. Those who came found that the people already here owned the homes, the land and the businesses. These people with money and power spoke English.

3) *Keeping the Old Religion Alive.* Most Americans who settled here before 1880 were Protestants. Protestants from England held the greatest power in the early days of the United States. Their churches were the most powerful. Most of the new immigrants came from countries other than England. They wanted to keep their own religion. Some were Protestants whose religion was similiar to that of the Protestants already in the United States. They quickly set up their own churches. Often their ministers had also come as immigrants and spoke the language of the church's members. Within a few years such Protestant churches began to use English. They became much like the older American Protestants.

Other immigrants had very different religious beliefs. Catholics found that they were often disliked because of their religion. Jews found that some towns would not approve the building of synagogues. The Greeks and Russians followed the religion called Greek Orthodox. It was new to the

Immigrants studying English in a New York public school night class. Why would it have been so important to them to learn English quickly?

United States; they had to set up their own churches.

Immigrants learned that differences in religion meant special problems. Americans discriminated against those of different religion. Many still do. However, each immigrant group has fought hard to keep its own form of religion alive.

4) *Fighting Prejudice.* Every immigrant group comes from a country with its own language and culture. The members of this group are proud of their culture. They try to keep it alive. They did this in the cities by trying to move into neighborhoods where others of their group lived. There the old language was spoken by the immigrants and often by their children. There the old customs were kept alive in social clubs, churches and many small businesses. Each immigrant group tried to keep its identity, at least during the lifetimes of those born in the "old country."

Other Americans have often been prejudiced against immigrant groups who have tried to keep their identity. Name-calling has been one form of such prejudice. Other forms have included discrimination in housing and employment. There has also been much social prejudice against many minority groups. Hotels have often refused to admit guests of a certain race, color or religion. Restaurants have refused to seat people. Many social clubs have admitted only white Protestants. Each immigrant group has had to set up its own organizations to fight the many kinds of prejudice from which it suffered.

Puerto Ricans Seeking Jobs. Many of the Puerto Ricans who came to the mainland cities after 1940 had job skills. Tens of thousands of women were trained clothing workers. The ILGWU, one of New York's largest unions, had already worked with clothing workers in Puerto Rico. This was one trade in which a woman could get a job. Men who had been trained in Puerto Rican vocational schools also found jobs. New York City needed trained workers for ten years after World War II ended in 1945. But more than half of those who came from

There are many successful
Puerto Rican-owned
businesses in New York City.
This busy food market is an
example.

Puerto Rico were young and untrained. They took any jobs
they could find. Many had to receive public assistance while
they looked for work. Sometimes the jobs they found paid so
little that they received some public aid even while they were
working.

By the 1950's so many Puerto Ricans had come to the mainland that each city had its Puerto Rican neighborhoods. The
people in these neighborhoods spoke Spanish. By 1970 Puerto
Ricans in New York City had opened more than 7,000 small
businesses in Puerto Rican neighborhoods. They owned groceries, restaurants, tailor shops, bookstores, records shops, drug-
stores, clothing stores and the many other small businesses that
any neighborhood needs. Bit by bit a Puerto Rican middle class
began to appear.

Yet job and housing discrimination did not end. Much of
the work of groups like the New York State Commission on
Human Rights has been to fight discrimination against Puerto
Ricans. Still, Puerto Ricans were luckier than earlier minority
groups. They began to come to the United States at the time
new laws against discrimination were first passed. Puerto Ricans
and black Americans were the first groups in the cities to get
government help in fighting discrimination.

Housing. Housing discrimination was hardest to fight. Puerto
Ricans tried to move into neighborhoods where other Puerto
Ricans already lived. There was not enough housing in these
neighborhoods. Landlords broke up apartments into single
rooms. Then they rented single rooms to whole families for
as much rent as they could get. The rent became even higher

The street is the only playground for these children in the East Harlem neighborhood known as *El Barrio*.

when the landlord added a few pieces of furniture and called it a furnished apartment. Puerto Rican neighborhoods grew more and more crowded. They had begun as slums. As landlords failed to keep them repaired, they were soon among the worst ghettos in the city.

Puerto Rican families who in time made a better living often tried to move into newer neighborhoods. Landlords refused to rent to them or offered them apartments at very high rents. Few Puerto Ricans were willing to wait the long months it took to get help from city or state anti-discrimination agencies. More often they remained in the slums.

Many problems come with living in a slum. There is more crime. Drugs are often sold and used openly. Old buildings, often with broken pipes and improper garbage collections, present health problems. Some landlords, to increase their profits or simply because they don't care, fail to keep their buildings in good repair or even to provide heat and hot water. Housing problems have been an important reason for the return of many people to Puerto Rico.

English or Spanish? Other immigrant groups have in time learned English. Puerto Ricans have been slower to do this. Spanish is their language. Why give up Spanish when you may at any time return to Puerto Rico? Why give up Spanish when you need it to get along in your neighborhood? In 1970 a group of Puerto Rican adults attending an evening school in

New York City explained this to their teacher. They needed English only when they left their neighborhoods to go to work. Often their employers had learned enough Spanish to get along with them. If not, there was always some Puerto Rican worker who spoke enough English to translate for others who spoke only Spanish.

Puerto Ricans are American citizens. This means that they have the right to vote. Yet the laws of most states have required each voter to speak, read and write English. The Voting Rights Act of 1965 had ended such state laws. It ordered all states to permit any person who had finished the sixth grade in a public school to vote. It also stated that people educated in Puerto Rico could not be barred from voting because they did not speak English. New York State would not accept this change in its voting laws. It wanted all voters to be able to read and write English. The matter came to the United States Supreme Court in 1966. The decision in the case, *Katzenbach v. Morgan,* was a great victory for Puerto Ricans.

—The Fourteenth Amendment guarantees all citizens equal protection of the laws.
—States cannot deny the right to vote because a citizen was educated in a public school that does not teach in English.
—In the past, states had the power to require new citizens to know English before they received the right to vote. Now, however, hundreds of thousands of Puerto Rican-American citizens are living in our cities. They are not *new* citizens. All citizens have the right to vote. To insist that these citizens must be able to read and write English would deny them their rights.

Two of the justices of the Supreme Court dissented. They believed that it was proper for states to require literary tests in English:

—All voters should be able to read and write. It is proper for a state to give its new voters a literacy test.
—Most candidates make their speeches in English. A person who reads and writes only Spanish cannot get the information a voter needs to make wise decisions. The New York State literacy test is simple. Any Puerto Rican can attend free evening schools. There he can learn enough English to take and pass this test.
—Americans who do not speak English should learn it to fit better into American life.

Congress passed a new Voting Rights Act in 1970. It stated that no person who had finished six years of schooling had to take a literacy test in any state. Meanwhile, Puerto Ricans have entered big-city politics. They have set up their own political organizations to try to elect Puerto Rican candidates to public office.

In the Public Schools. In 1970 New York City had more than 250,000 Puerto Rican students in its public schools. Most had been born in New York City; many had been born in Puerto Rico. Their families spoke Spanish. The people in their neighborhoods spoke Spanish. When these children entered public schools, they too spoke Spanish more often than English. The city's teachers spoke English. Their students had to begin their educations in what to them was a foreign language. In 1970 New York City had only about 500 Puerto Ricans among its more than 50,000 teachers. Perhaps one teacher in ten knew enough Spanish to speak to Spanish-speaking students! There were even fewer Spanish-speaking teachers in other large cities where Puerto Ricans had settled.

City school systems have tried to help their Spanish-speaking students. Teachers are taught the simple phrases they need to keep their classes going. New York City's City University trains most of the city's new teachers. Students in these programs now must study Spanish as part of their training. Other teachers are being trained to teach English as a second language. Many classes have begun using books in both English and Spanish.

However, Puerto Rican children in New York and other large cities have often failed in school. Until 1970 eight of every ten in New York dropped out before finishing high school. Boys and girls who needed years to learn English fell far behind English-speaking students. Then, in 1970, New York City approved a plan for "open admissions" to its colleges. Any student who completed high school would be admitted to one of the city's colleges. If he or she needed help to do college work, that help might be provided. At that time one student in four in the public schools was Puerto Rican. Only one in twenty-five of those in the colleges was Puerto Rican! With the promise of a free college education, it was hoped that more Puerto Rican students would remain in school and go on to higher education. As part of the change in the colleges, some courses would be given in Spanish and other courses would deal with Puerto Rican history and culture.

What Can Open Admissions Mean?

In September, 1970, the City University of New York opened its doors for the first time to all high school graduates wishing to enter. What this meant to black and Puerto Rican students can be seen by looking at the following chart.

ENTERING FRESHMEN

	Black	Puerto Rican	Others	Total
1967	1,104 (6.5%)	680 (4%)	15,200 (89.5%)	16,984
1969	2,699 (13.8%)	1,154 (5.9%)	15,706 (80.3%)	19,559
1970	7,595 (21.7%)	4,095 (11.7%)	23,345 (66.6%)	35,035

From 1967 to 1970, black enrollment increased nearly seven times. It almost tripled from 1969 to 1970. Puerto Rican enrollment increased from only 680 freshmen in 1967 to over 4,000—more than six times what it had been. It increased almost four times from 1969 to 1970!

Black and Puerto Rican students now have become a larger part of each entering class. If this continues, and if these students complete their college education, their chances for the future must be greatly improved.

It is hoped that more Puerto Rican students will go to college under the "open admissions" program. Why is it so important that they continue their education?

The Problem of Religion. Most Puerto Ricans are Catholics. The Catholic Church is strong in many American cities. Most American Catholics have been English-speaking. Few priests spoke Spanish. Most who did were in the Southwest, where the Mexican-Americans live. Then 1½ million Puerto Ricans came to the mainland cities. Those who joined English-speaking Catholic churches felt out of place. They also found that they were not always welcome.

Most people want to attend churches in their own neighborhoods. Puerto Rican neighborhoods grew rapidly. There were few Catholic churches in them. Puerto Ricans were facing a problem that Protestant black Americans had known for a hundred years—the need for new churches in the cities. If a neighborhood has no Catholic church, its people must wait until the Catholic Church builds one. Some Puerto Ricans changed their religion rather than wait years for a church to be built for them. Protestant churches, some in stores or small buildings, have become important in many Puerto Rican neighborhoods.

A Special Fear of Prejudice. Many Puerto Ricans are darker-skinned than the white Americans already living in the cities. The United States Census reports that one Puerto Rican in five is "non-white." White Americans have long discriminated against other Americans of different races or darker skin color. Puerto Ricans often found that they were suffering the same discrimination that black Americans, Mexican-Americans, Indians, Chinese-Americans and Japanese-Americans have known.

They tried to avoid such discrimination. One way was to speak only Spanish. To do this, they remained in their own neighborhoods as much as they could. Puerto Ricans kept alive their desires and plans to return to Puerto Rico. At the same time, they made use of the anti-discrimination laws. In 1969 the New York State Division of Human Rights reported that it had handled more than 1,100 cases of Puerto Ricans seeking an end to some form of discrimination.

Solving Some Problems. New York State has kept careful records of the progress made by its one million Puerto Rican citizens. Here are some of the facts about them it reported in 1970.

—Most Puerto Ricans in the state were young. Their average age was in the twenties.

— Puerto Rican children were finishing more years of schooling than their parents had.

— More than half of all Puerto Rican workers had found jobs in which they were able to make a living. Thousands in New York City alone were college graduates. It was hoped that the new open admissions plan would bring tens of thousands of Puerto Rican boys and girls into the colleges in the years ahead.

— Two-thirds of Puerto Ricans were living in apartments rather than in single rooms. Their housing had begun to improve.

— Puerto Ricans were taking part in training programs that would help them get higher-paying jobs. Much of this job training was being handled by Puerto Rican groups like the Puerto Rican Forum.

Many problems remain for Puerto Ricans in the cities. Still, they see the road ahead. They hope it can lead them to equality with other Americans, and to a life far better than the poverty they knew in their island home.

I. WHAT ARE THE FACTS?

Write the letter of the choice that best completes each statement.

1. The ILGWU is (a) a labor union, (b) a department of the government of Puerto Rico, (c) an agency of the United Nations.

2. In 1934 Puerto Rican clothing workers earned as little as (a) $5 a week, (b) $25 a week, (c) $50 a week.

3. Many Puerto Ricans in the cities have entered the middle class by (a) working in hospitals, (b) opening small stores, (c) becoming clothing workers.

4. Many Puerto Ricans have returned to the island because they (a) found few people in the mainland cities who spoke Spanish, (b) could not place their children in schools, (c) could not find good housing.

5. In 1970 the number of Puerto Rican students in the public schools of New York City was (a) 100,000, (b) 250,000, (c) 500,000.

6. In 1970 Spanish was spoken by one New York City teacher out of (a) 10, (b) 100, (c) 1,000.

7. Under open admission plans in colleges, students are admitted if they have (a) finished elementary school, (b) passed entrance examinations, (c) finished high school.

8. Puerto Rican students have most often fallen behind in their studies because (a) they are not permitted to attend school, (b) their schools are overcrowded, (c) they do not know English when they begin school.

9. By 1970 the housing conditions of Puerto Ricans in the mainland cities had (a) grown worse, (b) not changed, (c) improved.

10. The 1970 Voting Rights Act gave Puerto Ricans the right to vote in their states (a) only if they could speak, read and write English, (b) if they could read and write English or Spanish, (c) if they had lived in these cities for at least five years.

II. EXPLAINING WHY.

Explain why each of these conditions has been a problem to the Puerto Ricans.

1. Puerto Ricans try to live in neighborhoods where other Puerto Ricans already live.

2. Industry in the mainland cities is often more advanced than similar industries in Puerto Rico.

3. Some church groups have not built churches in Puerto Rican neighborhoods.

4. Puerto Rican boys and girls have often dropped out of school.

5. American election campaigns are usually run in English.

III. THINKING IT THROUGH!

Discuss.

1. Why have the Puerto Rican businesses in Puerto Rican neighborhoods been successful?

2. Explain why some immigrant groups have quickly learned English, while Spanish-speaking Americans have not.

3. Why should (or should not) the public schools in Puerto Rican neighborhoods teach in Spanish? What other steps would solve the problems of teaching Spanish-speaking children?

What Progress Have Puerto Ricans Made on the Mainland?

4 How can Puerto Ricans in the mainland cities solve their problems? Often they find life different from what they had expected. Work is hard to find without training or the ability to speak English. Living conditions may be very bad. For many young Puerto Ricans, school is a place in which they cannot succeed and do not know where to turn for help.

The Puerto Rican Forum is an organization started in 1957 by Puerto Rican leaders to do something about these and other problems in the mainland cities. Working with government agencies, private organizations and universities, the Puerto Rican Forum is involved in many areas and activities. It founded *Aspira*, Inc.—now a separate, national organization—to offer guidance and training that will enable Puerto Rican students to go to college. With the New York Urban League and Cornell University, it created Skill Advancement, Inc., to improve the skills of low-paid workers. It began the Agency for Business and Career Development, which aids Puerto Rican businessmen in many ways.

Today the Puerto Rican Forum is involved in helping to increase the number and types of Puerto Rican-owned businesses in mainland communities. It helps many other organizations. And it continues to provide the job training, language skills and leadership training that can bring Puerto Ricans in the cities a better and happier life.

How Well Have Puerto Ricans Fit into American Life?

In What Ways Have Puerto Ricans Brought Changes to the United States?

The Melting Pot. For perhaps a hundred years Americans seemed to believe in an idea called the "melting pot theory."

It was a way to describe what happened to the country's immigrants. Many Americans even demanded that new immigrants act in the ways this theory said they should act.

The idea was that people who came here from other countries should quickly become like other Americans. They should give up their old language and speak English. They should forget about the kinds of government they knew in their old countries. They should give up their old cultures and accept "American" ways.

New immigrants are called first-generation Americans. Their children, born and raised here, are called second-generation Americans. This second generation is educated in the public schools. Boys and girls bring the ideas of American life into their homes. They may still speak the old language with their parents, but more often they speak English. By the third generation the old language and culture are almost forgotten. The immigrant group has become American. One could imagine a giant pot filled with a rich soup. Add something new to the pot, and its flavor changes a little. Still it remains the same soup, for no one addition can change it much. Each new immigrant group changed American culture and life a little. It did not change it much, for its members became Americans in the end.

The melting pot theory is believed less today than it used to be. Many immigrant groups have not become Americanized. They have remained different in important ways. We have seen this with the Chinese. It is also true of the Syrians, Poles, Greeks, Italians and others. Groups like the Amish and Mennonites came here to find religious freedom. They have kept themselves apart from others so that their way of life could continue. Other groups live among Americans but refuse to lose their identity. This is truest in the large cities. A group can move into neighborhoods with other members of that group. There they can speak the old language and keep the old culture alive. They can even set up special schools to pass their way of life on to their children and grandchildren. They can form organizations to keep them from dying out as a separate group.

Many Contributions. Each new group mixes with other Americans in many ways. Ideas from each culture pass along to others. This changes and enriches all of American life. Americans eat and enjoy the foods of many lands. They enjoy the music and art brought here by different peoples. They add bits of foreign speech to their language. The more they are willing to do these things, the easier it is for different groups to live together in the crowded cities.

Puerto Ricans have made many contributions to American life. They came to the cities bearing an old and rich culture. Slowly, they have passed it on to other Americans.

Music. Puerto Ricans added a new spirit to American music. Two of their dances, the cha-cha and the merengue, were quickly accepted by young people all over the country. Their concert artists were soon well known. Julio de Arteago, world-famous composer and organist, appeared all over the United States. María Centeno became a leading concert pianist. Graciela Rivera and Justino Díaz sang with the Metropolitan Opera Company. Rafael Hernández, Puerto Rico's greatest musician, was widely accepted in the United States before his death in 1965. Pablo Casals, the great cellist, lives in Puerto Rico, where his mother was born. Each year he leads the Casals Music Festival. Outstanding musicans from all over the world join him. The concerts are recorded and then heard in every land.

Puerto Rican folk music has become well known in the United States. Noro Morales, the band leader, was one of the first to introduce it to Americans. Ansela Menchaca sang songs in Spanish and became popular. Bobby Capó became the leading Puerto Rican television star. His singing and acting are well known to millions of Americans. Florencio Ramos, called "Ramito," and Yomo Toro made many appearances playing Puerto Rican music for American audiences.

The great cellist Pablo Casals gives a music festival in Puerto Rico each year.

Art. Art has been important in Puerto Rico for more than 200 years. José Campeche was a well-known painter before the United States gained its freedom from England. Francisco Oller's paintings were well known in Europe before many United States artists were accepted there. Carlos Irizzari, a world-famous artist, moved back and forth between Puerto Rico and New York. Four Puerto Rican artists in New York City became famous—the first of many who made New York a center of Puerto Rican art. They are Roberto Lebrón, Ramón Carrasquillo, Rafael Ferrer and Wilfred Labiosa. Their work is found today in many American museums, and also in those of San Juan and Ponce in Puerto Rico. There their paintings

Actress Rita Moreno received an Oscar award for her outstanding work in films.

Batting champion Roberto Clemente is one of baseball's best players.

share space with the work of Puerto Ricans, such as the painter Julio Rosado and the sculptor Lindsey Daen. Lincoln Center is one of New York's cultural centers. A Puerto Rican, José A. Fernandez, was one of its chief architects.

Literature. Puerto Rican writers have been important since the early 1800's. They are known chiefly among Spanish-speaking peoples. Today some of their works are being translated into English. Enrique A. Laguerro's novels and stories are known all over the world. Luis Palés Matos was the leading poet in the 10-line form called the *décima*. René Marqués has written plays performed wherever Puerto Ricans live. Piri Thomas, a New York Puerto Rican, is known for his autobiography as well as for his poetry. One of the first Puerto Rican organizations in New York City was the Circle of Spanish-American Writers and Poets. In 1968 New York City alone had more than thirty Puerto Rican poets who were important in the Spanish-speaking world. Their work was widely spread by the Institute of Puerto Rican Culture and the Atheneum of Puerto Rico, both in New York City.

Stage and Screen. Puerto Ricans had loved the theater for more than 100 years before their great move to the mainland. Some of them became important in American theater. Best known was José Ferrer. Actress Rita Moreno has had many starring roles. Juano Hernández played many important roles. As motion pictures began to deal with minority problems, Puerto Rican actors and actresses became better known to the American public.

Sports. Most members of minority groups were barred from organized sports until the 1940's. Since then, Puerto Rican athletes have reached the "big leagues" together with black Americans. Hiram Gabriel Bithorn was the first. In 1942 he joined the Chicago Cubs and became one of that team's stars. Other Puerto Ricans have done as well. Among the best known are Roberto Clemente and Orlando Cepeda. Both were chosen best player in the National League. Three Puerto Rican pitchers have been great stars. They are Rubén Gomez, José Santiago, and Juan Pizarro. Each year more Puerto Ricans gain fame in baseball.

Puerto Ricans have also done well in boxing. José Torres'

appearances always brought large crowds. Sixto Escobar was a world champion. José Gonzalez was an American champion.

Keeping Identity. Puerto Ricans are not new to the world of culture. Thousands of well-trained, educated people were among those who moved to the mainland cities. They have added much to the United States. Many feel that they are part of two cultures at the same time. They are Americans. They are also Spanish-speaking carriers of an old culture. This may explain the large number of special groups they have organized. New York City, for example, has Hispanic (Spanish-speaking) societies in its police and fire departments. There are organized groups of Puerto Rican teachers, salesmen and merchants. Doctors have formed a Spanish-American medical society; lawyers join a Puerto Rican bar association. Joseph Monserrat has explained the need for such groups. They teach Americans to respect the differences among peoples. At the same time they help Puerto Ricans keep these differences alive even while becoming part of American life.

Puerto Ricans want to remain Puerto Ricans. They also want to help one another. *Aspira* is an organization set up by Puerto Rican professionals. Its goal is to help students and to improve their schools. It is run by Puerto Ricans for Puerto Ricans. Such self-help has been used by minorities throughout American history as they tried to improve their lives in their new country.

Puerto Ricans refuse to give up their culture. They keep their language alive. They read Spanish-language newspapers and books. Young children even read Spanish-language comic books. Puerto Ricans do not want their group to lose its identity. They believe they have much to offer even while remaining themselves.

Lessons from Puerto Rico. Puerto Ricans come from a quieter life to the busy life of the cities. They bring such ideas as their island's Operation Serenity. *Serenity* is a sense of peace and restfulness. Luis Ferre, governor of Puerto Rico, has explained that his people want to be modern without being torn apart by the pressures of modern life. Industry should be used to make life better and easier, not to push hard for more and more products. Puerto Rico spends tax money for art and culture, for dance and music, for "things of the spirit." Few American states do the same.

José Torres is a well-known boxer.

Luis Ferre, governor of Puerto Rico.

Puerto Rico's government offers a new way to give minority ideas a voice. The island's constitution permits losing political parties to have some seats in the legislature. This means that people can always hear many points of view. Even unpopular ideas have a chance to be heard.

The Puerto Rican idea of *compadre*, or fellowship, is important. Each man accepts the responsibility of helping others. A newcomer in a mainland city is helped by others until he has a job, a home and friends. Those who help him may never have met him before. Still, he is a *compadre*, a fellow Puerto Rican in need. In the same way, people who are related stay closer together than most Americans do.

The Puerto Ricans have had great problems. So many came so quickly. They are learning how to get along in their new city homes. The people of the cities are learning to get along with them. They are a different people; they are unlike any other immigrant group in America. Their success in the United States will depend largely on the willingness of other Americans to accept their differences.

I. WHAT ARE THE FACTS?

Answer each question in a sentence or two.

1. What is the difference between a first-generation American and a second-generation American?

2. What is the Puerto Rican Forum?

3. What is meant by "becoming Americanized"?

4. Why is the Casals Music Festival important?

5. What is the difference between *Puerto Rican* and *Hispano*?

6. What is a Hispanic society?

7. What is Operation Serenity?

8. How is the idea of *compadre* important to Puerto Ricans?

II. WHAT DO THEY DO?

Write the word MUSIC, ART, LITERATURE or SPORTS after each of these names to show the field in which the person has been most important.

1. Rafael Hernández

2. Roberto Clemente

3. Pablo Casals

4. Sixto Escobar

5. Bobby Capó

6. José Campeche

7. Enrique Laguerro

8. Piri Thomas

9. Rubén Gomez

10. Carlos Irizzari

III. THINKING IT THROUGH!

Discuss.

1. How has living in the United States changed the culture of Puerto Ricans?

2. How has the culture of the United States been changed by the Puerto Ricans?

3. What lessons in government can we learn from the Puerto Ricans?

4. How does the United States gain or lose when an immigrant group tries to keep its own identity? What problems face an immigrant group when it tries to keep its own identity?

James R. Smith

THE POOR

The United States is one of the richest countries in the world. Yet perhaps one-fourth of all its people can be called poor. This unit tells about poverty in our country. It shows how poverty has been a special problem for minorities and for other Americans as well. Poverty has grown steadily since the United States began. By the middle 1800's it had become so widespread that local and state governments had to take action to help the poor. From 1933 on, the national government has also taken steps to aid poor Americans. Poverty remains a great national problem today. This unit tells how poverty affects the lives of the poor, and what has been done to help them. In the 1960's the national government set up plans to end poverty. These plans have not yet succeeded. Some have been helped. Still, a growing number of poor Americans remain trapped for many reasons. Poor education leads to low-paying jobs. Changes in industry have brought many kinds of work to an end. Family life weakens when a family is poor. Meanwhile, older people live longer and cannot make a living when old. The cost of living keeps rising. As the 1970's began, Americans were seeking better ways to control the problems of poverty. New ideas appeared as the nation took steps to reach this goal.

How Great a Problem Has Poverty Been in the United States?

1 Think how it would feel to be so poor that you could not pay even for food or a place to live. Think how it would feel to be put in prison just because you were so poor. Most American cities and counties used to have a special kind of prison for the poor. It was called a poorhouse; sometimes it was called a workhouse or an almshouse. Near it there might also be a debtors' prison —a jail for people who could not pay their debts. It was 1832 before Congress passed a law to end debtors' prisons, and ten years later before the states passed their own laws to end them.

An English debtors' prison in the 1700's. Why is it considered wrong today to put a man in prison because he can't pay his debts?

Today we have no poorhouses or debtors' prisons. But it is one of the puzzles of our time that poverty grows greater from year to year even as our country grows richer. We know how much an American family needs to keep out of poverty. We say that a person is poor if he does not have enough food, clothing and shelter.

The history of the United States since 1890 has been filled with efforts and laws to help the poor. However, all have failed to end poverty. Today the poor are of all races, all religions and all national origins. Ending poverty is one of the most important of our local, state and national government activities. Yet in 1970 perhaps one American in four remained poor—owning nothing and having no future in the cities or on the land.

How Great a Problem Has Poverty Been in the United States?

How Did the United States Try to Solve This Problem?

A Crime to Be Poor. In the years before the colonies were settled, English law punished the poor. Those who could not pay their debts were placed in debtors' prisons. Many of the early English settlers came from such prisons. Some became indentured servants. They had to work for years to pay their debts and the cost of their passage to the New World. Runaway indentured servants, like runaway slaves, were caught and returned to their masters.

Richer Americans, and their governments, did not feel they should have to aid the poor. Men like Benjamin Franklin complained that rich people had to pay to support the poor. No matter how much help they gave, there were still more poor. Higher wages, said Franklin, would not end poverty. The poor would spend the money on drink or other foolish things. The charities set up in the colonies and later in the states never had much money. The rich would not spend their money to help poor people.

Low wages remained the rule for about 200 years. In 1832 the average wage of a worker was a dollar a day. One dollar bought a great deal more then than it does today, but it was not enough for a family's needs. The cities built poorhouses. Thousands might die of cold and hunger each winter, yet little was done to end poverty.

The cities of the United States soon developed terrible slums. Dr. John H. Griscom described one in New York City in 1845:

> ... The tenements ... are divided into small apartments. ...
> These closets, for they deserve no other name, are then rented
> to the poor ...
>
> ... The walls and windows ... become broken, the doors
> and floors become injured, the chimneys filled with soot ...
>
> We [permit] the [landlord] to stow them, like cattle, in
> pens ... they are allowed, may it not be said required, to live
> in dirt. ...

Working conditions were also bad during the 1800's. In
1845 workers in Lowell, Massachusetts, worked from sunrise
to sunset. This was more than eleven hours in winter and more
than thirteen hours in spring and summer. Some of these
workers made $3 a week or less!

Poverty Grows. The cities grew rapidly after 1850 as millions
came from Europe. Poverty grew as well. In 1857 a report to
New York's legislature described life in the city's slums:

> We could tell of one room, twelve feet by twelve, in which
> were ... twenty persons, of both sexes and all ages, with only
> two beds ... of another apartment, still smaller ... inhabited
> by a man, a woman, two girls, and a boy ... of another, an
> attic room, seven feet by five. ... We were told of a colony of
> 300 [people] who occupied a single basement. ...

Jacob Riis, a New York City newspaperman, told the country in 1890 that housing conditions had grown even worse:

> In Essex Street, two small rooms in a six-story tenement were
> made to hold a "family" of father and mother, twelve children
> and six boarders.

Poverty was widely discussed in the 1870's and 1880's. Richer
Americans said that poor people had only themselves to blame
for their poverty. The Reverend Henry Ward Beecher spoke
for this point of view:

> Is not a dollar a day enough to buy bread with? Water costs
> nothing; and a man who cannot live on bread is not fit to live.

Times were bad in city and farm areas by 1890. Millions of
poor farmers had become tenant farmers or sharecroppers. They
rented or used land owned by others; these owners took most

of what a farmer earned. Such farm families kept $100 a year or less for their labor. Many went into deep debt to their landlords.

New York City has kept the best records of its living conditions. Here is what one report in 1890 told:

—150,000 people were out of work.
—150,000 more people earned less than 60¢ a day.
—100,000 people had been evicted from their tenement apartments.
—One-tenth of all those who died that year had to be buried by the city, for their families had no money.

Child labor—work by children as young as five—spread through the country by 1890. More than 23,000 children worked in the new factories of the South. Most states did not require children to attend school for more than twelve to sixteen weeks a year. Even these rules were not enforced. In 1891 a report from Chicago said:

In one room ten feet by forty, 39 girls, twelve children ten to twelve in age and eleven men worked. . . .

State and Local Help for the Poor. Something had to be done to help the poor. In 1864 Massachusetts set up a state board of charities. Thirty years later, nineteen states had such agencies. By 1900, 138 cities had groups like today's Community Chests. Many charities worked together to raise money and to provide help in emergencies. The Red Cross was begun in 1881. It, too, offered help, chiefly in emergencies.

Henry George told the country in 1885 that poverty should not exist. The country was rich enough to provide for all:

I say that all this poverty . . . is unnecessary; I say that there is no natural reason why we should not all be rich . . . in the sense of having enough to completely satisfy all physical wants; of all having enough to get such an easy living that we could develop the better part of humanity . . . no one should think of such a thing as little children at work. . . .

Men like Henry George could speak, but few listened. By

Child labor was widespread throughout the United States by 1890. Would you like to have been this boy?

1904 poverty had grown greater. None could deny the truth of the facts offered by Robert Hunter, a social worker:

— There were ten million poor Americans—"underfed, under-clothed and poorly housed."
— This was one-eighth of all the people in the United States.
— Nearly half of all families owned nothing except their clothing and furniture.
— About four million Americans would starve without aid from public and private charities.
— Two million men were out of work from four to six months of each year.
— 1,700,000 children worked instead of going to school.
— One million workers were injured or killed each year. This made their families poor and in need of aid.

Poverty and the Great Depression. By 1930 most cities, counties and states had passed laws to help their poor. These governments were paying for three-fourths of all the help given to poor people. Small towns still had poorhouses, but most of the country gave direct aid—money to help poor families. Then, beginning in 1930, the country was hit by the greatest depression it had ever known. By 1932 ten million people were out of work. One-fourth of the country's families had no income. At least thirty million Americans suffered from poverty.

Local and state governments soon ran out of money. Most cities gave $4 to $5 a week to a family of four people. By the end of 1932 they could not give any aid at all. Oscar Ameringer, a newspaperman, told Congress what poverty was doing to people:

> . . . The last thing I saw on the night I left Seattle was numbers of women searching for scraps of food in the refuse piles of the principal market of that city . . . I saw men picking for meat scraps in the garbage cans in the cities of New York and Chicago. . . .

The Depression hit the white and black tenant farmers and sharecroppers of the South hardest of all. As late as 1938 most were earning as little as ten or twenty cents for a day's work. During the Depression years other workers also came close to starving. Children in Connecticut earned a dollar a week; workers in Pennsylvania earned less than ten cents an hour; women in Tennessee earned five cents an hour!

Help from Washington. Franklin Delano Roosevelt became President in 1933. One-third of the people in the country then did not have enough food and clothing or proper housing. Roosevelt's program to deal with the problems of the Depression was called the New Deal. For the next six years he made the relief of poverty one of his chief goals. By 1935 New Deal laws were helping twenty million Americans. It was giving them half or more of the money they needed to end their poverty.

Money for the Poor. As 1933 began, the average family receiving public assistance (often called "relief") was given about fifty cents a day. In some places four families out of every five needed such help. Congress quickly passed an emergency relief law. Money was sent to state relief agencies. They then gave it to the poor.

Jobs for the Poor. In 1933 and 1934, four million people were given jobs by the Civil Works Administration. They worked on roads and highways. They built schools and taught in them. They worked on a thousand airports. Three thousand writers and artists received special jobs. They wrote guide books and plays, painted murals and helped keep the cultural life of the country alive. The jobs program cost a billion dollars—more than the government had ever spent on a relief program.

Food for the Poor. The New Deal also gave food to the poor. It set up the Federal Surplus Relief Corporation. This agency helped farmers by buying some of their crops. It then gave this food to relief agencies in the states, who gave it to poor people. Farmers were also given loans to keep them going until their next crop had grown.

Helping Communities. The Public Works Administration (PWA) and the Works Projects Administration (WPA) were often attacked and often defended. These agencies helped build seven of every ten new school buildings during the years of the New Deal. They built two-thirds of the country's new courthouses and other public buildings. The six billion dollars they spent helped millions of people.

Jobs for Young Men. One of the important new pro-

These men were able to find work in a government caisson plant, thanks to a PWA contract. What would have happened to them if there had been no programs such as the PWA during the Depression?

grams was called the Civilian Conservation Corps, or CCC. Young men from families on relief were put to work improving the land. About 2½ million of them (500,000 at a time) planted trees, built reservoirs and dams and worked on beaches, parks and other needed improvements. About one-tenth of these young men were black. This was the first time the United States government had ever run an integrated national program. As one of the lasting results of the CCC, the young men planted 200 million trees—most of them now part of the country's natural wealth!

Helping the Farmers. The New Deal tried to help farmers make a better living. It made loans to help them bring electricity to their farms. It paid them for growing less of a crop if the supply was already too great. The Tennessee Valley Authority began the building of dams that gave electric power, fertilizers and water to poor farmers. Today the power produced by TVA dams helps communities all over the country when they must have more electricity.

Social Security. President Roosevelt realized that relief could not go on forever. He had to offer the country

Young men build an irrigation ditch as members of the CCC. How did their work help both themselves and the nation?

a way to prevent the kind of poverty it had known in the Depression years. A group of laws passed by the New Deal beginning in 1935 have become known as the Social Security System. It was the President's goal to help people "from the cradle to the grave."

a) Unemployment Insurance. The first problem was the danger of losing your job. This had happened to more than ten million Americans. Once their savings were gone, they had no way to provide for their families. A law set up a national unemployment insurance system. Only about half of those in the country were covered by the law at first. Today most workers, except farm, restaurant, hotel and hospital workers, are covered. Each worker and his employer pay money into a fund. When a worker loses his job, he can apply for weekly unemployment payments. Each state has set up its own system of paying this insurance. The amount is less than the worker's regular pay, but at least he does have some income while out of work. Payments can continue for as long as half a year.

b) Old-Age Pensions. Old people without savings or jobs were a large part of the country's poor. A law set up a system of old-age pensions. Today a worker covered by the law can "retire" at age 62 or age 65. He (or she) then receives a monthly check for the rest of his life. The amount in this pension is small; few people can manage with it alone. However, it means some regular income to people who would otherwise have to live only on public assistance.

c) Survivors' Insurance. An important part of the law provided some money to the children and wives of workers covered by the pension plan. If the covered person died, his wife then received a smaller payment each month as long as she lived. She also received extra money to help care for her children.

Minimum Wage Laws. The years of very low wages for workers came to an end during the New Deal. One of the New Deal agencies got employers to agree to pay a minimum wage. Many industries did this. Wages in all industries began to rise. Later laws passed by states and by Congress slowly raised the lowest wage paid workers all over the country. Today minimum wages in most occupations are $1.60 an hour or more.

Special Help for Students. The New Deal tried to help students remain in school. Millions of young Americans had left school to find work when their families were in great need. A National Youth Administration was begun. It paid students up to $15 a month for work they did in their high schools or colleges—record-keeping, working in libraries, marking papers or doing special jobs. This money helped them remain in school. It was often half of what they could earn if they left school and took full-time jobs.

Poverty Remains. These and many other laws slowly brought the Depression to an end. But there were still millions out of work in 1941, when the United States became involved in World War II. The New Deal had made great changes in our country. Now it came to an end. The need to fight a great war brought many new changes. After the war ended in 1945, the United States saw ten years of almost steady growth. New products, new jobs and new ways to produce changed the life of its people.

But by 1955 new problems had appeared. Unemployment again began to grow, even though the country was producing more every year. Machinery took the place of farm workers.

Unemployment continues, although the country grows richer each year. What can be done to help men like these find jobs?

Many tenant farmers and sharecroppers lost their farms. Greater use of machinery put half the country's miners out of work. Automation—the use of machines to run machines—destroyed jobs in every industry. Since 1955 we have had from three to five million unemployed workers each year. Poverty has grown again. The number of poor people grows greater each year. Prices rise, and the cost of living rises with them. The many laws passed during the New Deal do not fully protect people from poverty.

President John F. Kennedy saw this national problem in 1963:

> Poverty in the midst of plenty . . . must not go unchallenged in this country. Ours is the wealthiest of nations, yet one-sixth of our people live below minimal levels of health, housing, food and education—in the slums of cities, in migratory labor camps, in economically depressed areas, on Indian reservations.

President Kennedy did not live to solve these problems. Lyndon B. Johnson, who followed him as President, made a beginning. We will examine that beginning in the next chapter.

I. WHAT ARE THE FACTS?

Write the letter of the choice that best completes each statement.

1. Before 1832 poor people received help chiefly from (a) private charities, (b) local governments, (c) the national government.

2. Before 1900 most cities helped poor people (a) whenever the head of the family lost his job, (b) only in emergencies, (c) when the state government ordered the help.

3. In 1933 the part of the country's population that did not have proper food, clothing or housing was (a) one-half, (b) one-third, (c) one-eighth.

4. The CCC gave work to (a) all men and women farm workers without jobs, (b) men ready to work at building city schools and other public buildings, (c) young men from families on relief who were ready to work on projects to improve the land.

5. Unemployment insurance is part of the larger plan called (a) direct relief, (b) public assistance, (c) social security.

II. WHAT DO THEY MEAN?

Explain the meaning of each word or phrase in a sentence or two.

1. debtors' prison
2. charitable organization
3. poorhouse
4. child labor
5. social worker
6. direct aid
7. public assistance
8. New Deal
9. public works
10. minimum wage

III. THINKING IT THROUGH!

Discuss.

1. Tell which statement you agree with in each pair. Be sure to give reasons for your opinions.

a) Child labor can help end poverty, because families then have more money to spend.
b) Child labor leads to ever greater poverty, because children who work become uneducated adults with little hope for the future.
c) All Americans should have the right to guaranteed protection against poverty.
d) The more aid the poor receive, the less they try to improve their lives themselves.

2. Why do you think poverty has been a national problem since colonial times?

What Can Be Done to End Poverty?

2 About one-tenth of the people in the United States live in "poverty areas," large regions of great poverty. The best known of these is called Appalachia. It runs from New England south to Mississippi and Alabama, following the line of the Appalachian Mountains. Its farms are poor. It has small factory towns and few large cities. Much of Appalachia has coal mines and iron or steel plants. It has never been a rich area. Today it is poorer than it used to be. Farmers have not been able to buy the machinery they need. About half the miners and other workers have lost their jobs. The work they used to do can now be done by fewer men using new machines. Many small factories have lowered wages or closed.

Poverty has driven young people out of Appalachia. More than two million of them have moved away, mostly to the country's larger cities. There they have often become part of the cities' poor. A report in 1970 stated that at least eight of every ten young people remaining in the area planned to leave it. In 1965 Congress passed the Appalachian Regional Development Act. It was a plan to help 360 counties in the area. Each state asked for the help it needed. New roads and new

A poor farmer and his family on the porch of their Arkansas home. What kind of future do you think his children will have?

businesses were to be developed. Yet the program has not solved the problem of poverty in Appalachia.

> *Who Are the Poor in the United States Today?*
> *What Programs Are Trying to End Poverty?*

Who Are the Poor? In 1968 the Citizens' Crusade Against Poverty issued a report called *Hunger, USA*. It said most of the poor now were among groups that had been here a long time—Indians, Negroes, Appalachian whites and Spanish-speaking residents of the Southwest. By 1970 there had been many such reports about poverty in the United States. Here are some of the facts they presented:

— More than 25 million Americans received public assistance.
— Two-thirds of these poor people were white. One-third were "non-white," chiefly black Americans.
— In the eyes of the United States government, a family of four earning less than $310 a month ($3,720 a year) was poor. On this basis three of every ten Americans were poor!
— Millions of farm families had moved to the cities since the 1930's. Most of them had remained poor. There were still about one million small farms in the country. Most small farmers were also among the poor.
— Some of the worst poverty was found in the large cities. About half the cities' poor were blacks and Puerto Ricans.
— Between one-third and one-fourth of the poor received little or no public assistance. Most of these were older people, chiefly women, who lived with their relatives. There were about eight million elderly poor.
— One-eighth of all white people were poor; two-fifths of all "non-whites" were poor.
— The largest number of poor people were families headed by women. This was more than one-third of all poor white families and more than three-fifths of all non-white families. About eleven million children under eighteen were in these families.
— One-fourth of all American families had less than $1,000. This included all savings and the cash value of whatever a family owned.

A wood stove provides the only heat in the drafty shack of this mother and her six children.

Business Week magazine looked at poverty in 1968 and told its readers:

— Over thirty million Americans live in poverty.
— Thirty million more are close to poverty.
— Cities do not have the money "to do the job that must be done."

Helping the Poor. Dozens of relief programs try to help the poor. Some are federal programs. State and local governments run others. The federal government pays about three-fourths of the cost of public assistance. It gives the money to state or local governments. A state government must often pay part of the cost if it is to receive federal aid. The federal government usually requires that help be given to poor people of all races, colors and national origins. Some states have refused to accept this rule. To avoid it they have refused some federal aid.

How Much Aid? In 1970 half the states were giving a poor family of four at least $200 a month. Ten states were giving them more than $250 a month. Five states in the North were giving more than $275 a month. On the other hand, ten states in the South were giving a poor family less than $30 a week. Payments were as low as $13 a week! This led more and more poor families to leave the South for the cities of the North. Most had remained there during long years of poverty because other states would not give them public assistance for up to a year after they arrived. This was changed by a United States Supreme Court decision in 1969 (*Shapiro v. Thompson*). The Court ruled that a state with a public assistance plan must give aid at once to anyone who moved into the state if that person was poor enough to receive aid. This decision meant that poor people could move freely to other parts of the country where they might receive the help they needed.

What Kinds of Aid? The most important assistance received by poor people is the money they need to make some kind of living. There are also dozens of special kinds of assistance in states and communities all over the country:

— Blind people receive training and pensions, are taught how to read Braille, get medical treatment and can get trained dogs.
— Older poor people receive free medical care. This can be in hospitals or at home. They can also be trained and given jobs working in hospitals.
— Mentally retarded people receive education, job training and money if they need it to live.
— People in prisons are trained for jobs they can take after they leave prison.
— Crippled people are trained for special jobs and are given equipment they need to move around.
— Veterans can receive job training or be paid while they continue their education. They can receive free medical care in veterans' hospitals.
— Medicare and Medicaid offer medical aid to older people and those receiving public assistance.

It is important that poor people learn about the many programs that can help them. This is most true of poor people with such special problems as those listed above.

Why Are So Many People Poor? The United States is a rich country. Why, then, are so many of its people poor? These reasons are often given to explain poverty:

— American industry has changed. Workers need more and more education and training. One American in ten has had less than eight years of schooling. Many such Americans are among the poor. Poorly trained workers receive lower wages.
— Poor people cannot afford to remain in school. Young boys and girls often drop out of school to try to make some money to help their families. Their lack of education then keeps them as poor as their families were.
— Discrimination has kept people in minority groups out of better-paying jobs. Even when there is little job discrimination, the jobs require more education and training than poor people have received.
— Poor people in cities live in poorer neighborhoods. The schools are older. For many reasons, students in them do not learn as much as they could. They then find it harder to make a living.
— Poor families suffer more than others from diseases that proper medical care could prevent.
— Millions of poor people are not members of the unions and are therefore not protected by them. This means that they receive lower wages, can be fired more easily and do not receive the extra benefits unions have won for their members.

In 1964 President Lyndon Johnson began the War on Poverty. Do you think poverty can ever be ended?

The "War on Poverty." On January 8, 1964, President Johnson spoke to the country about some of its problems. "Poverty," he said. "There is the real enemy." He asked Congress to pass laws to change life for poor Americans. Later that year it passed the Economic Opportunity Act. The law stated its goals:

> . . . poor people can and must be provided with opportunities to earn a decent living and maintain their families on a comfortable living standard. Poor people in the United States are now often set apart from society. . . . This act will help to provide the poor people of our nation with the human skills and resources with which they, themselves, will earn their rightful place in society.

By the end of 1970 it was possible to see what changes this law had brought. Perhaps its goals could have been reached if the country had spent more in its war against poverty. How-

ever, the great cost of fighting a war in Vietnam had left less for the country's other needs. Still, much had been done. Let's look at the chief programs begun under President Johnson's plan.

Young men learn to operate a lathe at a Job Corps training center. Why do they need such training?

This North Carolina woman is paying for groceries with low-cost food stamps. How will it help her family have a more balanced diet?

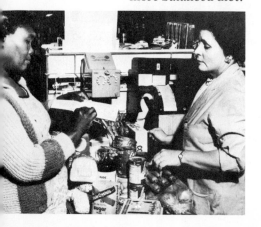

1) *Appalachia and Other Poor Areas.* Some new industries have been begun in the poverty areas. Many new roads have been built. In some areas poor people have helped plan the projects needed to improve their lives. However, there has been little real change in the two chief problems of places like Appalachia. a) Young people are still leaving for the cities. b) The leading industries, such as coal mining and iron and steel, do not employ more workers than in 1964.

2) *Jobs for Young People.* Much has been done to help young people get training that can lead to better jobs. A Job Corps program has tried to train 500,000 young people. Since students have had to leave their cities or farm areas to be trained in centers far from home, many have not finished the program. Still, more than 100,000 Job Corps graduates found jobs in the first two years of the program. Summer programs have given jobs to hundreds of thousands of boys and girls, helping them to stay in school the rest of the year. More money has been given to state employment agencies. They have improved their services to people in need of work. However, young people often remained out of work in times of poor business conditions.

3) *Food Stamps.* A food stamp program has helped more and more poor families. People with low incomes can buy food stamps. In most states, one dollar spent on food stamps can buy two to four dollars' worth of certain foods. By 1970 this program had spread to most of the country. Some states and counties had refused to take part in the program.

4) *VISTA.* VISTA is a program called Volunteers in Service to America. Trained people agree to spend

a year or two at very low pay helping people in poor areas. They move into the areas and add their special skills to the work being done to end poverty. They have opened community centers, taught, worked with community groups and have helped young people stay in school.

5) *Better Minimum Wage Laws*. Since 1964 Congress has tried to place more workers under minimum wage laws. The minimum wage is still low. A person earning less than $2 an hour will take home less than the $3,720 set in 1970 as the poverty level for a family of four. Unions and many leaders of Congress have been asking for a higher minimum wage. However, by 1971 four of every five workers in the United States were protected by unemployment insurance.

6) *Better Schools*. Great amounts of money have been given to the states to improve their schools. Head Start classes have helped hundreds of thousands of poor children aged three to five to prepare for their regular schooling. School lunch programs have given

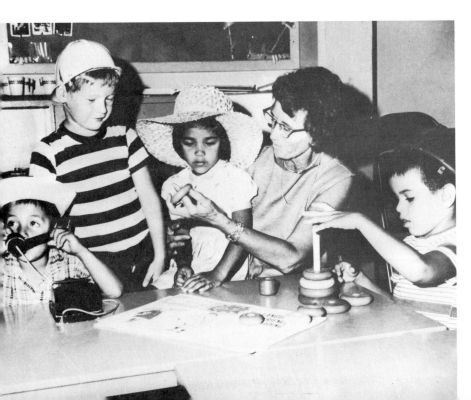

Head Start helps very young children get ready to begin school. Why is its name a good one?

free or low-cost lunches to the children of poor families. By 1971 no poor child in such a program had to pay more than $1 a week for well-balanced lunches. Federal money gave extra books and supplies to most public schools from 1965 to 1970. Thousands of schools were able to hire teacher aides, extra teachers and guidance counselors, and to offer summer school and other special programs. One such program has been after-school tutoring for students who need extra help. Students who wished to go to college were helped by College Bound programs. Those who went on to college could also receive loans and other help.

7) *Hospitals and Nursing Homes.* Hospitals received help if they admitted all poor people in need of medical care. Some hospitals refused to join this program. Medical care for the poor, chiefly the aged poor, has improved. Health clinics were begun in city slums. Nursing homes were built with federal and state aid. Medical schools and hospitals received money to train more doctors and nurses. The Medicaid plan paid medical costs for millions of poor and aged Americans. By 1971 most Americans could expect better medical care wherever their communities had accepted these services.

8) *Housing.* More than sixty cities were given money for the Model Cities Program. The poor people of an area helped plan the needed changes. State and federal money was then to be used to build new houses or repair older housing. The program has been less successful than was hoped because of the rising costs of building.

9) *Better Travel.* By 1970 the suburbs of large cities had as many people as the cities themselves. Poorer people could not move out of the city slums unless the cost of travel to their city jobs remained low. The national government made many studies of how to improve transportation. One study led to a plan for high-speed trains between cities and their

suburbs. Another set up aid to cities to improve roads and highways. Such plans will not be of great help until years have passed, for improving travel is slow and costly.

Being Part of the War on Poverty. Poor Americans have helped plan and run many aid programs. They have come to see that something can be done. Many have joined groups to demand the aid and services promised by the country's laws. Here are some of the results of community-run and -planned programs in cities throughout the country.

— Job-Mobile buses in Philadelphia go to poor neighborhoods. There they advise people of jobs that are available and that they might be able to fill.
— Toledo, Ohio, and Washington, D.C., have set up programs to clean up poor neighborhoods. City and federal money has paid young people for the work they do in such programs. Such work has also created community pride.
— "Operation Breadbasket" in Chicago began under the leadership of Dr. Martin Luther King, Jr. In its first two years it found 1,500 jobs for poor black citizens of that city. In 1970 its leader was the Reverend Jesse Jackson.
— Poor people in most parts of the country have elected community councils who play a large part in planning new programs.
— Groups such as the National Urban League and the Urban Coalition work all over the country to help members of minority groups find jobs and learn about the many services offered under new laws. In 1966 alone the National Urban League found jobs for 40,000 people and helped 8,000 black workers gain promotions to better jobs.
— Urban task forces in New York bring together the people working in poverty and other programs in each neighborhood. They can then join to ask for what their people need most.

Why Does Poverty Grow? Studies made under the War on Poverty program have helped us understand why poverty does not end even though so much is being done to try to end it. Here are four of the reasons for our ever-growing poverty:

The Reverend Jesse Jackson is head of Chicago's *Operation Breadbasket.*

More older people. Better medical care and advances in medicine help people live longer. The more older people we have, the more aged poor we have.

Not enough education or training. Millions of Americans have had little or no education or training. There are few jobs today for untrained workers. The jobs they can find pay minimum wages. People receiving such low pay cannot rise above the poverty level. They remain poor.

Dependent children. The largest program of public assistance is called Aid to Dependent Children. A dependent child is one whose family is too poor to provide needed food, shelter and clothing. The number of broken families continues to grow. This means that more and more children have to be helped by public assistance.

Rising prices. Inflation is a national problem. Prices keep rising. Wages rise too, but usually after prices have risen first. Higher costs mean that families are not able to save. Rising costs of living can keep families poor even though they may make more money each year. Prices are often higher in poor areas. Poor people who buy on installment plans pay even more.

1950's

1970's

Twenty dollars used to buy more food than it does today. When prices rise faster than wages, inflation results— and the poor are hurt more than others.

Solutions for the '70's. No large country in the world's history has ever really ended poverty. Poor people have suffered, and have felt that they were trapped by their own poverty. Yet a new idea appeared after 1945. Adlai Stevenson, twice candidate for President of the United States, called this idea the "revolution of rising expectations." People all over the world have come to believe that they can expect their lives to improve. Poor Americans know that most people in the country are not poor. Why should others have everything they need while millions cannot escape from poverty?

Poor Americans ask such questions with ever louder voices. They know that their government has, since 1933, provided many kinds of public assistance. Such aid had not ended poverty. By 1970 some other ways to attack the problem were being discussed in the United States. Some or all of them may be tried in the years ahead. Perhaps they will make possible an end to the poverty that spoils so many lives, young and old.

1. *Income Maintenance.* President Richard M. Nixon offered a plan to attack poverty. In 1970 it was widely discussed all over the country and was being studied by Congress. President Nixon said that our system of public assistance should be changed. All American families should instead have a minimum income. It would be at least half of what a person could earn if he received a minimum wage. A family of four would be guaranteed $1,600 a year. Food stamps and other aid would really make this family's income greater. The plan would not end poverty in itself. But it would lower the cost of running aid programs. This would leave more money for direct payments to poor families.

2. *Family Assistance.* Another plan has been tried in other countries and has been suggested by some Americans. Parents would receive cash payments each month for each of their children. If this amount were $100 a month, then a family with three children would receive $300 a month. If the family could make a living without this aid, they would repay the money when they paid their income taxes.

3. *Negative Income Tax.* A plan discussed at public meetings all over the country offered another way to attack poverty. Poor people who made less money than they needed would receive money from the government to make up the difference. Suppose the poverty level were set at $4,000 a year. Those families making less would receive half or more of the amount they needed to reach $4,000. Instead of paying an income tax, they would receive money at tax time.

4. *Work and Public Assistance.* Most programs of public assistance end when a family begins to earn more money. This has kept these families just as poor as they were under public assistance. One plan discussed by the country's large city mayors was to continue public assistance even when a poor family begins to earn money from jobs. The amount of

public assistance would be smaller, but would continue for a while. This would give poor people an extra reason for gaining more education, learning job skills and then going to work.

5. *Family Services.* As part of the War on Poverty, many city neighborhoods opened day-care centers. Working parents could leave their children there and pick them up at the end of the working day. More such centers would make it possible for children in families with one parent to escape from poverty. The cost of the day-care centers is a great deal less than the costs of public assistance for whole families. Other family services have also been suggested. Housekeepers can care for aged people or very young children while parents work. Consumer experts can help train poor people to use their money wisely.

6. *Protection in the Courts.* Poor people have often found that the laws harm them as often as they help them. They often lack the money to pay a lawyer when they are sued or charged with a crime. As late as 1941 the Supreme Court had ruled that poor people did not have to be provided with the help of a lawyer (*Betts v. Brady*).

   — Each state can decide for itself when a defendant must have a lawyer to receive a fair trial.
   — The Fourteenth Amendment guarantees due process. However, this does not always mean a defendant must have a lawyer.

The Court changed its position in 1962. It decided in the case of *Gideon v. Wainright* that all persons charged with crimes must be given the aid of lawyers.

   — Any person charged with a crime who is too poor to hire a lawyer must be given one by the state so that a fair trial can be held.
   — This right to have the aid of a lawyer may not be found in some countries, but it must exist in ours.

Thousands of people in prisons all over the country were freed or given new trials after this decision. Some cities have also taken the step of having a public defender. His job is to help people who have been charged with crimes or who need help in a court.

It later became part of the War on Poverty to give poor people the help of lawyers. By 1970 nearly 2,000 lawyers were spending all their working time in this way. They had helped a million poor Americans who had never before had the services of a lawyer.

An End to Poverty? Before his death Robert Kennedy called for a new set of national goals. One of these would be to end poverty. This is what he and others said:

— Discrimination and segregation have helped cause poverty. They have kept millions of Americans from receiving fair treatment and their "fair share" of all that the country can provide for its citizens.
— Poor housing traps the poor, leaving them with little hope.
— Poor education keeps the poor from escaping their poverty.
— Public assistance keeps the poor alive, but does not help them end their poverty.
— Problems of poverty make the cities problem centers in other ways. Cities cannot themselves raise the money needed to solve these problems.

Poverty, then, is part of many other problems. To end it we must have a new set of solutions based on new goals for the future of the United States.

I. WHAT ARE THE FACTS?

Answer each question in a sentence or two.

1. Describe the area called Appalachia.

2. What name was given to President Johnson's program to lessen poverty?

3. What is the food stamp program?

4. What work is done by VISTA?

5. What is "Operation Breadbasket"?

6. How many Americans received public assistance in 1970?

7. What has caused so many farm families to move to the cities?

8. What is the goal of the Job Corps?

9. How do Head Start classes help the children of poor families?

10. What is a "dependent child"?

II. EXPLAINING WHY.

Answer each question in a short paragraph.

1. Why have some states refused some federal aid programs to help their poor?

2. Why has poor housing been called a cause of poverty?

3. Why are private charities so active when there are so many government programs to aid the poor?

4. Why have cities such as New York set up urban task forces?

5. Why did the Supreme Court order all states to provide lawyers to poor people charged with crimes?

III. THINKING IT THROUGH!

Discuss.

1. Why do you agree or disagree with this statement? *No country can ever end poverty, for there will always be rich people and poor people.*

2. How important is each of these in the attack on poverty? Why?
   a) better schools
   b) guaranteed minimum income
   c) ending discrimination and segregation

3. What is meant by "national goals"? How would these have to be changed before poverty could be ended in the United States?

Marcia Kay Keegan

Unit Nine

MINORITIES AND GOVERNMENT

We live under three levels of government—local, state and national. Local and state governments have often seemed to permit or even to favor discrimination against minority groups. The national government did little to improve the life of the country's minorities until the 1950's. Supreme Court decisions began the change. Then came new federal laws and changes in state and local laws. Minority groups learned that change was possible. They looked for ways to bring it about. This unit describes the chief ways in which minorities have worked for and gained greater equality. Their greatest success has come through changes in the laws and in the meaning of these laws as viewed by the courts. Segregated housing has been weakened. Presidents have attacked segregation in the armed forces. States have passed laws against discrimination because of race, religion or the country from which a person or his family came. Laws against the discrimination of women, notably in the world of work, have also been enacted. Yet the problems of discrimination, prejudice and segregation remain. As the 1970's began, it was clear that the new laws of the United States could in time end these evils. However, laws will mean little unless they are really enforced by all levels of government.

Does a State Law Weaken Discrimination?

1 In April, 1950, the small town of Elmont, New York, needed seventeen more teachers for the new school year. Dorothy Brown hoped to be one of them. She was experienced enough, since she had already taught for ten years in Washington, D.C. She was certainly well trained, for she had been a successful graduate student at New York University. The principal who interviewed Mrs. Brown asked whether she would mind teaching Negro children. She said that she would not, as she herself was a Negro.

After several weeks' wait Dorothy Brown was told that all the positions had been filled. The truth, she soon found out, was that the town would not hire a Negro teacher. New York's Long Island, where Elmont is located, contains hundreds of thousands of school children in its two counties. In 1950 not one of these children was being taught by a black teacher.

Mrs. Brown went to the New York State Commission Against Discrimination. This group had been set up under the first state law to fight discrimination in hiring. She complained that she had not been hired because of her race. The Commission said it would take action. But it seemed to work very slowly, for the new school year began without any results.

Mrs. Brown tried the N.A.A.C.P. Its lawyers went to court to get the head of the Elmont school system to present her name to the local school board. The case dragged on for years; finally a decision came from the highest court in New York State, the Court of Appeals. The Court ordered the Elmont school board to consider Mrs. Brown as a possible teacher.

The board refused, and a new case was begun in the federal courts. Here it was charged that Mrs. Brown had been denied equal protection of the laws (Fourteenth Amendment). The case ended with an agreement by Long Island school officials to stop discriminating against black teachers. Five years had passed from Dorothy Brown's first interview to the decision by a federal court! Since 1955, Negro teachers have been able to find work in any school in New York State.

> *What Are "Fair Employment Practices"?*
> *Have State and Local Laws Weakened Discrimination?*
> *What Was the New York State Anti-Discrimination Act of 1945?*
> *What Changes Could Such a Law Bring?*

Fair Employment. The National Urban League, founded in 1910, is one of the most important Negro organizations in the country. Its chief goal is to help black Americans find better jobs. It does this by getting white employers to end discrimination in hiring. The civil rights movement had been working for fair employment since 1905. The Niagara Movement had asked for it. The N.A.A.C.P. has always urged it. Some white and Spanish-speaking groups have also worked to end unfair hiring. These include the Workers' Defense League, the interracial Urban Coalition and the Puerto Rican Forum.

Examples of the problems these groups attack can be found all over the United States:

— A person is refused a job because the employer won't hire a person of a race different from his own.
— A person is refused a job because of his religion, or creed.
— A person is refused a job because his skin color is dark or is not like that of the people who own the business.
— A person is refused a job because he or his family came from a certain country. He is being discriminated against because of his *national origin.*

Fair employment means the ending of these reasons for not hiring a person. A worker's race should not matter. His religious beliefs should have nothing to do with his getting a job. The color of a person's skin does not affect his ability to work. The country from which he or his parents came is not related to his skill on the job. Yet people have been denied jobs for such reasons during most of American history.

Governments and Fair Employment. No one person or group of people can end job discrimination. It is the kind of problem that can be solved only by the power of government. Most local, state and federal governments did nothing until the 1940's. World War II had begun in Europe and Asia. Defense industries—those businesses that make the weapons and supplies needed by the armed forces—grew quickly with government aid. But these businesses denied jobs to members of minority groups.

A. Philip Randolph, the most important black labor leader in the United States, announced plans for a great March on Washington. People from all over the country would go to Washington to demand fair employment rules, made and enforced by the federal government. A meeting like this would show how strongly Negroes and others felt about being denied the jobs for which they were trained. President Franklin D. Roosevelt asked Randolph and other leaders of the planned event to come to Washington to speak to him. The result was an order from the President to all defense industries—Executive Order 8802. It promised an end to discrimination against black workers in businesses doing defense work for the government. The March on Washington was called off.

Later that year the United States entered World War II. The government had not really enforced its new order. But there was such a need for workers during the war that many defense companies did hire minority-group workers. When the war ended, discrimination because of race, color, creed and national origin appeared again all over the country.

A First Fair Employment Law. In 1945 New York became the first state in the nation to pass a law to end discrimination in

A. Philip Randolph planned a March on Washington to demand fair employment for all Americans. How could such a march have helped win more jobs?

Blacks and whites eat together at an integrated lunch counter. Federal and state laws now bar discrimination in places of public accommodation.

employment. The law made rules that every employer in the state was to obey:

— No employer could refuse to hire any person because of race, creed, color or national origin.
— No employer could fire any person for any of these reasons.
— No labor union could keep out any person for any of these reasons.
— No labor union could make a person leave the union for any of these reasons.
— A state commission would hear any complaints of discrimination. It could then order the practice stopped. Its rulings could be reviewed by a court.

Thirty-four states and the District of Columbia have passed laws to prevent discrimination in employment. Do such laws bring about fair employment? Only when they are really enforced. In too many states government leaders have been unwilling or unable to make the laws work.

The Slow Path to Equal Treatment. The weakening of all types of discrimination has been slow. Many states have laws similar to New York's. Laws have also been passed to prevent discrimination in housing—one of them a federal law in 1968. We have laws in many states to prevent discrimination in places of public accommodation—that is, places that sell services to any people who want them. This means hotels, restaurants, movie houses, bowling alleys, stores, ice cream parlors and all other places that admit the public. Yet we know that discrimination continues even where such laws have been passed. Many businesses find ways to refuse service to members of minority groups. In certain neighborhoods blacks, Jews, Puerto Ricans and others find they cannot rent or buy housing. Some employers still do not hire people because of race or color. Some labor unions—like those in the building trades (plumbers, electricians and so on)—admit few black workers.

How can discrimination continue when there are laws against it? There are many reasons. State and local laws have not been enforced as well as they could have been. The same laws that try to end discrimination also provide protection for a person accused of discrimination. Suppose a member of a minority group needs a house. He tries to buy one but meets open discrimination. He goes to his state commission for help. Months and even years may pass while the commission studies the matter and tries to get the person accused of discrimination to change his ways. Meanwhile the person who began the case will have found another place to live. If he meets discrimination again, he remembers that he really was not helped by the commission the first time. He may not go back to it. Perhaps the commissions are right in trying to get people to change through quiet discussions. But this takes time. Ending discrimination is a slow, difficult job.

Meanwhile, people who have been guilty of discrimination believe in their prejudices and hold onto them. Often groups of such people are powerful enough to keep their state from acting against discrimination—even when there is a law against it. Businessmen may say that the state is telling them how to run their businesses. Labor unions may claim that there is not enough work for all. They may fight efforts to add new members. Politicians may say that they favor laws against discrimination. This helps them get votes. But most men who run for office need the money contributed by businessmen to help them get elected. They then owe favors to these men. One favor that many politicians have granted is to enforce laws against discrimination weakly.

Change has come slowly. The struggle for equal treatment goes on. Equal rights have become part of state laws. But until they are truly enforced, until they have become part of the thinking of all people, Americans of all races, colors, creeds and national origins will not be treated equally.

I. WHAT ARE THE FACTS?

Write the letter of the choice that best completes each statement.

1. Dorothy Brown was not hired because she (a) had no experience, (b) did not want to teach Negro children, (c) was a Negro.

2. Fair employment problems are found (a) only in big cities, (b) only where there are many members of minority groups, (c) all over the country.

3. The National Urban League tries to assist (a) all workers, (b) all members of minority groups, (c) black workers.

4. The first state to pass a fair employment law was (a) New York, (b) Virginia, (c) Ohio.

5. The work of A. Philip Randolph led to (a) Executive Order 8802, (b) the camping of thousands of people on the White House lawn, (c) an end to discrimination in hiring.

II. WHAT DO THEY MEAN?

Explain the meaning of each of these words or phrases.

1. fair employment

2. creed

3. national origin

4. 1941 March on Washington

5. law enforcement

III. WHY IS IT IMPORTANT?

Answer each question in a short paragraph.

1. Why is it important to other people when a woman like Dorothy Brown gains the right to teach in the public schools of one small town?

2. Suppose the members of one minority group are able to end job discrimination against them. Why would or wouldn't this be important to other minority groups?

IV. THINKING IT THROUGH!

Discuss.

1. Why is it right or wrong for employers to hire people because of their race, creed, color or national origin?

2. Many companies have hired only white workers. Suppose one of these companies decided to hire only black workers. What might a state Fair Employment Commission then do? Why?

3. Why haven't fair employment laws ended job discrimination?

4. What is prejudice? What makes some people prejudiced against other people? Do you think you yourself should work to break down prejudice? Why? What could you as a student do if you believed there was prejudice in your school or community?

5. What difference does it make to you when your teacher is of a different race, creed, color or national origin? Why do you think it makes a difference to many children of minority groups?

Can the Government End Discrimination in the Armed Forces?

2 The people of France have long believed that all French citizens are equal. In 1918 the United States Army was in France, fighting in the First World War. More than 100,000 of the American soldiers were black. All of them were in segregated units. Most of these units were commanded by white officers. The Negro units were attached to the French army and fought under French command. Soon black American soldiers were mixing with white French soldiers. They were also meeting and being accepted by the French people. Thousands were honored with medals by the French government.

A segregated unit of black soldiers during World War I.

White Southerners held the highest posts in the American army. They objected to so much freedom and so many honors for American Negroes. They were able to get the heads of the French army to send a *directive*, or set of orders, to the French officers. This *French Directive* meant an end to the fair and equal treatment the French had been giving black soldiers.

In What Ways Have the Armed Forces Been Segregated?

When Did This Segregation Begin to Weaken?

How Did President Truman Weaken Segregation in the Armed Forces?

The French Directive. Black soldiers and sailors have been important in every war fought by the United States. In World War I Negroes were a key part of the armed forces. They were tightly controlled by Jim Crow rules. No black man could serve in the Marines. No black man could become a fighting sailor; the Navy made him a cook or some other kind of worker. All black men in the Army were in segregated units. The Army tried to use them as laborers whenever possible.

The French had never treated their black citizens in such ways. American Negro soldiers fighting under French command in 1918 were used like any other fighting men. Their bravery helped the French win important battles. The French began to treat them as friends. But then came the French Directive. This is what it said:

— All white Americans believe Negroes should not be treated as well as whites.
— White Americans do not want soldiers, officers or other Frenchmen to be friendly to Negro soldiers. These black soldiers might then expect equality when they return to the United States.
— White Americans have little to do with black Americans except in business or when black people are their servants.
— Negro soldiers cannot be trusted; they might attack French women or commit other crimes.
— For such reasons, French officers may not eat with blacks. They are not to shake hands with them in public. They are

not to spend time with them except as part of the work of the army.
— It is also important that French officers stop praising black soldiers when white Americans are present.

Such advice from the leaders of the American armed forces to the French was not surprising. Woodrow Wilson was then President. In his view, segregation was a benefit to Negroes. The Presidents who followed Wilson also accepted segregation in the armed forces. It continued during World War II just as it had in all earlier wars.

Truman and the Armed Forces. Except for a few battles in which every soldier or sailor had to join in defending against some enemy attack, black soldiers remained segregated during World War II. Only a few changes were made. A small number of Negro officers were trained and appointed for the first time. A small group of black pilots saw action. One black officer, Benjamin O. Davis, Sr., became the first Negro general in American history. But segregation in the armed forces continued even after the end of World War II. It was not until 1948 that President Harry S. Truman took the first real steps to weaken it.

President Truman had been an officer during World War I. He later reported that he had been disturbed by the way black soldiers were treated in France. Much of the change in the way minority-group Americans have lived in the United States since 1945 begins with the efforts of Harry S. Truman.

President Truman made a report to the nation in 1947. It told of the great damage done to the United States and its people by the denial of equal rights to the members of minority groups. It reminded the country that white officers, soldiers and sailors had seen Negroes treated badly in the armed services. As a result they "were given reason to look down on their fellow citizens." This, President Truman said, was wrong. It had to be changed. It was time to bring equal rights to the armed forces.

Truman was a candidate for President in 1948. But his party, the Democrats, seemed ready to fall apart. One group in the North, led by Hubert H. Humphrey (later a Senator, Vice-President and candidate for President), wanted the party to fight against discrimination and segregation. The Southern

Benjamin O. Davis became the first Negro general in the United States. Why was this an important step toward equality in the armed forces?

Many of the changes toward equal treatment for all began with President Harry S Truman.

leaders of the Democratic Party said that they would not permit civil rights to become an important goal of their party.

The Democrats accepted the civil rights path. The Southern Democrats walked out of the party. The voters of the country, for the first time, could decide on a candidate because of his position on civil rights.

Keeping the Promise. Black and white voters who believed in equal rights for all voted for Harry S. Truman. He won the election of 1948. But he found that Southern Democrats remained the heads of most of the important committees that decide what laws are to be discussed by Congress. What was the President to do? He had promised action to try to bring equality to American life. Yet he knew Congress could hold back the rights of minorities by refusing to pass the laws he wanted. He had to find some other way to keep the promise his party had made.

The President of the United States is the commander-in-chief of the country's armed forces. He can make the rules under which these forces are run. Congress has little power here. This was the change President Truman could bring to the nation! In 1949 he gave his orders to the commanders of each of the armed services:

— They were to assign soldiers and sailors to work according to their ability, not because of their race.
— They were to give each person the same right to be promoted or to hold any special job in the armed services.
— Blacks and whites were to be placed in the same units. All segregated units were to be changed to integrated units.
— These changes were to be made as quickly as possible.

The changes had been ordered, but they did not come quickly. The armed services had thousands of officers from the South. Many of them would not accept an end to segregation. They failed to carry out the new orders. Some resigned rather than carry them out. Some towns in the South objected to equal treatment for soldiers stationed in nearby camps. The career soldiers stationed in army camps were slow to change their way of treating members of minority groups.

General Dwight D. Eisenhower became President in 1953.

How would he feel about changing the old segregated army he had known? The country was weary after three years of war

A former general, President Eisenhower continued to integrate the armed services.

in Korea; the spirit of the armed forces was very low. Negroes had begun to volunteer in large numbers. The armed services needed them. President Eisenhower continued the steps President Truman had begun. In 1954 he reported that the integration orders had been carried out in all of the services.

Minority-group Americans knew this was not true. However, they had to agree that much had been done. The treatment of minority groups in the armed forces had changed. But there were still large numbers of officers who did not believe in equality. There were still too many Army, Marine and Air Force bases located in the South, where black Americans have never known equal treatment. And there were still very few officers from minority groups.

An End to Discrimination? The armed forces have been called the mirror of the country. This means that all soldiers will not achieve equal treatment until all people outside of the armed forces also achieve it. Still, the rules have been made, ready to be carried out. Any President who really wants to do so can now push ahead to end discrimination in the armed forces.

I. WHAT ARE THE FACTS?

Answer each question in a sentence.

1. Why hadn't France passed Jim Crow laws before 1918?

2. From what part of the country did most high-ranking Army officers come in 1918?

3. Who was the first Negro general in United States history?

4. How did Southerners control Congress, even though they were a minority?

5. In what year did President Truman order the integration of the armed services?

II. EXPLAINING WHY.

The five statements in the second group below are the reasons for the truth of the first five statements. Match each statement with its reason.

STATEMENTS

1. In 1918 officers of the United States Army arranged for the French Directive.

2. President Wilson did not try to end segregation in the armed services.

3. In World War II white men in the armed forces had reason to look down on black servicemen.

4. Most black voters supported Truman in 1948.

5. The armed services ended segregation slowly after the President had issued his new orders.

REASONS

a. They saw black soldiers receiving poor treatment only because of their color.
b. Leading officers still believed in a Jim Crow army, even after 1949.
c. They believed Truman would act to bring greater civil rights to all Americans.
d. He thought segregation was a benefit to Negroes.
e. They did not want the French to treat black soldiers as equals.

III. THINKING IT THROUGH!

Discuss.

1. Why do you think black soldiers have fought so well in the wars

of the United States, even when their lives in the armed services were segregated?

2. For what reasons do you think President Truman decided to order an end to segregation in the armed services?

IV. A CLASS RESEARCH PROJECT.

Think of men you know who have served in the armed services. Try to find men who have served in World War II, the Korean War (1950–1953) and the war in Vietnam. Ask each to answer these questions: How much segregation did you find when you were in the armed services? What forms did it take? Report your findings to the class. With this information, the class can discuss the question: What progress has been made to end segregation in the armed forces?

How Can Laws Help
Minorities Gain Better Housing?

3 St. Louis is a crowded city. For years, it has not had enough homes for all its people. Many of the buildings are old and run down. Whole neighborhoods have become slums. St. Louis County, however, is large and important. As St. Louis has grown, new towns and developments have been built just outside the city. One of the newest of these is the giant Paddock Woods. The Alfred Mayer Company, builder and owner of Paddock Woods, has sold thousands of lots.

In 1965 Joseph Lee Jones came to see Paddock Woods. He and his family liked it. They decided to buy a lot and order one of the new-style homes. But the Mayer Company was not selling land to Negroes, and Mr. Jones was black.

Mr. Jones sued to get for himself and members of all minority groups the clear right to live wherever they wished. Three years later his case reached the United States Supreme Court.

Joseph Lee Jones and his family decided to buy a home in Paddock Woods.

350

In What Ways Have People Discriminated Against Minority Groups in Housing?

How Was Such Discrimination Weakened by the Courts?

What Have the Laws Done to End Discrimination in Housing?

The Story of Housing Discrimination. American cities began to grow rapidly after the Civil War. There is always a shortage of housing when a city grows quickly. New neighborhoods take time to build. In the forty years after the Civil War, city transportation was not good enough for people to travel far to work. So people crowded together in the old neighborhoods near their places of work.

Many new groups came to the growing cities. They came from Europe and Asia, from South America and Mexico. People left American farms to live and work in the cities. The shortage of homes grew worse. But jobs were waiting in the cities, and more people poured in. One neighborhood after another became crowded. Buildings grew old and were not rebuilt. Today's big-city slums developed.

Since housing cost less in the slums, the poorest people moved in. Those who came from the same country, spoke the same language or had the same religion often wanted to live together. Large cities soon had German, Irish, Italian and Jewish neighborhoods. Most landlords preferred to rent to these white groups. In every city black people could rent homes in only a few neighborhoods. These became black neighborhoods. In Europe Jews had been forced by law to live together in walled parts of cities called *ghettos*. People in the United States began to speak of Irish ghettos, Jewish ghettos, Italian ghettos and Negro ghettos.

Each city had its minority-group citizens. Most landlords were people who had lived in the cities for a long time. They were chiefly white and Protestant. Some of them were very prejudiced against any group but their own. But as the number of minority-group citizens grew larger, prejudices began to weaken. Most white groups could in time move out of the slums.

Prejudice against some groups did not weaken. Chinese, Japanese, Mexicans, Filipinos, Puerto Ricans, Indians and especially Negroes still could rent only in neighborhoods where their people already lived. White landowners (many of them church groups or colleges) believed that their property would be worth less if "colored" people lived there. Some white landlords were racists. They did not want to deal with "colored" tenants. They sometimes feared their white tenants would move away if minority groups moved in.

Step One—State and Local Laws. Jim Crow laws became part of life in every Southern state after the Civil War. Large numbers of freedmen left the land where they had been slaves. Many moved to towns or cities. Laws were soon passed stating where they could live. This happened even though Congress had passed a law in 1866 that said:

> All citizens of the United States shall have the same right in every State and Territory, as is enjoyed by white citizens thereof to inherit, purchase, lease, sell, hold, and convey real and personal property.

Little was done to enforce this law after Reconstruction ended in 1877. *Plessy v. Ferguson* (separate but equal) came in 1896. The Supreme Court seemed to approve Jim Crow laws. State after state in the South passed laws to keep black citizens from living in the same neighborhoods as whites. By 1915 every large city in the South had its "black" section. These were ghettos, as tightly ruled as the ones Jews had known in Europe.

The N.A.A.C.P. had been organized in 1910. One of its first cases—*Buchanan v. Warley*—was an attack on a housing law. Louisville, Kentucky, had a law to keep Negroes in separate blocks and neighborhoods. The law said its goal was ". . . to prevent conflict and ill-feeling between the white and colored races . . . and to preserve the public peace and general welfare by . . . requiring . . . the use of separate blocks for . . . white and colored people. . . ." There could be no change. Where most homes were occupied by black people, no white person could move into a block. Where most people on a block were white, no black person could move in. In 1915 Moorfield Storey, the famous Boston lawyer and N.A.A.C.P. president, took the case and won it! The Court made a clear decision in 1917:

—Each citizen has a right to buy or sell property. Laws like the one in Louisville deny this right.

—Louisville says that this law is a proper use of its police power—the power to act to keep peace and to protect its citizens.

—No city or state can take away any right guaranteed by the Constitution of the United States. Police power does not give any city the right to deny a right in the Constitution. "The Fourteenth Amendment protects life, liberty, and property from invasion by the States without due process of law. . . . Property . . . includes the right to acquire, use, and [sell] it."

—The Fourteenth Amendment ". . . denied to any State the power to withhold from (the colored race) the equal protection of the laws. . . . What is this but declaring that the law in the United States shall be the same for the black as for the white . . . ?"

—No city or state can solve its problems by denying any citizen

In 1917 the Supreme Court said no law could force people to live in segregated housing. Then why do ghetto slums such as this still exist?

353

his Constitutional rights. The Louisville law is not permitted by the Constitution.

This was an important first step. State and local laws could no longer force minority groups to live in ghettos. Arizona and New Mexico could no longer pass laws segregating Mexican-Americans and Indians. California could not keep its Chinese, Japanese, Filipino and Mexican citizens separate. Southern governments could no longer keep black citizens in black neighborhoods. At least such things could no longer be done by law.

Step Two—Private Agreements. This did not mean that all neighborhoods suddenly were opened to all people. The same white groups who had wanted the housing discrimination laws found a new way to keep minority groups out of certain neighborhoods. The new way became known as the "restrictive covenant."

A *covenant* is an agreement. Something is *restricted* when it is not allowed. A *restrictive covenant* is an agreement that does not allow something to be done. Every neighborhood in the United States that wanted to keep minorities out began to make such agreements after 1917. Property owners put them in their deeds—the legal papers that proved they owned their homes or land. For the next thirty years, state courts agreed that property owners had the right to make these agreements. They even helped enforce them. Suppose that a group of white Protestants live in a certain neighborhood. They want only white Protestants to live there. They agree that none of them will ever sell his property to anyone who is not a white Protestant. Most of the agreements simply said "white Christian" or listed those groups to whom property could not be sold. If a house was sold, the new owner had to accept the agreement as part of his contract to buy the house. He had to obey it if he later sold the property. Restrictive covenants meant that members of minority groups who wanted to leave the city slums just could not find any other place to live.

N.A.A.C.P. lawyers tried many times to have state courts rule that such agreements denied the right of all Americans to buy and sell property. They failed. Finally in 1945 they brought two cases to the Supreme Court. Three years later the Court made its decision in the case of *Shelley v. Kraemer*. It meant an end to restrictive covenants! Thurgood Marshall of the N.A.A.C.P. presented the case. It was so important that many other civil rights groups also offered opinions to the Supreme Court. Among them were the American Federation of Labor, the American Jewish Congress, the American Indian Citizens League, the American Civil Liberties Union and several groups of churches.

The Shelley family lived in St. Louis, Missouri. Mr. Shelley contracted to buy a home on Labadie Avenue and was ready to move in. Other property owners on the block went to court to keep him out. They had made a restrictive covenant in 1911. It stated that the property could be sold only to a white person. The Shelleys were black. The state court agreed that the Shelleys could not buy the home they wanted.

The second case came from Detroit, Michigan. Another Negro family, the Sipeses, bought a home, moved in and were then ordered to move out. A restrictive covenant made in 1934 said this property could be used or occupied only by a white person.

The Supreme Court decided the two cases together. It ruled that restrictive covenants were not permitted by the Fourteenth Amendment!

— The Court had ruled in 1917 that no state could deny any citizen the right to own or sell property.
— Restrictive covenants could keep minority groups out of a neighborhood only if state courts enforced them. This meant that the power of the state was being used to deny citizens the right to own or sell property.
— A State cannot use its power to deny any right guaranteed by the Constitution.
— People can make restrictive covenants if they wish, but no court has the power to enforce them.

Who was helped by the Shelley decision? It seemed that now all members of minority groups could live where they pleased. Some did begin to move out of the ghettos and slums. But this did not mean an end to ghettos. Most members of minority groups were still poor. They could not afford to live in the newer or better neighborhoods. Millions of black and Puerto Rican people moved into the Northern cities after 1940. Most of them moved into the slums; these areas grew larger.

Those who could afford to looked for better housing. They found a new problem. Supreme Court decisions protected them against state and local laws and restrictive covenants that segregated neighborhoods. But they still found that they could **not** always buy the homes they wanted. A house might be for sale. They might have the money needed to buy it. Yet they often found that the owner or real estate company just would not sell it to a member of a minority group. A new series of court cases had to be won before this new wall could be torn down.

Step Three—Private Refusals. White Christian Americans have been most responsible for segregated housing. Some have wanted to live only among white Christians. Some have said that the value of their property would fall if minority groups moved into their neighborhoods. They have pointed out that many white people are so prejudiced that they would sell their homes cheaply and move away rather than live next to a person from a minority group. Some white people fear that minority-group families will bring special problems. They fear white and black children will grow up together and marry. They blame Negroes for crime and noise in their neighborhoods. Fears such as these grow when the people who hold them are already prejudiced.

Real estate companies buy and sell property for homeowners. Some of the larger companies build homes and even whole new neighborhoods. Some of them try to make money from prejudice. They may work together secretly to keep property values high in a neighborhood. They refuse to sell property to anyone who is not "white and Christian." The prejudiced people who live in the area, or who move into it, are willing to pay more to live in a "white and Christian" neighborhood.

Other real estate companies have made money through "blockbusting." They sell one or two homes in a block to members of a minority group. They then spread stories that frighten "white Christian" families. The neighborhood, they say, is going to become Negro, or Jewish or Puerto Rican. The value of property is going to fall quickly. Sell now, while you can still get a good price. If a homeowner is already prejudiced, he may easily be frightened into moving away. The real estate companies buy up whole blocks this way. They then sell or rent the homes at high prices to members of minority groups who want to escape from the ghettos. Once one block in a neighborhood has been "busted," the companies move on to other blocks. They pay less and less for the homes people sell them. Then they make large profits when they sell or rent these houses.

It is the real estate companies and home builders who have often kept neighborhoods "restricted." The story of Joseph Lee Jones in Paddock Woods, St. Louis County, is important to every American. It led to the end of the power of real estate companies and property owners to decide to sell only to one group of people. The case of *Jones v. Alfred H. Mayer Co.* was decided by the United States Supreme Court in June, 1968.

This New Jersey woman and her husband are about to become the only black family in a formerly all-white neighborhood. What kind of treatment do you think they will receive from their new neighbors?

— Congress passed a law in 1866 giving all citizens equal right to rent, buy or sell property.
— The Mayer Company refused to sell Joseph Lee Jones a lot and home only because he was a Negro.
— Any Negro citizen who is denied the right to rent or buy a home is being denied a right guaranteed by the Constitution and laws of the United States.
— Private persons cannot act in ways that deny equal treatment to any citizens wishing to rent or buy property.

The Supreme Court had spoken. Mr. Jones could buy the home he wanted, in the community he had chosen. Since this 1968 decision, no real estate company or property owner can refuse to rent or sell a home or apartment just because the person who wants it is a member of a minority group.

Step Four—A Fair Housing Law. Congress passed a fair housing law only a few days before the Supreme Court announced its decision in the Jones case. This law listed a number of actions that would now be crimes. People guilty of these actions could face a year in jail, a fine of $1,000 or both.

> To refuse to sell or rent . . . a dwelling to any person because of race, color, religion, or national origin.
>
> To discriminate against any person in . . . the sale or rental of a dwelling, or in the provision of services [in that dwelling], because of race, color, religion, or national origin.
>
> To make, print, or publish . . . any notice, statement, or advertisement, with respect to the sale or rental of a dwelling, that indicates any preference, limitation, or discrimination based on race, color, religion, or national origin. . . .
>
> To represent to any person because of race, color, religion, or national origin that any dwelling is not available for inspection, sale, or rental when such dwelling is in fact available.
>
> For profit, to [try to get] any person to sell or rent any dwelling by [talking about] the entry . . . into the neighborhood of a person or persons of a particular race, color, religion, or national origin.

Many banks had refused to lend money to members of minority groups who wished to buy homes. Another part of the Fair Housing Law made it unlawful for any bank to do this only because of race, color, religion or national origin. It also became unlawful for any real estate company to refuse to look for or sell a home for any person because of his race, color, religion or national origin.

Suppose that a person believes he has been refused an apartment or house because of his race, color, religion or national origin. He can write to the Secretary of Housing and Urban Development, a member of the President's Cabinet in Washington, D.C. The law states that the Secretary must then investigate the complaint. He must try to get the discrimination ended. If he cannot, he must ask the Attorney General, the government's chief lawyer, to take the matter into a federal court. It can *order* an end to the discrimination. Any person who then disobeys this order is guilty of contempt of court. He can be fined or jailed.

The Fair Housing Law is still new. Many years may have to pass before it ends housing discrimination in the United States. We can expect the greatest success in those states that already have state laws against discrimination.

What will happen in the South? Housing segregation has remained strong there. Negroes, Indians and Mexican-Americans have not been allowed to live in "white" neighborhoods. Even where they know they have a right to do so, fear has kept them away. White mobs and groups such as the KKK have wrecked homes and shot into them whenever a "non-white" person has moved into a "white" neighborhood. Much the same has happened in many neighborhoods in the North when a minority-group family has been the first to move into a neighborhood.

Will Fair Housing Be Delayed? More than 100 years have passed since Congress passed the law giving all citizens equal rights to buy, sell, rent or own property. We are just beginning to make certain that this law is carried out! The fight for fair housing has been long and hard. State and local laws to segregate housing were not ended until 1917. Private restrictive covenants lasted until 1948. They are still a problem in some towns. Until 1968 private refusals to rent or sell property could keep any person out of a desired home or neighborhood. Today no citizen can be refused a home because of his race, color, religion or national origin. How strongly will the government of the United States enforce its Fair Housing Law? The answer to this question will decide how long it takes before housing is open equally to all Americans.

I. WHAT ARE THE FACTS?

Write the letter of the choice that best completes each statement.

1. Paddock Woods is near (a) Detroit, (b) St. Louis, (c) New Orleans.

2. The case begun by Joseph Lee Jones gave all Americans the right to (a) sell their property to anyone they pleased, (b) buy property wherever they pleased, (c) make any agreement they pleased about selling or not selling their property.

3. Irish, Italians, Jews and Southern Negroes came to the North and settled chiefly in (a) small towns, (b) farming areas, (c) large cities.

4. Today the right to buy, sell or rent property is given by law to (a) white citizens only, (b) all citizens, (c) black citizens only.

5. Restrictive covenants tried to (a) keep certain groups out of a neighborhood, (b) open a neighborhood to all, (c) get some people to move out of a neighborhood.

6. The chief N.A.A.C.P. lawyer in the *Shelley v. Kraemer* case was (a) Thurgood Marshall, (b) Moorfield Storey, (c) Earl Warren.

7. The right to rent or buy a home is now guaranteed by (a) the Supreme Court, (b) a federal law, (c) all landlords.

8. The Fair Housing Law makes it a crime to (a) buy property in a restricted neighborhood, (b) engage in "blockbusting" for a profit, (c) refuse to sell or rent to a person who cannot pay a month's rent in advance.

9. If you believe you have been discriminated against in buying or renting a home, you should complain to (a) your mayor, (b) your district attorney, (c) the Secretary of Housing and Urban Development.

10. Open housing means that (a) any person should be able to live anywhere, (b) buildings should be open to visitors of any race, color, religion or national origin, (c) the courts should be open to all law suits about any housing problem.

II. THINKING IT THROUGH!

Discuss.

1. Why do members of a minority group tend to move into the neighborhood in which other members of that group already live? How does this cause ghettos to develop? Should steps be taken by city governments to break up these ghettos? Why or why not?

2. Present the arguments for and against permitting the people of a neighborhood to have the right to control the services provided that neighborhood by the city, such as education, hospitals, police, sanitation, fire departments.

3. Why have so many neighborhoods remained restricted, even though court decisions and the Fair Housing Law have ordered open housing?

4. What is "blockbusting"? Why has it been made a crime?

III. A SUMMARY ACTIVITY.

How have these three kinds of housing discrimination been weakened during the past 100 years?

a) State and local laws forced neighborhoods to be segregated.
b) Restrictive covenants kept many neighborhoods "all white."
c) Real estate companies often refused to rent or sell housing to members of minority groups.

How Are Our Civil Liberties Growing?

4 A person charged with a crime has certain rights that are set by laws, the Constitution and Supreme Court decisions. The story of a crime in Phoenix, Arizona, brought this fact to world attention. A woman had been attacked during a robbery. The police arrested a young Mexican-American named Ernesto Miranda. They held him under arrest, and questioned him for days. Finally he signed a confession. It became the most important evidence against him at his trial. He was found guilty.

Ernesto Miranda (right) talks with his lawyer after the Supreme Court decided he had been denied civil liberties by the police.

Some people believed that Ernesto Miranda had been denied important rights. They appealed his conviction. The case was decided by the Supreme Court in 1966. Chief Justice Warren and a majority of the Court found that Miranda had been denied his rights as a citizen—those rights we call civil liberties:

—He had been arrested on suspicion.
—He was questioned for days in a room in which he was cut off from the outside world.
—He was not told that he did not have to answer ques-

tions, that it was his right to have a lawyer present, that any statement he made could be used against him.

— He finally broke down under questioning, signed a confession and was convicted because of it.

Miranda was freed. He could not be convicted of a crime if he had been denied the rights promised by the Constitution.

How Do Americans Secure the Rights Promised by the Constitution?
Why Haven't All These Rights Always Been Secure for All?
How Have New Laws Begun to Make the Promises Come True?

Gaining Civil Liberties. Minority-group Americans have had to wage a long fight to gain a goal that their country has promised all of its citizens—equal treatment under the laws. Black Americans, our largest minority, have fought this struggle hardest of all. Each time they have won a small victory, all other Americans have gained with them. All live under the same laws; all share in any growth of human rights.

Racism has been sharp, bitter and lasting. Somehow, minority Americans have learned to depend on the law. Most of the gains they have made in their lasting drive for equality have come because laws and their enforcement have changed. The goal remains the fair treatment promised all Americans by their country's Constitution. The Constitution explains what "fair treatment" means. It lists the rights no government may deny. These rights guaranteed to all citizens are called *civil liberties.* They are stated in nine Amendments, and further explained by dozens of Supreme Court decisions.

People today have become keenly aware of their promised civil liberties. The years 1883 to 1954 saw a great national silence about the rights of the country's minorities. Little was done to correct injustices. These were the years of Jim Crow. "Non-white" minorities knew they were being denied many of their rights. The white majority knew these rights were being denied. The great change began with the Supreme Court decisions of the 1950's. The courts began to act to protect the rights of all Americans. Congress began to pass the laws needed to secure the rights promised by the Constitution.

Court decisions and new laws have been the road to fair and equal treatment for all. Let us look at four of the problems Americans have faced. How have minority-group Americans gained the right to vote? How have Jim Crow laws and customs been weakened? How have all Americans gained more secure rights in the courts? What happens when a state or community denies civil liberties to some of its people?

1. The Right to Vote. Two Amendments to the Constitution give citizens equal rights to vote. The Fifteenth Amendment, adopted in 1870, states that:

> The right of citizens of the United States to vote shall not be denied or abridged by the United States or by any state on account of race, color or previous condition of servitude.

The Nineteenth Amendment, adopted in 1920, gave women the right to vote.

> The right of citizens of the United States to vote shall not be denied or abridged by the United States or by any State on account of sex.

Black Americans did vote during Reconstruction. They could no longer do so after the Supreme Court ended the civil rights laws in 1883. Jim Crow laws were passed in every state of the South. White supremacy became the way of life in much of the country.

Congress finally passed its first civil rights law since Reconstruction in 1957, under President Eisenhower. It set up a United States Commission on Civil Rights. This group had the task of studying cases in which people were denied equal protection of the laws. The government could then begin a court case against the person or persons who had denied someone the right to vote. The Commission gained a little more power from a second civil rights law in 1960. By 1960 it had begun more than thirty cases to protect the right of black citizens to vote in five Southern states.

Still, this was a slow way to secure the right to vote for millions of Americans. Literacy tests—tests to find out if a person can read, write and understand the laws—were still used to keep

President Johnson hands a pen to Martin Luther King, Jr., after signing the 1964 Civil Rights Act. How could the law make it harder for Southern officials to keep black people from voting?

blacks, Indians and Mexican-Americans off the lists of voters. Racist white officials gave these tests; they failed most black people and even some whites. By 1960 only three of every ten black citizens of voting age in the South were voters. In Alabama it was only one in seven; in Mississippi it was one in twelve.

President Lyndon B. Johnson made real efforts to end such denial. His greatest success came in 1964. In that year Congress finally passed a strong Civil Rights Act. The law made it harder for white election officials in the South to keep black people from voting. All literacy tests and any other tests for voters had to be written. The same test had to be used for black and white

Federal officials registered Negroes in Birmingham, Alabama, in 1966 after the government decided local officials had not done enough to aid would-be black voters.

365

A member of the Georgia state legislature, Julian Bond has become well known nationally for his demands for black equality.

In 1969 Charles Evers became the first black man to be elected mayor of a Southern town. How do you think he was able to be elected?

voters. Any man or woman who had finished the sixth grade did not have to take a test. Indians and Mexican-Americans would also benefit from this law.

The law would mean nothing unless it was enforced. A Voting Rights Act was added in 1965. Federal examiners could go to any town or county. If an examiner found that a person had the right to vote under the new law, then that person's name had to be placed on the list of voters. Examiners went into every part of the South. They brought a quick change. By the end of 1965 the number of black citizens voting in the South had doubled! The number of black voters has grown steadily since then. Except for some small towns where fear still keeps Negroes from demanding their rights, black Americans can now vote all over the South.

One change brings other changes. Before 1965 there were only a handful of black officeholders in Southern state or local governments. By 1970 the country was reading about more than 300 Southern Negroes who held public office. Among these were Julian Bond and Grace Hamilton in the Georgia state legislature; Charles Evers, mayor of Fayette, Mississippi; Maynard Jackson, vice-mayor of Atlanta, Georgia; Barbara Jordan in the Texas State Senate; Walter Washington, who was appointed mayor of Washington by Presidents Johnson and Nixon.

2. The Weakening of Jim Crow. The Fourteenth Amendment includes these promises:

> . . . No State shall make or enforce any law which shall abridge the privileges or immunities of citizens of the United States; nor shall any State deprive any person of life, liberty, or property, without due process of law; nor deny to any person within its jurisdiction the equal protection of the laws.

The Civil Rights Act of 1964 ordered an end to discrimination in most public places against any person because of his race, color, religion or national origin. This meant that any person could enter and be treated equally in a hotel, motel, restaurant or theater. It meant an end to "White Only" waiting rooms and railway cars. It meant that black and white Americans could expect equal treatment in all public parks, swimming pools, beaches and stadiums.

The changes ordered by the Civil Rights Act have been made

in most parts of the South. Some white people have refused to accept them. Once the changes ordered by this law have been enforced all over the country, the Jim Crow way of life may end. Civil rights organizations still bring hundreds of cases before the courts each year. Most of these are in the South. The rights of people often depend on such actions by citizens and their organizations.

One important part of Jim Crow has been the failure of some unions to admit black workers, or of businessmen to hire them. The 1964 law also barred discrimination against any race. This part of the law can be used when a business or a union group has 25 or more workers. Enforcement has not been easy. Few black workers had the training needed for the jobs union members held. Federal and state programs were begun to train black workers. The problem remains to get the members of the white majority to accept and work with members of minority groups.

3. Equal Treatment in the Courts. The Sixth Amendment to the Constitution spells out some of the protections each citizen should have in the courts.

> In all criminal prosecutions, the accused shall enjoy the right to a speedy and public trial, by an impartial jury of the State and district wherein the crime shall have been committed . . . and to be informed of the nature and cause of the accusation; to be confronted with the witnesses against him, to have [ways] for obtaining witnesses in his favor and to have the Assistance of Counsel for his defense.

These rights have not always been protected. Supreme Court decisions have spelled out two important protections. In the *Gideon* case, the Court ordered that no person be tried for a major crime unless he has been provided with the help of a lawyer. It also ordered lower courts to grant new trials to persons who had been jailed after trials where they did not have lawyers.

The second protection had to do with the taking of confessions. The Fifth Amendment to the Constitution protects a person from being a witness against himself. Many people have been convicted and jailed because of confessions they made without really knowing their rights. In the *Miranda* case the Court ordered a fairer way to handle confessions. Today each person charged with a crime must be told his rights before the police question him. He has a right to refuse to answer any questions and to have a lawyer as soon as he is arrested. He must be warned that any statement he makes may be used against him. All police and courts in every part of the country are expected to obey these rules. Failure to do so may mean that a conviction can be reversed if the case is appealed to a higher court.

Congress added another protection in the 1964 Civil Rights Act. Many Southern federal judges had delayed decisions in civil rights cases. They often sent them back to state or local courts to be "reviewed." This meant that a denied right would not be protected, sometimes for years. The law gave higher federal courts the power to order quicker decisions of such cases.

4. Protecting Civil Rights. The members of Congress who wrote and voted for the 1964 Civil Rights Act knew that the changes they hoped for might be slow in coming. They continued the Civil Rights Commission. People who feel their civil rights are being denied can ask this group for help. The Commission has heard hundreds of cases. Its orders have brought many peaceful changes to towns that realize there is really no way to escape obeying the country's laws.

The 1964 law also began a federal Community Relations Service. Its job has been to try to settle problems between the races before they become serious. Members of the CRS staff visit any town where such problems appear. They try to help both sides settle their differences.

Money is the final weapon in the struggle to gain equal rights for all Americans. Most communities now have many programs paid for by the federal government. Such money comes for schools, housing, clearing slums, transportation, public buildings, welfare, free food plans and many other government activities. The 1964 law ordered that none of these programs could permit discrimination because of race. If it is found, then the money can be denied.

Cities and states need more help from the national government each year. Without this help, their problems grow worse. In time this part of the Civil Rights Act may become the way finally to destroy Jim Crow and other kinds of discrimination in places that would otherwise fight on to keep it alive. Yet here again the decision must be made by the President. It is he and the officials he appoints who must declare that town or state has been guilty of discrimination.

The Constitution, the laws, the courts, citizens ready to demand their rights—these are the keys to civil liberties. Governments are made of people. People change their ways slowly. Discrimination and prejudice are the targets of our time. Their ending has come slowly; it will come faster when all citizens know their rights and are ready and able to defend them.

I. WHAT ARE THE FACTS?

Write the letter of the choice in COLUMN B that best matches each statement in COLUMN A.

Column A

1. A defendant is denied his rights. He confesses. The judge rules that his confession cannot be used against him.
2. A citizen's right to vote cannot be denied because of his race.
3. Women cannot be denied the right to vote because of their sex.
4. The United States Commission on Civil Rights helps citizens secure their rights.
5. Black and white voters must be given the same literacy test.
6. All citizens should receive equal protection of the laws.
7. The defendant in the criminal case could not be tried unless he had the help of a lawyer.
8. The federal examiner added many names to the list of voters.

Column B

a) Civil Rights Act of 1957
b) Fourteenth Amendment
c) *Miranda* Decision
d) Voting Rights Act of 1965
e) Nineteenth Amendment
f) Fifteenth Amendment
g) *Gideon* Decision
h) Civil Rights Act of 1964

II. EXPLAINING CIVIL LIBERTIES.

Explain how a civil liberty has been denied in each of these situations.

1. A young man is arrested and charged with a crime. The police

place him in a small room. They keep him there for days and question him day and night. A bright light shines in his face. He is not permitted to speak to anyone but the detectives who are questioning him. Finally he admits that he committed the crime and signs a confession.

2. A poor man is charged with a crime. He is told he can hire a lawyer to defend him. He replies that he has no money to pay a lawyer. The judge then orders him to defend himself, for he has a right to act as his own lawyer.

3. A man who lived in a Communist country in Europe becomes a citizen of the United States. He is told by a local election official that he cannot vote because he comes from a country that is an enemy of the United States.

4. The mayor of a town announces that all voters will now take the same literacy test. White voters can take it orally; black voters must write their answers.

5. A hotel refuses to admit any persons who do not agree to attend church services in the hotel.

III. THINKING IT THROUGH!

Discuss.

1. What is a literacy test? Why do you agree or disagree with the idea that all such tests for voters should be abolished?

2. How has the increase in the number of black voters in the United States led to an increase in the number of black office-holders?

3. What reasons could any state or community give for trying to deny civil liberties to some of its citizens?

4. How has the Fourteenth Amendment made possible most of the advances in civil liberties in the United States?

5. What steps do you think are still needed to strengthen the civil liberties of all Americans?

How Has Government
Acted Toward Minority Groups?

5 The Bill of Rights of our Constitution lists the chief ways in which citizens can tell their government what they want it to do. They can write, speak and publish their opinions. They can meet freely. They can petition the government to pass or change laws. Such rights are especially important to minority groups. Their problems have been most pressing—often questions of life and death.

The United States government once tried to destroy the Bill of Rights. In 1798 Congress passed the Sedition Act. Sedition is an action intended to destroy the government. The law made it a crime to "write, print, utter or publish . . . writings against the government of the United States . . . Congress or the President. . . ." A person could be fined $2,000 or be sent to jail for up to two years if found guilty of breaking this law.

Twenty-five men were arrested under the Sedition Act. Newspapers were shut down. Ten men were found guilty and sentenced. The law shocked the country. In 1800 the people voted the men who had passed it out of office. The Act died in 1801. Congress has never again passed another like it. Minority groups, like other Americans, have kept their right to ask for changes in the country's laws. Congress has not always listened to their

Newspapers were shut down under the 1798 Sedition Act when they criticized the government. Why was the act unconstitutional?

voices. Still, they have again and again made it consider their many problems.

How Have State and Local Governments Differed in Their Treatment of Minority Groups?

What Changes Have Come in the Way Congress Has Treated Minority Groups?

Our Three Governments. We live under three different kinds of government—local, state and national. A local government makes laws for a community. It can be a village, a town or township, a city or a county. A county may have several towns or cities within it. Local laws deal with the needs and problems of the small area within the community. They are made and enforced by that community. One community does not make laws for other communities. Each local government has its own police, judges and other officials. It is their duty to enforce local laws.

Laws made by state governments are enforced all over the state. These laws usually replace local laws that deal with the same subject. State governments enforce their laws through

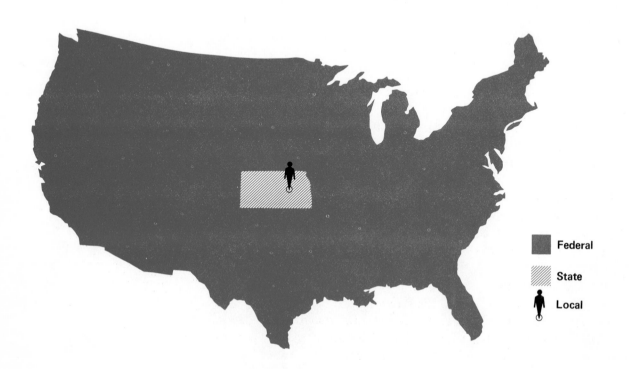

Federal

State

Local

Our Three Levels of Government

state police, judges and other officials. Each local government must also enforce state laws.

Congress passes laws for the whole country. These laws can replace state or local laws on the same subjects. A community can make its own rules about such matters as voting. A state law can force changes in the local rules. A law passed by Congress can change both the state and the local laws.

The Constitution lists the powers of Congress—the kinds of laws it may pass. These laws must be obeyed all over the country unless the Supreme Court rules in a case that a law is unconstitutional (not permitted by the Constitution).

State or local governments have again and again refused to obey certain laws passed by Congress. This has often happened when Congress has acted to improve the rights of minorities through laws affecting civil rights, voting, fair housing and other areas of discrimination. Federal courts can then order local officials to obey the laws. A federal judge has the power to order these officials to enforce the law. If they fail to do so, they can be punished by that judge. If the local or state government still refuses to obey the law, the President can use federal marshals or soldiers to make certain the law is enforced.

This happened in Little Rock, Arkansas, in 1957. It happened when mobs refused to permit black students to enter schools or colleges in other parts of the country. It has happened when soldiers were needed to protect groups of citizens, permit civil rights groups to march, keep the post offices open and end strikes. The President has used his police power to carry out laws whenever danger faced the government or any group of people in the United States. *Police power* is the power of any government to use force to enforce its laws. Such power has been used against minority groups many times in American history. It has also been used to help and protect minorities.

Discrimination by Local and State Governments. Minority groups often suffer from discrimination permitted or even planned by local or state governments. Local and state officials see to it that members of minority groups do not receive equal protection of the laws. Their actions may be approved by the majority of people in the state or community. The result is that the members of one or more minority groups are denied the rights they should receive. Schools may remain segregated. Groups such as the Ku Klux Klan may be permitted to operate freely. Due process may be denied in courts.

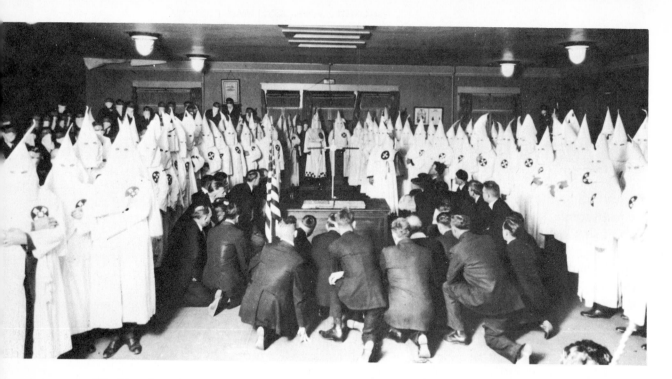

The Ku Klux Klan still operates freely in many communities. Here new members swear their loyalty in a secret ceremony. If discrimination is against the law, how can such groups remain active?

Such unfair treatment can be ended by a state government. It has the power to make local governments treat all citizens equally. Some state governments have done this; some have not. It was the governor of Arkansas who tried to keep the schools of Little Rock segregated. It was the governor of Mississippi who blocked the admission of black students to the state university. It was the governor of Alabama who insisted that segregation in all its forms would never end in that state. In some states governors and other officials work to keep discrimination against minority groups alive. In others state officials have led the struggle to end discrimination.

Minority groups know that they cannot always depend on their state governments to end unequal treatment. Some states have passed laws to end many kinds of discrimination. When these laws are enforced, members of minority groups can hope for fair treatment. But they know that a state-by-state plan to end discrimination is very slow. They have therefore turned to the national government for help.

The National Government and Minorities. The national government ended slavery at the close of the Civil War. It brought the country a short period of equal rights during Reconstruc-

374

tion. But it has done little for its minorities through most of the country's history. It was the national government that helped destroy the Indians. The national government protected slavery until the Civil War. It did not prevent the spread of Jim Crow laws after Reconstruction. It permitted the stealing of land from Mexican-Americans. It barred some minorities from entering the United States. It caused Japanese-Americans to be imprisoned during World War II. It failed to pass a law to end lynchings. State and local laws denied equal rights in many parts of the country; for years Congress did not pass laws to end such denial of rights.

There were always some men in Congress who wanted it to pass the laws that were needed to protect minorities. These men spoke out, but there were always too few of them to get the laws passed. It was not until the 1940's and 1950's that the changes finally began.

The real change in Congress came when the Supreme Court began to favor equal rights in its decisions. Minority groups began to challenge unfair laws in the courts. From 1950 on, the Court took a stand in favor of civil rights in case after case. Slowly Congress, the states and more and more communities have accepted the Court's rulings.

The Court's decision in the Brown case in 1954 led to a national drive to end Jim Crow laws and other kinds of discrimination. One part of this drive was the wider use of the Bill of Rights by minority groups. Congress at last listened to the calls for equality. It passed new laws to guarantee civil rights. It increased the number of voters through new voting laws. Housing laws attacked open discrimination. Federal officials were sent to states and communities to help enforce the laws.

Most present members of Congress have entered public life since 1945. This was the year of the first state law against discrimination. Most Americans have come to accept the need for laws to guarantee equal rights. A majority of Congress has voted for the laws that protect the rights of minorities. They are doing what the people who elected them demand. In this way the majority of Americans have made the great decision—to bring justice to the country's minorities.

Enforcing Laws for Equality. Equal rights do not come just because a law has been passed. The law must be enforced. Each community must accept it and obey it. Most Americans respect laws and obey them. Yet some communities refuse to change the ways they have treated their minorities. Sometimes whole states refuse to accept changes. This has been most true in the matter of school desegregation.

The courts then become the road to change. New cases are begun to make sure officials enforce the laws. Such cases can be very slow. Sixteen years passed between the Brown decision and the integration of most of the school systems in the South in 1970. Other changes have also been slow—in housing, job discrimination and other moves toward equality. Many more years may pass before the rights now guaranteed by the country's laws are shared equally by all Americans.

The people of the United States have become more willing to end denials of rights to the minorities. The task of enforcing the new laws remains. Will these laws really be enforced? The national government holds the greatest power. It also has the great responsibility of seeing to it that its laws are enforced. The President's power is great. He can enforce laws in many ways, from the use of the courts to the cutting off of funds to a state or community. He can use federal marshals or the armed forces. Just as important, he can show by his speeches and actions that the country really means to end the poor treatment of its minorities. In time the actions of the national government will show how equality for minority groups can become a way of life in the United States, as well as a part of the country's laws.

I. WHAT ARE THE FACTS?

Answer each question in a sentence or two.

1. How did the Sedition Act weaken the Bill of Rights?

2. How did the people of the United States force the ending of the Sedition Act?

3. What are the three levels of government in the United States?

4. How does a government enforce its laws?

5. What is the meaning of *police power*?

6. Why have minority groups turned to Congress for help in ending discrimination?

7. Why have minority groups brought equal rights cases to the United States Supreme Court?

8. How has Congress changed its position on equal rights for all?

9. Why have changes in the rights of minorities been so slow?

10. Why is the President called "the key to equality"?

II. THINKING IT THROUGH!

Discuss.

1. Some communities and states have insisted that they have the right to decide for themselves how minority groups should be treated. List the reasons they might give. Then list the answer to each.

2. What problems might the country face if the President made quick use of police power to enforce laws for equality? Why do these laws contain ways in which people affected by the laws can turn to the courts?

How Have Minorities Dealt with Government?

6 The Civil Rights Act of 1964 set up ways for black people in the South to register and vote. The officials of Selma, Alabama, refused to obey the law. They did not permit black citizens to register. Thousands of people from all over the United States came to Selma to join in a great protest. Two thousand were jailed.

Dr. Martin Luther King and other civil rights leaders then turned to the state government. They planned a march to Montgomery, the state capital. Governor

The march from Selma to Montgomery, led by Martin Luther King, Jr. How could such a march help black people win the right to vote?

Wallace ordered them to remain in Selma. State police attacked them when they tried to begin the march. President Johnson ordered the United States Army to protect the marchers. Two weeks later 20,000 people finished the march to Montgomery.

Congress passed a new Voting Rights Act in 1965. Under it, federal officials came to Selma. They added black citizens to the city's list of registered voters. The story of Selma shows how members of a minority group had to move from local to state to national government to gain a right that had long been denied to them.

What Do Minority Groups Want From Governments?
What Methods Have They Used?

Goals of Minority Groups. American minority groups have known great discrimination. They want equality, fair treatment and a better life. They ask for three things in the 1970's:

1. *Fair Law Enforcement.* Congress, the Supreme Court and many states and communities have passed laws that can improve the rights of all Americans. Minority groups know that equal protection of the laws can improve their lives. They want these laws to be enforced.

2. *A New Goal for the Nation.* Minority groups want the country to pay greater attention to the goal of improving life for all its people. Education, housing, jobs, poverty and other problems facing minorities may then be solved.

3. *An End to Discrimination.* Discrimination has lessened, but it still remains a problem. Minority groups ask for more laws against discrimination. They want equal rights to become part of all American thinking. By 1970 it was clear that this was happening. Women had added their voices to the cry for equality. They had even asked for an amendment to the Constitution to guarantee an end to any discrimination based on sex.

Women marched in Washington, D.C., in 1970 in what they called the "Women's Strike for Equality." How have women been discriminated against?

Working for Change. Minority groups have set up many self-help organizations to provide needed services. Among these are social clubs, medical plans, sports clubs, burial associations and social agencies. Such self-help activities can make life a little better. They cannot solve the larger problems of discrimination, poverty, housing, education and equal rights. Minority groups have had to seek ways to have the power of government work toward these goals for them and for all other Americans.

By the 1970's minority groups had used a number of methods to reach their goals. Not all groups work in the same ways. Yet all use one or more of these methods to bring about the changes they believe important.

1. *Gaining Positions in Government.* Every minority group wants its members to hold elected or appointed jobs in government. Such men and women can then use their positions to help add to the rights of all minorities. If members of minority groups are among those who enforce the laws

380

and work in the government, all Americans may know greater equality. Leaders of minorities want to see minority members as police and school officials. They want them to be in charge of housing and welfare offices. They would like them to be commissioners and inspectors in local and state governments. Then, the minorities believe, they will find greater fairness in their daily dealings with government.

Minority-group Americans have gained more government positions. By 1970 one-fourth of those holding jobs in Washington, D.C., were members of minority groups. The largest part of these were black Americans. The same kind of change has also come to many city and state governments.

2. *Working for Community Control.* The drive for community control may grow during the 1970's. It had its beginnings in the big-city move toward community school boards. It has been part of the War on Poverty programs. Each minority group wants to have a voice in decisions about its life. By 1970 some groups were asking for community control of police, fire departments and other services.

Minority-group Americans, especially blacks, have gained more elected positions. Left: Senator Edward Brooke of Massachusetts. Middle: Newark, New Jersey, mayor Kenneth Gibson. Right: Congresswoman Shirley Chisholm of New York City.

3. *Receiving Equal Treatment*. Minority groups have often asked that they be treated as persons, not as part of a minority. They want each man or woman to be judged as a human being, not for reasons of race, color, religion or national origin.

4. *Using Voting Power*. Minority groups have become more active in the country's political life. When the members of a group vote for one candidate, they can expect that person to help them if he is elected. Such support of a candidate has brought needed changes when an election is close. Then the votes of the minority group make a difference in who is elected. Group voting has brought real improvement in many cities where large numbers of minority-group voters live.

Black Americans made great use of their voting power in the 1960's. By 1970 there were black mayors or high officials in such cities as Cleveland, New York, Newark, Gary and Atlanta. Other minorities had long used their voting power to gain greater rights and fair treatment. Among these were the Irish, the Jews, the Italians and the Poles.

5. *Using Civil Disobedience*. Civil disobedience is the open refusal to obey a law you believe is unfair. Minority groups have used this method to improve their rights many times since the United States began. A person or group decides to disobey a law to show how unfair it is. They know they then face punishment for what they have done. They expect to receive wide public attention. They hope a court will decide that the law they broke is unconstitutional. Otherwise, they hope the majority will agree that the law is unfair and will support efforts to change it.

The story of Selma, Alabama, shows how civil disobedience can bring changes. Those who came to Selma marched in its streets even though local officials told them they could not. They were ready to be jailed. They marched to Montgomery even though Governor Wallace was ready to use force against them. By the end of their march, the whole country knew they had been unfairly treated. It also knew that the black citizens of Selma were being denied the right to vote. Congress then passed the Voting Rights Act of 1965. Civil disobedience in one city had led to a change that improved civil rights in the whole country.

Those who came to Selma acted peacefully. Their kind of civil disobedience is called *nonviolent*. It was the method used by Dr. Martin Luther King. It is the method still used by most minority groups.

6. *Using Violence.* Sometimes members of a minority group believe peaceful protest will not bring the changes they wish. They then turn to violent civil disobedience. They occupy a building, close a street, begin a riot, use guns or use bombs. Those who act in such ways know that the majority of Americans fear the use of violence. Those who are using violence hope that it will make the rest of the people agree to some demanded change.

Such use of violence has grown greatly since 1965. Minority-group organizations such as the Black Panthers say that the minorities and the rest of the country are at war. This war, they say, must be fought with any and all weapons. The quick use of violence has become a national problem.

With the growth of organizations such as the Black Panthers, the use of violence has increased. How do you feel about this move toward violence as a way to gain needed changes?

Young Lords occupied this East Harlem church to demand better treatment for the Puerto Rican community. Do you think they had a right to do so?

College student groups have used it to gain their demands. Groups such as the Young Lords have occupied churches and hospitals to bring about changes in the way they are run. Mexican-Americans have shot at Anglos who tried to settle on land the Mexican-Americans claimed. Such groups point out that violence has often been used against their minority. They say their own use of violence will make the majority understand how wrongly it has treated them.

The majority has answered such use of violence in three ways. 1) It has met force with force to end violent civil disobedience. Police or soldiers have shot at those who were breaking the laws. People arrested for acts of civil disobedience were fined or jailed. 2) Sometimes the majority has given in and has made the changes demanded by those who are breaking the laws. 3) Most often the two sides have met and have come to some agreement. In these cases the demands were met in part, and the violence came to an end.

7. *Defending the Minority.* Minority groups have sometimes come under attack. Groups within the minority then take steps to defend homes, property and lives. By 1970 there were many self-defense groups among American minorities. The Deacons for Defense, a black group in the South, promised to fight back against attacks on black Americans. The Black Panthers openly gathered weapons for their promised use of force to defend black citizens. The Brown Berets trained themselves to defend fellow Mexican-Americans. The Jewish Defense League patrolled the streets of Jewish neighborhoods.

Police and other government officials view such defense groups as dangerous. They believe citizens should depend on their government for safety. They believe people and their government should try to work together.

8. *Using the Power of Money.* Minority groups know that businessmen have great power in American life. They have used pressure against these businessmen as part of their drive for equal rights. A group may agree not to buy from stores that do not give up job discrimination. It may refuse to advertise in newspapers that do not report fairly about minorities. It may decide to buy only from businesses owned by members of its own minority group. Most often the goal of such actions is to show that discrimination is poor business.

9. *Using the Courts.* Black American organizations have had the greatest success in improving rights through the courts. Other minority groups have also used the courts. Cases are begun for two chief reasons. A minority group may want to get a court order that will make officials enforce laws for equality. Or a case may be a challenge of some law that is believed to deny equality.

Sometimes the threat of a court case is enough to get an official to do his job better. Leaders of minority groups attend public meetings. There they point out that a law is not being enforced properly. They explain that they will bring cases before the courts unless changes are made. Many changes in government have come after members of minority groups spoke out for them in public.

10. *Separatism.* Members of some minority groups have decided

Malcolm X at first taught that separatism was the best way for black Americans to solve their problems. Shortly before his death he began to speak of blacks and whites working together to improve civil rights. Which of the two beliefs do you think wisest? Why?

they cannot gain equality from the majority. They have decided to separate themselves from the rest of the country. Such a move is called *separatism*. It was a goal of those who followed Marcus Garvey. It is a belief of the group called the Black Muslims. They separate themselves from others in every way possible. They set up their own businesses, schools and farms. Groups within other minorities have also tried some form of separatism. This has been true of Indians, Mexican-Americans, Japanese-Americans, Chinese-Americans, Jews, Catholics, Russians, Poles and others.

Malcolm X, a leader of the Black Muslims, spread ideas of separatism in the black communities. He later left the Muslims but continued to teach that white Americans would not solve the problems of black people. He said black Americans would have to understand themselves. They would have to work out their own plans to improve their lives. Malcolm X was killed in 1965. In the years since then, many other black leaders have also spoken out for separatist ideas. Among the best known is Roy Innis, leader of the organization called CORE. Separatist ideas have gained the greatest following in the question of community control of schools.

The most successful example of separatism in the United States is the city of Hamtramck, Michigan. This city is surrounded by Detroit. The people of Hamtramck are chiefly Polish Catholics. They speak Polish, follow Polish customs and remain separate from Detroit in every way they can.

Most civil rights groups do not believe in separatism. They still seek an integrated world of citizens enjoying equal rights. Still, movements for separate communities appear again and again. They have often been started by religious groups that wanted to keep their religion unchanged. Utah, a state first organized by the religious group called the Mormons, is still a Mormon area. Other religious groups have also set up communities within many of the states.

Minorities and Government in the 1970's. American minorities have learned that equal protection of the laws comes slowly. The majority is slow to give up prejudice and discrimination. Much of the use of civil disobedience has been aimed at speeding up desired changes.

Minorities have come to realize that their greatest protections can come from the national government. They believe that the President of the United States can do most to improve their lives. They have asked him to lead in the full enforcement of the laws for equality. They call upon him to use the power of his position as the country's leader to help all Americans receive fair and equal treatment under the laws.

The courts remain an important road to equality. Here again minorities have offered a challenge to the President. They have asked him to appoint federal judges who will work to help enforce laws for equality. In this way the Constitution can remain the path to the justice they seek.

I. WHAT ARE THE FACTS?

Write the letter of the choice that best completes each statement.

1. The events at Selma, Alabama, led to a change in (a) local laws, (b) state laws, (c) national laws.

2. By 1970 minority-group workers in Washington, D.C., held (a) one-fourth of government jobs, (b) one-half of government jobs, (c) three-fourths of government jobs.

3. The civil rights leader best known for his belief in nonviolent civil disobedience was (a) Rev. Dr. Martin Luther King, (b) Roy Innis, (c) Marcus Garvey.

4. A Mexican-American defense group is the (a) Black Panthers, (b) Brown Berets, (c) Deacons for Defense.

5. Self-help activities by minority groups provide members of these groups with (a) equal rights, (b) needed services, (c) political power.

II. THINKING IT THROUGH!

Discuss.

1. What are the chief goals of the minority groups in your community? What methods are they using to gain them?

2. How can each of these improve the lives of members of a minority group?

a) One of its leaders is made Commissioner of Human Rights.

b) One of its members becomes a school principal.

c) One of its members opens a department store.

d) One hundred of its members finish college and decide to remain in their home community.

3. What steps are being demanded of the national government today to improve the rights and living conditions of the country's minorities?

When They Came

The only native Americans were, of course, the Indians and, later, the Mexicans of the Southwest. All others came here from another land. They came for many reasons—to live and work as they pleased; to be able to worship as they chose; to build lives for themselves and their children that were somehow better than the lives they had known in "the old country." All, except for the Africans, came with hope. Only the black Africans came against their will, to be sold as slaves in the nation called "the land of the free."

The following chart shows about when most of our minority groups came to America. While some members of each group may have come before or after the dates listed, the chart shows when most members of that group first came.

1600's through 1800's	French and Spanish (to lands that became part of the United States) English, then Scottish and Welsh
1620's through 1820's	Black Africans (slaves)
1840's and 1850's	Irish French
1830's through 1880's	Germans, including some German Jews
1850's through 1880's	Chinese Scandinavians
1900—1910	Austrians and Hungarians Greeks Russians, including many Russian Jews Japanese Filipinos Italians
early 1920's	Poles Rumanians West Indians
1930's and 1940's	German Jews and other victims of World War II
1945 on	Puerto Ricans
1950's	Hungarians, Czechs
early 1960's	Cubans Dominicans West Indians

GLOSSARY

Unit 1

council: group of people elected to make laws for the community.

forefathers: ancestors; ones who lived before you, long ago.

frontier: area beyond which there are no large settlements.

frontiersman: person who lives and supports himself in a frontier area.

genocide: planned killing of an entire people because they are members of a minority, most often done by governments.

Great Spirit: Indian term meaning God.

Homestead Act: Morrill Act of 1862, under which settlers could receive 160 acres of land in the West.

hunting grounds: area used by Indians for hunting rather than as places to live.

Indian Removal: planned, forced movement of Indians from their homes to new areas and later to reservations in the West.

lawsuit: case brought before a court by someone in order to get something he claims a right to.

massacre: cruel, violent killing of a large number of people.

missionary: minister or other representative of a religious group who tries to spread his religion among people of another religion.

moccasins: soft shoes made of animal hides often worn by Indians.

nomad: one who has no permanent home but travels alone or in a group in order to find food and other necessities.

poverty: condition of being so poor that one hasn't enough to live on.

reservation: area set aside for Indians and belonging to them as a community.

sacred: special to members of a certain religion; holy.

termination policy: government policy of ending control of reservations by the Indians who lived on them.

territory: large section of land controlled by a nation but without the full rights of a state.

trading post: store on a reservation in which Indians bought the goods they needed.

treaty: agreement between nations concerning peace, trade or other matters.

truce: agreement to end fighting.

voter registration: process of adding voters to the list of those permitted to vote, usually by putting their names on the official list or register.

ward: person considered by law to be unable to care completely for himself, and who therefore does not have certain rights.

Unit 2

abolition: doing away with something, such as slavery.

amendment: addition to a constitution or law.

black codes: state and local laws passed after the Civil War to keep freedmen from gaining equality.

busing: bringing children by bus from their neighborhood to a school in another neighborhood, used to aid integration.

civil rights: rights that all citizens are entitled to have.

colored person: person with one or more black ancestor.

community control: plan in which the people living in a community have the power to decide how schools and other services are managed.

compromise: situation in which each side gives up part of what it really wants so that agreement can be reached.

decentralization: taking control of a government activity from the central government and giving it to local government groups.

de facto segregation: segregation that takes place because of conditions other than law.

de jure segregation: segregation that takes place because it is the law.

discrimination: treating a person or group in ways that keep them from having equality.

dissent: not in agreement with the majority; in the Supreme Court, a written opinion about a case by one or more justices that disagrees with the decision reached by the majority.

due process: carrying out rules and laws in a just and equal way, no matter who is involved.

emancipation: giving freedom to someone, such as a slave.

equal protection of the laws: promise in the Fourteenth Amendment that all citizens would be treated equally by the laws of all states.

freedmen: former slaves.

ghetto: at first a neighborhood in which a minority group is forced to live; later any neighborhood in poor condition in which members of a minority group live.

grandfather clause: part of the voting laws of some states that permitted voting only by those whose grandparents had had the right to vote.

indentured servant: one who agreed to be someone's servant for a certain number of years and whose services could be sold by that person.

integration: mixing in daily life of people of different groups, usually those of different races.

Jim Crow: body of laws and customs designed to keep black Americans and "non-white" minorities from having equal rights and equal treatment.

judicial review: power of courts to decide whether or not a law is constitutional.

Ku Klux Klan: national secret hate group, begun in 1865, whose members work to deny equal rights to minority groups.

lynching, lynch law: murder of a person thought to be guilty of a crime, usually by a mob taking the law into its own hands.

N.A.A.C.P.: National Association for the Advancement of Colored People, largest and oldest organization speaking for black Americans.

open enrollment: plan permitting a parent to decide to send his child to school in another neighborhood, usually with children of another race or national group.

prejudice: dislike or distrust of a person or group because of race, religion or national origin.

proclamation: announcement by a government or government official.

public housing project: group of buildings built and owned by a government to provide housing for a given group of citizens.

racist: one who hates people of another race, or whose actions are designed to take away the rights of those people.

Reconstruction: the years 1865-1877, during which the federal government tried to solve the problems in the South after the Civil War.

segregation: actions that force a minority group to remain apart from other groups in their daily lives.

"separate but equal": rule set by the Supreme Court in *Plessy v. Ferguson* (1896) permitting segregation of facilities for blacks and whites if those facilities were equal in quality.

serf: farm worker, largely in the Middle Ages, who was almost like a slave and could be sold with the land on which he worked.

slave: person owned by another person and having no freedom or rights of any kind.

slave codes: state and local laws passed before the Civil War to help slaveowners keep control of their slaves.

supremacy: being better, or having more rights or power, than another group.

unanimous: everyone agreeing.

Underground Railroad: secret organization that helped runaway slaves escape to the North.

UNIA: Universal Negro Improvement Association, "Back to Africa" organization active in the 1920's, led by Marcus Garvey.

Unit 3

Alianza: organization headed by Reies Tijerina that tries to regain lands lost by Mexican-Americans to Anglo-Americans.

Anglo: term meaning "white American," used chiefly in areas containing large numbers of Mexican-Americans.

Aztec: Indian tribe that ruled Mexico when Spain conquered that land.

barrio: "neighborhood," usually one in which Spanish-speaking Americans live.

bracero: farm worker, usually one who comes from Mexico to work on a farm in the United States.

campesinos: Spanish word meaning farm workers.

Chicano: word often used to describe a Mexican-American.

colonias: areas in the Southwest, usually rural, in which large number of Mexican-Americans live.

culture: the ideas, skills, arts and ways of life of a people.

huelga: Spanish word meaning strike.

La Causa: strike of grapepickers led by Cesar Chavez in California from 1965 to 1970.

La Raza: "The Race," or those sharing the culture developed by mixing of Spanish, Indian and later Mexican peoples.

Manifest Destiny: idea popular in the nineteenth century that it was God's will for the United States to control all land between the Atlantic and Pacific Oceans.

migrant worker: farm worker who moves from job to job and has no single place of work.

mission: group of buildings, usually including a church and school, operated by representatives of a religion in order to bring their religion and other aid to the people of the area.

N.F.W.A.: National Farm Workers Association, organization formed and led by Cesar Chavez.

rancho: large farm or landholding, most often used for raising cattle or sheep.

smuggler: one who secretly brings things into or out of a country in a way that is against the law.

Unit 4

benevolent society or association: self-help group formed by members of the same group, usually Chinese-Americans.

concentration camp: camp in which a government keeps some special group of prisoners.

coolie: term used to describe Chinese or other Asian unskilled workers.

coolie trader: usually a Chinese who organized the migration of Chinese unskilled workers to the United States in the nineteenth century.

Exclusion Act: immigration law of 1882 that barred Chinese immigration into the United States.

immigration law: law setting rules for immigration into a country, such as how many can come per year and from what countries.

infamy: great wickedness.

Nisei: Japanese-Americans born in the United States whose parents came from Japan.

queue: long braid of hair worn hanging down the back by Chinese and other Asians.

Unit 5

archbishop: Catholic bishop of the highest rank, head of an archdiocese.

bishop: Catholic priest who is head of a diocese.

cardinal: member of the highest-ranking group of Catholic bishops, next in importance to the Pope.

diocese: Catholic Church district that may include several churches.

immigrant: person who leaves his own country to settle in a new one.

Know-Nothings: members of a secret political group in the 1800's who wished to deny rights to immigrants and especially to Catholics.

Nativist: one who favors denying rights to immigrants or to persons of a non-Protestant religion.

nun: woman who has chosen to spend her life as a member of a religious order, giving up worldly goods, never marrying and, usually, living in a convent.

parish: district served by a single Catholic church.

parochial: having to do with a church parish; usually describing a school organized and run by a religious group for its own children.

persecution: plan or action under which a group of people is denied its rights or made to suffer unfairly.

Pope: head of the Catholic Church, elected by the College of Cardinals.

priest: religious leader of a Catholic church.

sweat shop: factory with unsafe or unsanitary working conditions, paying low wages for long hours of work.

Unit 6

Anti-Defamation League: organization devoted to fighting anti-Semitism and other forms of discrimination, a part of B'nai B'rith.

anti-Semitism: hatred of Jews.

bigotry: prejudice.

B'nai B'rith: American Jewish organization founded in 1843.

fugitive: one who is running away.

Israelite: originally someone in the Biblical kingdom of Israel: used in the early United States to mean any Jew.

Jewish Defense League: militant Jewish American group engaging in defense and other direct actions.

Judaism: religion of the Jews, based on the belief in one God.

pogrom: organized massacre of a group, such as the many attacks on communities of European Jews.

Protocols of the Elders of Zion: false set of documents describing a so-called Jewish plan for world control.

refugee: person who flees from his home or country to gain refuge from war or persecution.

scapegoat: person or group blamed for the troubles of others.

swastika: symbol used by the Nazis in Germany and by pro-German or anti-Semitic groups in other lands.

synagogue: Jewish house of worship.

Talmud: religious books containing the laws of Judaism and the explanations of those laws; the basis of Jewish religious thought and practice.

vagabond: homeless wanderer.

Yiddish: language most similar to German, used by European Jews and written with Hebrew letters.

Unit 7

Arawak: Indian tribe most important in the Carribbean and the mainland of northern South America.

Boriquen: early Indian name of Puerto Rico.

cacique: Indian chief, such as those in early Puerto Rico.

commonwealth: country or state with powers of self-government but still part of and under some control by another nation.

compadre: comrade of fellow-countryman; the feeling of togetherness among Puerto Ricans.

El Barrio: name given to some Puerto Rican or Spanish-speaking neighborhoods.

Fomento: Puerto Rican organization whose aim is to help develop the island.

Hispano: Spanish-American; a white Spaniard living in one of the areas conquered by Spain, or anyone who considers himself Spanish rather than American.

ILGWU: International Ladies' Garment Workers Union, a large union organized by Jewish immigrants in New York City, now a national group.

jibaros: poor farm workers in Puerto Rico.

La Boriquena: Puerto Rican national anthem.

mainland: original 48 states of the United States, as compared with Puerto Rico or other islands.

melting pot theory: idea that immigrants would in time become like other Americans and share the rights held by earlier settlers.

non-voting representative: one who sits in a legislature with the power to speak for those he represents but without the right to vote.

open admissions: policy of admitting all high school graduates who apply to college.

Operation Bootstrap: plan under which Puerto Rico has developed new industries with little outside aid.

Operation Serenity: a plan to improve the cultural and social life of the people of Puerto Rico.

Puerto Rican Forum: organization of Puerto Ricans in New York City that works to solve the economic problems of that minority.

San Juan Bautista: "Saint John the Baptist," name first given to Spanish settlements near present-day San Juan, Puerto Rico.

Tainos: Indian tribe living in Puerto Rico when Spain conquered the island.

veto: power of a government or government official to prevent a law or decision from going into effect.

Unit 8

Appalachia: thirteen-state poverty area along the Appalachian Mountains running south from New York.

CCC: Civilian Conservation Corps, started by President Franklin Roosevelt to help create jobs for unskilled workers during the Depression.

child labor: work by children under the age set by law for required school attendance; usually, work by children under 14.

food stamps: offered by the federal government to people in need so that they can obtain food at low prices.

Head Start: program under which pre-school children receive training to help prepare them for school.

income maintenance: plan to guarantee each person or family a definite income each year.

Job Corps: government program to train young people and then place them in jobs.

Model Cities Program: federal program to aid cities with slum and other problem neighborhoods.

National Urban League: nation-wide black organization whose chief task is to break down job discrimination against black Americans.

negative income tax: the paying of money to the poor at income tax time, so that all Americans have some minimum income each year.

New Deal: programs and laws offered by President Franklin Roosevelt beginning in 1933.

NYA: National Youth Administration, New Deal organization designed to provide income and work for students.

Operation Breadbasket: job-training and job-finding program begun by Dr. Martin Luther King, Jr., and later headed by Reverend Jesse Jackson.

pension: payment to a person who has reached a certain age.

public works: building projects planned and carried through by a government.

sharecropper: one who farms someone else's land and gets part of the crop in return for his work.

Social Security: laws designed to guarantee income or provide services to people; the laws passed by Congress beginning in 1935 providing old-age and survivors' insurance, unemployment insurance and aid to older people.

suburbs: outer parts of a city, or the communities just outside a city.

survivors' insurance: payments to the family of a someone who dies and was covered by social security laws.

tenant farmer: farmer who farms land belonging to another person.

TVA: Tennessee Valley Authority, government agency created during the New Deal to develop and run dams providing cheap electric power.

Urban Coalition: national integrated group whose goal is the ending of discrimination based upon race or color.

VISTA: Volunteers in Service to America, federal program under which trained persons spend a year or two aiding the poor people of an area.

War on Poverty: set of laws passed by Congress since 1964 designed to end poverty or ease its problems throughout the United States, begun by President Lyndon Johnson.

WPA: Works Progress Administration, started by President Franklin Roosevelt to help create jobs during the Depression.

Unit 9

Black Muslims: black separatist group following the Muslim religion.

Black Panthers: militant black self-defense group that also demands changes in the way of life of the United States.

blockbusting: actions by real estate companies to change a neighborhood by frightening one group out and then bringing another group in.

Brown Berets: Mexican-American self-defense group.

civil liberties: the rights guaranteed to every citizen.

CORE: Congress of Racial Equality, a civil rights group that was integrated at first but later became a separatist black organization.

fair employment: all persons working at whatever jobs they are trained to fill, without suffering discrimination.

fair housing, open housing: housing in which any person can live, whatever his race, religion, color or national origin.

nonviolent protest: peaceful actions planned to show disagreement with a law or custom, or with some action by another group or organization.

restrictive covenant: agreement not to rent or sell property to the group of persons named in the agreement.

sedition: treason or betrayal of your country.

separatism: belief that your group should remain separate from other groups in every possible way.

Workers' Defense League: national group working for the improvement of civil rights, and especially the right of the poor and those holding unpopular political beliefs.

Young Lords: militant organization of young Puerto Ricans in the United States.

INDEX

Brown, John, 79.

Brown v. Board of Education of Topeka, 136, 138, 143-144, 150, 152, 261, 375, 376.

Buchanan v. Warley, 352-354.

Buffalo, New York, 231.

Bureau of Indian Affairs, 35, 41, 55, 57-58.

Burger, Justice Warren E., 146.

Burleigh, W. A., 39.

Burlingame Treaty, 196, 197.

busing, 146, 152-154, 155;
    Anti-Busing Law, 155-156.

C

cacique, 271.

Caguas, Puerto Rico, 279.

Campeche, José, 301.

campesinos, 181.

Capó, Bobby, 301.

Cardozo, Justice Benjamin, 258.

Carib Indians, 271.

Carrasquillo, Ramón, 301.

Carroll, Father John, 221.

Caruso, Enrico, 236.

Casals, Pablo, 301.

Castro, Fidel, 225.

Catholic Church, 27, 162, 163-164, 182, 218-220, 222, 226, 230, 231-232, 235, 244, 274, 296.

Catholics, 218-227, 230-238, 242, 245, 255, 259, 260, 289, 296, 386.

Catron, Thomas B., 182.

Caucasian race, 98.

Celebrezze, Anthony, 236.

Centeno, María, 301.

Central Pacific Railroad, 190, 191, 223.

Cepeda, Orlando, 302.

Chao, Dr. Ramman.

Charleston, South Carolina, 246.

Chavez, Cesar, 180-182, 184.

Chee Dodge, 53-54.

Cherokee Indians, 18-21, 28-29.

Cheyenne Indians, 32, 33, 34.

Chicago, Illinois, 155, 176, 213, 231, 283, 285;
    Cubs, 302.

chicanos, 160.

Chickasaw Indians, 18, 28-29.

Childers, Ernest, 52.

child labor, 311-312.

China, 190, 191, 192, 193, 196, 197, 198, 199, 200, 205, 206.

Chinatowns, 195, 200-201.

Chinee, 190, 191.

Chinese-Americans, 151, 190-201, 213, 257, 300, 386.

Chinese Exclusion Act, 196, 197.

Chinese laundries, 198.

Chinese restaurants, 198-199.

Ching, Dr. Peter, 199.

Choctaw Indians, 18, 28-29.

Christian Front, 260.

Chu, Dr. Ju Chin, 192.

Circle of Spanish-American Writers and Poets, 302.

Citizens' Crusade Against Hunger, 320.

Civil disobedience, 382-383, 384.

Civil liberties, 362-369.

Civil Rights Act of 1964, 365, 366-367, 368-369.

civil rights, 92, 121, 122, 146, 233, 251, 258, 261, 273, 286, 337, 345-346, 375-376, 382.

Civil War, 28-29, 30, 85, 88, 90, 95, 143, 151, 171, 210, 227, 247, 289, 351, 352, 374, 375.

Civil Works Administration, 313.

Civilian Conservation Corps, 314.

Clay, Henry, 22.

Clemente, Roberto, 302.

Cleveland, Ohio, 382.

Cochise, Chief, 32.

Cohan, George M., 236.

Cold War, 233.

College Bound, 326.

Collier, John, 54.

Colombus, Christopher, 7, 47, 271.

colonies, 184.

colonies, 218, 220-221, 242-243, 245, 274-276, 309;
    and Indians, 8-9, 13-14, 218;
    and Jews, 242-243, 245;
    slavery in, 64-67, 68;
    Spanish, 164, 270-274.

Colorado, 32, 166, 171, 172, 197;
    Denver, 170.

Comanche Indians, 31.

Commonwealth Day, 276.

Communist, 256, 257, 261.

Community Chest, 311.

Community Relations Service, 368.

Community Service Organization, 184.

compadre, 304.

concentration camps, 27, 205, 208-212.

Conestoga Indians, 13-14.

Confederacy, 28, 29, 247;
    and Indians, 28-29.

missionaries, 3, 43.
Mississippi, 145, 146, 319;
    Fayette, 366;
    University of, 145, 374.
Missouri, Paddock Woods, 350, 357;
    St. Louis, 350, 355, 357;
    University of, 125-126.
Mitchell, James, 236.
Mitchell, John, 236.
Model Cities Program, 326.
Mongoloid race, 98.
Monroe, James, 71.
Monserrat, Joseph, 283, 303.
Montana, 31.
Monteux, Pierre, 236.
Montgomery, Jack, 52.
Montoya, Sen. Joseph, 176.
Moore v. Dempsey, 129, 131-132, 142.
Morales, Noro, 301.
Moreno, Rita, 302.
Mormons, 386.
Morse, Samuel F. B., 224.
Moscoso, Teodoro, 280.
Mulatoes, 99.
Muñoz Marin, Luis, 275-276, 284.
Muñoz Rivera, Luis, 274-275.
Murphy, Justice Frank, 210.
Muslims, 27, 64.

N

Napoleon III, 258.
Nash, Philleo, 56.
Nathan, George Jean, 236.
National Afro-American Council, 94.
*National and Private Advantages of the African
    Trade Considered, The,* 66.
National Association for the Advancement of Col-
    ored People, 111, 118, 122-126, 129, 131, 132,
    135, 337, 352, 354-355.
National Congress of American Indians, 54, 59.
National Council of Christians and Jews, 262.
National Council of Jewish Women, 250.
National Farm Workers Association, 180.
National Forest Service, 183-184.
National Guard, 144.
National Indian Education Conference, 58.
National Indian Youth Council, 57.
National League, 302.
National Urban League, 327, 337.
National Youth Administration, 316.

Nation of Immigrants, A, 236.
Nativists, 223-224, 227, 255, 259.
Navaho Community College, 57.
Navaho Council, 53.
Navaho Indians, 40, 53, 54, 56.
Nazi Party, 26-27, 260, 261, 264.
negative income tax, 329.
Negroes, 64-72, 75-79, 82-85, 88-95, 98, 104-108,
    110-118, 121-126, 128-133, 135-147, 150-156,
    195, 255, 273, 320, 336-337, 338, 343-347, 350-
    359.
Nevada, 40, 166.
New Amsterdam, 242-243.
Newark, New Jersey, 155, 245, 382.
"New Colossus, The," 248.
New Deal, 53, 233, 313-316, 317.
New England, 319.
New Hampshire, 245.
New Mexico, 40, 57, 163, 166, 171-172, 176, 354;
    Tierra Amarilla, 182.
Newport, Rhode Island, 246.
New York City, 66, 77, 110, 150, 153, 155, 156, 176,
    213, 223, 230, 231, 246, 249, 250, 251, 261, 263,
    273, 309-310, 311, 327, 382;
    busing, 146, 152-154, 155;
    Harlem, 110, 282, 283;
    open admissions, 294-295;
    open enrollment, 153-156;
    Puerto Ricans, 279-280, 282-283, 285-286, 288,
        290-295, 297, 301, 302, 303;
    school integration, 153;
    University of, 279, 294-295.
New York Philharmonic, 213.
New York State, 2, 56, 152-154, 155-156, 191, 230,
    251, 293-294, 310;
    anti-discrimination laws, 338-339;
    Commission on Human Rights, 152, 291, 296-
        297, 336-337;
    integration efforts, 152-153.
New York University, 336.
New York Urban League, 299.
Nez Percé Indians, 31.
Niagara Movement, 117-118, 337.
Nilus, Serge, 258.
Nineteenth Amendment, 364-366.
Nixon, Richard M., 146, 234, 366.
Nobel Prize, 192, 236, 252, 264.
Noguchi, Isamu, 213.
Nomads, 3.
North Carolina, 21, 245.

North Dakota, 57.
Norwegian-Americans, 250.
Notes on the State of Virginia, 71.
nuns, 219.

O

Oath of Supremacy, 220.
O'Brien, Lawrence, 236.
O'Connell, Cardinal, 259.
O'Dwyer, Paul, 236.
Office of Economic Opportunity, 176.
Oklahoma, 28, 31-32, 40;
    University of, 126.
Old Testament, 244, 263.
old-age pensions, 315.
Oller, Francisco, 301.
Omaha, Nebraska, 46, 190.
100th Infantry Battalion, 211.
open enrollment, 153-156.
Operation Bootstrap, 280, 284-285.
Operation Breadbasket, 327.
Operation Serenity, 303.
Oregon, 31, 55, 208.
Ormandy, Eugene, 265.
Orthodox Judaism, 263.
Osceola, 21.
O'Sullivan, John L., 161.
Ottawa Indians, 15.
Oyama v. California, 208.
Ozawa, Sejii, 213.

P

Pacific Railway Act, 190.
Paine, Thomas, 67, 68.
Paris, 273.
Pea Ridge, Battle of, 28.
Pearl Harbor, 204-205.
Pei, I. M., 192.
Penn, William, 13.
Pennsylvania, 13-14, 91, 218, 221, 245-246;
    Nativist riots, 224;
    Philadelphia, 66, 71, 75, 77, 176, 213, 222, 223,
    245, 246, 283, 327.
Pesotta, Rose, 288.
Philippine Islands, 270.
Phillips, Jonas, 246.
Pike, Gov. William A., 171-172.
Pine Ridge Reservation, 26.
Piñero, Jesus T., 276.

pirates, 272, 273.
Pizarro, Juan, 302.
    "Plans of the Jews." *See Protocols of Zion.*
Plessy, Homer Adolph, 97, 100.
Plessy v. Ferguson, 100-102, 123, 139, 143, 352.
pogroms, 257.
Poland, 225, 231.
Polish-Americans, 226, 250, 300, 386.
Polk, James, 166.
Ponce de Leon, Juan, 271.
Ponce, Puerto Rico, 301.
Pontiac, Chief, 15.
poorhouse, 308, 309, 312.
Pope John XXIII, 235.
Pope Paul VI, 218-219.
Portugal, 64, 242, 245.
Porter v. Hall, 52.
Postlethwayt, Malachy, 66.
poverty, 128, 233, 308-317, 319-331, 379-380;
    among Indians, 45, 50-51;
    Mexican-Americans, 174;
    Puerto Ricans, 281-282, 286, 288;
    reasons for, 327-328.
Power, Ramón, 273.
prejudice, 104, 130-131, 137, 174, 207, 247-248,
    259, 290, 340, 351-352, 356, 369, 386.
priests, 219, 221, 224, 225, 226, 235, 260.
Princeton, New Jersey, 264.
private schools, 145, 147.
Prophet, the, 15.
Protestants, 218, 219, 220, 221, 222, 223, 226, 234,
    244, 259, 260, 289, 296, 351, 354.
Protocols of Zion, 258-259, 260.
public assistance, 283, 286, 291, 313-314, 320, 321-
    322, 328, 329-330, 331, 368, 381.
public defender, 331.
public housing, 151, 381.
Public Works Administration, 313.
Puerto Rican Day Parade, 286.
Puerto Rican Discovery Day, 271.
Puerto Rican Federation of Labor, 288.
Puerto Rican Forum, 297, 299, 337.
Puerto Ricans, 151, 153, 155, 156, 236, 250, 270-
    277, 279-286, 288-297, 299-304, 320, 356;
    and courts, 275;
    and Spain, 270-274;
    art, 301;
    discrimination against, 286, 340, 355-356;
    in music, 301;
    in sports, 302;

403

literature, 302;
on stage and screen, 302;
voting, 293-294.
Puerto Rico, 225, 270-277, 279, 280-285, 290-291,
292, 293, 296, 301-302, 303-304;
and Spain, 270-274;
development, 284-285;
Operation Bootstrap, 284-285;
schools, 274, 281-282, 284;
self-government, 273-277;
University of, 284.

Q

Quakers, 64, 218.
Quanak Parker, Chief, 31.

R

races of man, 98.
racism, 352, 363, 365.
railroad workers, 190-191, 194.
Ramos, Florencio, 301.
ranchos, 163.
Randolph, A. Philip, 338.
Reconstruction, 88-95, 99, 100, 106, 123, 233, 252,
364, 374-375.
Red Cross, 311.
Reform Judaism, 263-264.
refugee, 242.
Republican Party, 83-85, 91, 227, 230, 233, 234,
260.
reservations, 16, 25, 31, 32, 34, 36, 40-46, 56, 57-58;
trading posts on, 42.
Ribicoff, Sen. Abraham, 258.
Rice, Elmer, 265.
Riis, Jacob, 310.
Rio Grande River, 163, 166.
Rivera, Graciela, 301.
Roberts, Justice Owen, 210.
Roberts, Sarah C., 135, 136-137.
Robinson, Solon, 70.
Rochester, New York, segregation, 153.
Rockefeller Institute of Medical Research, 264.
Rockne, Knute, 236.
Roman Empire, 243.
Rome, 27, 64, 218, 232, 243.
Rooney, Mickey, 236.
Roosevelt, Franklin D., 53, 121, 204-205, 251, 260,
313-316, 338.
Roosevelt, Theodore, 28, 206.

Rosado, Julio, 302.
Rose, Alex, 251.
Roybal, Rep. Eduardo, 176.
Russia, 27, 146, 205, 233, 248, 257, 258-259, 261.
Russian-Americans, 289-290, 386.
Ruth, "Babe," 236.

S

Sagayewatha, Chief, 9.
Salk, Dr. Jonas, 264.
San Antonio, Texas, 170.
Sandifer, Jawn A., 125.
San Francisco, 191, 198, 206.
San Juan, Puerto Rico, 270, 271, 280, 284, 301.
Santa Fe, New Mexico, 171-172.
Santiago, José, 302.
Sapiro, Aaron, 259.
Savannah, Georgia, 246.
schools, 300, 313, 316, 323, 325-326, 336-337, 368,
379;
big city, 150-156, 294-295;
Catholic, 219, 226-227, 235;
community control, 150, 381;
decentralization, 156;
freedmens', 91;
Indian, 45, 57-58;
integration of, 138, 139, 141, 142-147, 150-156,
376;
Japanese-Americans in, 206, 207-208;
Jews in, 244, 251-252;
Mexican-Americans in, 163, 174-175;
neighborhood, 150-152;
open admissions, 294-295, 297;
open enrollment, 153-156;
Puerto Rican, 274, 281-282, 284;
Puerto Ricans in, 279-280, 283, 292-293, 294-295,
297, 299, 303;
segregated, 57, 105, 117, 125-126, 135-147, 150-
156, 373, 376.
Schreiber, Moses, 248.
Schurz Carl, 35.
Scott, Dred, 82, 83, 100.
Second Amendment, 221.
Sedition Act, 371-372.
segregation, 97, 99, 101-102, 136, 180, 211, 244,
331;
in armed forces, 343-347;
de facto, 151, 152-156;
de jure, 151;

Thomas, Piri, 302.
Tijerina, Reies, 179, 182-184.
Tillman, Sen. Benjamin R., 107.
Tippecanoe, Battle of, 15.
Toleration Act of 1649, 220.
Toltec Indians, 160.
Toro, Jomo, 301.
Torres, José, 302-303.
Toscanini, Arturo, 236.
transcontinental railroad, 190.
Turkey, 27.
Truman, Harry S, 54, 55, 276;
    integrating armed forces, 344, 345-347.
Tsai, Gerald, 192.
Tubman, Harriet, 79.
Tuskeegee Institute, 110.

U

Underground Railroad, 76, 79.
unemployment insurance, 315.
Union Pacific Railroad, 190, 223.
United Farm Workers Organizing Committee, 180.
United Mine Workers, 236.
United Nations, 26.
United States Air Force, 204, 347.
United States Army, 15, 18, 21, 26, 29, 30, 31, 32,
    33, 34, 40, 41, 144, 145, 166, 171, 183, 184, 205,
    208, 274, 342, 379;
    discrimination in, 343-347;
    Japanese-Americans in, 207, 211, 212.
United States Commission on Civil Rights, 364,
    368.
United States Marines, 344, 347.
United States Marshals, 145, 373, 376.
United States Navy, 204, 344, 345, 346.
United States v. Wong Kim Ark, 207.
Universal Negro Improvement Association, 110-111,
    114-116.
Urban Coalition, 327, 337.
Utah, 40, 166, 197, 386.

V

Vatican Council, 222.
Venezuela, 271.
Vietnam, 146, 324.

Virginia, 65, 71, 72, 74, 78, 79, 135, 138-139;
    Richmond, 246.
VISTA, 324-325.
Voting Rights Act of 1965, 293, 366, 379, 382;
    of 1970, 294.

W

Wagner, Robert F., Jr., 236.
Wagner, Sen. Robert F., 236.
Walker, David, 78-79.
Walker's Appeal, 78-79.
Wallace, Gov. George, 378-379, 382.
War of 1812, 15.
War on Poverty, 57, 323-328, 330, 331, 381.
Warren, Justice Earl, 136, 139-141, 362.
Washington, Booker T., 110, 111, 112-113.
Washington, D.C., 121, 155, 161, 205, 232, 338,
    339, 358, 366, 381.
Washington, George, 71, 245, 246-247.
Washington, Walter, 366.
Watson, Thomas, 255.
Weld, Theodore, 69-70.
Wexler, Jacqueline Grennan, 238.
White, Rep. George H., 106-107.
white supremacy, 94, 99, 105, 108, 142, 236, 364.
Whitney, Eli, 76.
Willkie, Wendell, 260.
Wilson, Woodrow, 259, 345.
Wise, Rabbi Stephen, 263-264.
Woolman, John, 64, 66.
Workers' Defense League, 337.
World War I, 343-345.
World War II, 26, 52, 54, 204-205, 207, 208-212,
    233, 251, 258, 260, 290, 316, 338, 345, 375.
Wounded Knee, Battle of, 25-26.
Wyoming, 166;
    Rock Springs, 197.

XYZ

Yamasaki, Minoru, 213.
Yang, Dr. Chen Ning, 192.
Yiddish, 249, 250.
Young Lords, 384.
Yutang, Lin, 192.